# SHINING THE LIGHT VI

*THE END OF WHAT WAS . . .*

LIGHT TECHNOLOGY RESEARCH

# SHINING THE LIGHT BOOK VI

## THE END OF WHAT WAS

### THE TRUTH ABOUT

- End of 50-Year Earth/ET Secrecy
- Hacker Causes Titan 4 Explosion
- Oxygen-Eating Meteoroids
- All Humans Are Being Tested Now
- Why You're Tired and What to Do about It
- Humanity Chooses Species Consciousness

Light Technology Research

Cover art: Balance
by Robert Lewis Arnold

Thanks to Maxine Appleman of Boulder, Colorado,
for sharing her research material from channelings with Robert.
These make up chapters 1, 26, 34, 35 and 36.

ISBN 1-891824-24-4

Published by
**Light Technology Publishing**
P.O. Box 3540
Flagstaff, AZ 86003
(800) 450-0985

Printed by
**Sedona Color Graphics**
Sedona, AZ

Robert Shapiro has grown up with the experience of extraterrestrial and extradimensional contact. From age twelve he has had a series of personal UFO contacts. Throughout his life there has been communication with beings from several star systems and dimensions. The development of his career and lifestyle has come as a direct result of this communication. Robert has been a professional channel for over twenty years, and although he can channel almost anyone or anything with an exceptionally clear and profound connection, he most often channels Zoosh, who describes himself below. Robert's great contribution to our understanding of the history, purpose and destiny of humanity is his 13-volume epochal work, The Explorer Race series. He also has gifted us with the remarkable 3-book Shamanic Secrets series; *Material Mastery, Physical Mastery* and *Spiritual Mastery*. When he is not channeling, Robert is a shaman and spiritual teacher in his own right who lives in Hawaii. He is available for personal appointments and can be reached at (808) 926-4194.

Zoosh, a great being who is inspiring and guiding humanity, the Explorer Race, has been with us for "about a trillion years." He is witty, wise and compassionate. He says about himself, "It has been my job and my purpose in life to follow the birth of your souls on your journey to re-creating the universe. My job is to be your companion, your guide, occasionally your entertainer. I have to nurture that sense of mystery—it's not as if you're going to have it forever.

"It is my job to help you get there, to help you to understand your experience and to observe everything. And, in time, to remind you of the everything you are in one of my many guises."

## Other Books by Robert Shapiro

### THE EXPLORER RACE SERIES

1 • *The Explorer Race*
2 • *ETs and the Explorer Race*
3 • *Explorer Race: Origins and the Next 50 Years*
4 • *Explorer Race: Creator and Friends of the Creator*
5 • *Explorer Race and Particle Personalities*
6 • *Explorer Race and Beyond*
7 • *Explorer Race and The Council of Creators*
8 • *Explorer Race and Isis*
9 • *Explorer Race and Jesus*
10 • *Explorer Race and Lost Civilizations*
11 • *Explorer Race: ET Visitors Speak*
12 • *Explorer Race: A Leap of Faith—Gentle Steps to the Next Time Line*
13 • *Explorer Race: The Ultimate UFO Book*

### SHINING THE LIGHT SERIES

1 • *Shining the Light*
2 • *Shining the Light II: The Battle Continues*
3 • *Shining the Light III: Humanity Gets a Second Chance*
4 • *Shining the Light IV: Humanity's Greatest Challenge*
5 • *Shining the Light V: Humanity Is Going to Make It!*
6 • *Shining the Light VI: The End of What Was*

• *The Sedona Vortex Guidebook (with other channels)*

# Contents


1 • Pearls of Wisdom . . . . . . . . . . . . . . . . . . . . 1
*Zoosh—August 6, 1997—From a private research reading*

2 • The End of the 50-Year Earth/ET Secrecy Agreement. . . . 3
*Zoosh—January 20, 1998*
Pacts with ETs in the 1940s . . . . . . . . . . . . . . . . . . 4
Thank You for Your Help . . . . . . . . . . . . . . . . . . 6
The 1947 Contract . . . . . . . . . . . . . . . . . . . . 8
The Crafts and ET Engineering Help . . . . . . . . . . . . . 9
Trial Balloons in the Educational TV/Press . . . . . . . . . . 10
ET-Scientist Collaboration on an Asteroid Deflector . . . . . . . . 11
SSG's Success: Pitting People Against Each Other . . . . . . . . . 13
Area 51 Obsolete. . . . . . . . . . . . . . . . . . . . . 14
Bob Lazar . . . . . . . . . . . . . . . . . . . . . . . 15
Follow-up on the Xpotaz and the SSG . . . . . . . . . . . . . 16
MIB Says ET Info Being Dribbled out to Prepare for
Major Secrets to be Revealed in 1998 . . . . . . . . . . . . . 17
Art Bell Show Call-In for Area 51 Workers (9/11-12/98) . . . . . 17
Underground Bases, New Uses . . . . . . . . . . . . . . . . 19
Population Transfers. . . . . . . . . . . . . . . . . . . . 20
The Ground-Based Crafts to Be Openly Used in 15 Years . . . . . 21
Future Mars and Moon Bases . . . . . . . . . . . . . . . . 22
The Global Government. . . . . . . . . . . . . . . . . . . 24
Nations with the 50-Year Agreements . . . . . . . . . . . . . 25
Japan. . . . . . . . . . . . . . . . . . . . . . . . . . 26

3 • Don't Use Water for Fuel, or Earth Will Look Like Mars!. 27
*Zoosh—March 1998*

4 • Officials Often Ignorant of 50-Year-Old Files . . . . . . . 29
*Edgar Mitchell, Ph.D.*

5 • SSG Commands "Don't Read!" on U.S. TV Sets . . . . . . 33
*Speaks of Many Truths—April 16, 1998*
"Don't Read" and "Eat" . . . . . . . . . . . . . . . . . . 34
An Ongoing SSG Project. . . . . . . . . . . . . . . . . . . 35
TV-Set Circuitry Is Used Remotely. . . . . . . . . . . . . . . 36
Reading, Wisdom and Practical Application . . . . . . . . . . . 37
How It Works to Condition You. . . . . . . . . . . . . . . . 38
The Cycles of Experimentation and Control
through Visual Subliminals . . . . . . . . . . . . . . . . . 39
The Carrier Wave Alone Generates Discomfort, Nervousness . . . 40
Watch How You Feel . . . . . . . . . . . . . . . . . . . . 41
Shielding You Can Do That Breaks up the Visual . . . . . . . . 41
Hard Times for Publishers and Students. . . . . . . . . . . . 42

6 • More Subliminal Messages and the Sinister Secret Government . . . . . . . . . . . . 45
*Zoosh—April 17, 1998*
Addictive News and Subliminal Sales . . . . . . . . . . . . . . . . 46
From Satellite Broadcasts . . . . . . . . . . . . . . . . . . . . . 46
U.S. Government's Attempt to Stop It . . . . . . . . . . . . . . . 47
The Untraceable Source That Manipulates the Satellites . . . . . . 48
The Cumulative Impact . . . . . . . . . . . . . . . . . . . . . . 48
How Publishing Can Counteract the Trend . . . . . . . . . . . . . 49
"Don't Read" Phasing Out . . . . . . . . . . . . . . . . . . . . . 51

7 • How to Aid Whales Caught in Worldwide Sonar FM Radiation . . . . . . . . . . . . 55
*Zoosh—April 21, 1998*
Navy Sonar Testing on Whales off Hawaii . . . . . . . . . . . . . 55
From the Report . . . . . . . . . . . . . . . . . . . . . . . . . 55
What You Can Do: Send Love and Gold Light While You Exercise 57
Sonar as a Security System and Its Cumulative Impact . . . . . . . 58
Be Physical When Sending Strength . . . . . . . . . . . . . . . . 59
The Long-Range Effect . . . . . . . . . . . . . . . . . . . . . . 60
Electromagnetic Radiation and the Pineal/Pituitary Glands . . . . 61
A Protective Belt . . . . . . . . . . . . . . . . . . . . . . . . 61

8 • Electronic Reproduction of Sound Produces Stress . . . . 63
*Isis—April 23, 1998*
"Even" People in an "Odd" World = Stress . . . . . . . . . . . . . 64
Tinnitus and Electronic Sound . . . . . . . . . . . . . . . . . . . 64

9 • The Mechanics of the SSG Commands on U.S. TV Sets . . 67
*Isis—May 19, 1998*

10 • Nuclear Tests Could Aid Unification . . . . . . . . . . . 71
*Zoosh—May 19, 1998*
What Readers Can Do* . . . . . . . . . . . . . . . . . . . . . . . 73

11 • Sphinx in the Rockies . . . . . . . . . . . . . . . . . . . . 75
*Zoosh—May 28, 1998*
Underground Civilizations . . . . . . . . . . . . . . . . . . . . 75
Civilization's Star Origin and Culture Base under the Rockies . . . 76
Feminine Technology . . . . . . . . . . . . . . . . . . . . . . . 77
The Builders' Job to Track All Possible Futures . . . . . . . . . . 78
Visual Attractors . . . . . . . . . . . . . . . . . . . . . . . . 79
The Builders' Three Sources; Their Adoption of the Explorer Race. 79
The Importance of the Great Pyramid and the Sphinx . . . . . . . 81
Artifacts Elsewhere on Earth . . . . . . . . . . . . . . . . . . . 81
Connections with Tribal Peoples . . . . . . . . . . . . . . . . . 82
The Cat Connection . . . . . . . . . . . . . . . . . . . . . . . . 83

12 • Cats as Our Teachers . . . . . . . . . . . . . . . . . . . . 85
*Speaks of Many Truths—May 28, 1998*

13 • Living Prayer Gives to Earth . . . . . . . . . . . . . . . . 89
*Speaks of Many Truths—June 22, 1998*
How Manifesting Occurs, How to Ask . . . . . . . . . . . . . . . 89
Prayer for Peace . . . . . . . . . . . . . . . . . . . . . . . . 90
A Prayer for the Surrounding Life . . . . . . . . . . . . . . . . 90
Living Prayer* . . . . . . . . . . . . . . . . . . . . . . . . . 91
Welcoming Will Make a Big Difference . . . . . . . . . . . . . . 93
Use the Living Prayer for Weather . . . . . . . . . . . . . . . . 93

14 • The Physical Body Cries, "Show Me the Way!" . . . . . . 95
*Zoosh—June 29, 1998*
The SSG's Subliminal Messages and Your Natural Susceptibility . . 95
Result: A Slight Slide in Dimensional Level . . . . . . . . . . . 96
The Physical Location of the Body's Cry . . . . . . . . . . . . . 97
A Living Prayer, Something We All Can Do . . . . . . . . . . . . 98
Creator School, Where the Physical Self Seeks Constant Balance . 98
Prayer for Heart Healing* . . . . . . . . . . . . . . . . . . . . 99
A New Level of Cooperation . . . . . . . . . . . . . . . . . . . 100

15 • The Arrival of the Wisdom Seekers and Wisdom Givers. 101
*Zoosh—July 2, 1998*
You Will Suddenly Have to *Know*. . . . . . . . . . . . . . . . . 101
Wisdom Givers Soon to Arrive and Touch You . . . . . . . . . . . 102
The Wisdom Seekers . . . . . . . . . . . . . . . . . . . . . . . 103
Awakening Timed to a Specific Population Size . . . . . . . . . 104
The Snapback Has Begun . . . . . . . . . . . . . . . . . . . . . 104
The Touching and Its Results. . . . . . . . . . . . . . . . . . . 105
Media Subliminals May Increase, but You'll Begin to Notice . . . 107
The End of Suffering . . . . . . . . . . . . . . . . . . . . . . 108

16 • Zero Point and the Unified Field . . . . . . . . . . . . . 109
*Zoosh—July 9-10, 1998*
Mantras of Feeling and Optimistic Vision . . . . . . . . . . . . 109
A Deep-Space Explosion . . . . . . . . . . . . . . . . . . . . . 110
Pulses from the Galactic Center . . . . . . . . . . . . . . . . 111
Mantras of Feeling and Optimistic Vision* . . . . . . . . . . . . 111
The Sun's Disappearing Magnetic Poles and Unusual Flares . . . 112
SOHO's Silence . . . . . . . . . . . . . . . . . . . . . . . . . 113
An Unannounced Magnetic Storm . . . . . . . . . . . . . . . . . 114
Fires in Mexico . . . . . . . . . . . . . . . . . . . . . . . . . 114
North American Volcanoes and Earthquakes. . . . . . . . . . . . 115
Melting Ice in the Antarctic . . . . . . . . . . . . . . . . . . 115
Geomagnetic Field Changes . . . . . . . . . . . . . . . . . . . 116
Schumann Resonance Climbing . . . . . . . . . . . . . . . . . . 117

Magnetic-Field Measurements by Instruments Calibrated for 3.0 (not 3.458) Earth . . . 118
Wants: Unfulfilled Needs . . . 119
The Bible Code . . . 120
Serving the Essential Heart, Not the Expendable Mind . . . 120

17 • Hacker, an SSG Dupe, Causes Titan 4 Rocket Explosion 123
*Zoosh—August 13, 1998*
How Hackers Are Duped by the SSG . . . 126
Plutonium on Board the Rocket . . . 129
U.S. Embassy Bombings in Africa . . . 131

18 • Cowboy Diplomacy Not the Answer . . . 133
*Zoosh—August 20, 1998*
Afghanistan Bombing Regrettable . . . 133
International Terrorism and the U.N. . . . 135
The American Revolution . . . 136
Whitley Strieber's Visitor . . . 137

19 • U.S. Should Be No. 1 Ally of the United Nations . . . 141
*Zoosh—August 21, 1998*
Clouds as Messengers . . . 142

20 • Stock Market Flash . . . 143
*Zoosh—September 1, 1998*

21 • Bumping Dimensions Causes Discomfort . . . 145
*Zoosh—September 29, 1998*
The Remedy . . . 146
FLASH! Political Upheaval Part of Process . . . 148
Stepped-up Security Urged . . . 148

22 • Creator Flips the Switch . . . 149
*Zoosh—September 30, 1998*
Women Take on Violence as Men Release It . . . 149
Finally, a Resolution . . . 150

23 • Tunnels under Phoenix and White Light in New England 153
*Zoosh—October 1, 1998*
How to Relieve the Stress . . . 154
President's Behavior Was Self-Destructive . . . 156
Cynicism Makes Us Easier to Control . . . 157
Resistance to Life Lessons . . . 158
Time to Choose . . . 160
Healings through a Comatose Woman . . . 160
Message to New Englanders . . . 161

24 • Soul Mechanism: Weightlessness Equals Death . . . . . 163
*Zoosh—October 29, 1998*
Artificial Gravity Necessary in Space to Tether Soul to Body . . . 164

25 • No Mining! No Drilling! . . . . . . . . . . . . . . . . . . 167
*The Collective Consciousness of All Earth Guides—November 28, 1998*
The Recent Release of Three Organisms . . . . . . . . . . . . 167
Mining, Drilling and Benevolent Magic . . . . . . . . . . 168
*Zoosh—November 28, 1998*
ETs Bury an Enzyme near Europe about A.D. 1300. . . . . . . . . 168
Making Amends by Incarnating Here to Become Guides . . . . . 170
Your Unknown Hazards . . . . . . . . . . . . . . . . . . . . 171
Making "Impossible" Changes through Benevolent Magic . . . . 171
Native People Affected by Another ET Organism
Released from Underground . . . . . . . . . . . . . . . . 172
Mining Companies Need to Use Sensitives/Dowsers. . . . . . . 173
Another ET-Buried Hazard from Ancient Times . . . . . . . . . 174
The Most Hazardous Release of All—This Year in the U.S. . . . . 175
The Only Cure: Benevolent Magic and Mapping the Planet Anew 175
Toxic Dumps on the Moon and Mars . . . . . . . . . . . . . . 177
Recycling . . . . . . . . . . . . . . . . . . . . . . . . . . 178

26 • Need for Control Makes You Vulnerable to SSG . . . . . 179
*Zoosh—October 3, 1997*
An Exercise in Letting Go. . . . . . . . . . . . . . . . . . . 181

27 • A Lesson in Benevolent Magic . . . . . . . . . . . . . . 183
*Zoosh—January 23, 1999*
Hang onto That Smile* . . . . . . . . . . . . . . . . . . . . 185

28 • SSG Manipulations and a Temporary Astral Processing . 187
*Zoosh—January 23, 1999*
SSG Experiment with Benevolent Subliminals . . . . . . . . . . 187
A Bubble in the Astral Veil . . . . . . . . . . . . . . . . . . 188
Hate Anchors You to SSG's Enslaving Radio Wave . . . . . . . . 191
Broadcast from Undetectable Underground Caverns . . . . . . 192

29 • Crop Circles . . . . . . . . . . . . . . . . . . . . . . . 195
*Zoosh—February 26, 1999*
The Wiltshire Oval and Key Codes . . . . . . . . . . . . . . . 196
Walking Inside Depletes Their Energy . . . . . . . . . . . . . 196
Subliminal Messages, Sub-Key Patterns . . . . . . . . . . . . 198
Acceleration in Interacting with Spirit . . . . . . . . . . . . 199
The SSG's Reaction . . . . . . . . . . . . . . . . . . . . . . 200
An Exercise for Looking at Crop Circles . . . . . . . . . . . . 201
Angular Parts of the Pattern. . . . . . . . . . . . . . . . . . 203
New Overflight Problems. . . . . . . . . . . . . . . . . . . . 203
"Grapeshot" . . . . . . . . . . . . . . . . . . . . . . . . . 204
Gathering Crop Seeds and Compensating the Farmer . . . . . . 204
Addendum—March 26, 1999 . . . . . . . . . . . . . . . . . . 205

30 • Reach Out to a New Friend and Global Unity Will Follow . . . . . . . . . . . . . . 209
*Zoosh—April 7, 1999*

31 • Oxygen-Eating Meteoroids . . . . . . . . . . . . . . . . 211
*Zoosh—April 7, 8 and 20, 1999*
Tiny but Dangerous . . . . . . . . . . . . . . . . . . . . . . . . 211
Their Original Purpose . . . . . . . . . . . . . . . . . . . . . . . 212
The Space Coordinates for Detection . . . . . . . . . . . . . . . . 214
A System of Antennas Needed . . . . . . . . . . . . . . . . . . 214
Deploying a Deflector Shield . . . . . . . . . . . . . . . . . . . 215
Techniques Using Creativity . . . . . . . . . . . . . . . . . . . 218
Your Unexpressed Kinetic Energy . . . . . . . . . . . . . . . . 219
Exercise: Using the "Long Touch" to Deflect the Meteoroids. . . 220
More on the Original Purpose of the Meteoroids . . . . . . . . . . 221
The Zetas, Who Are the Receivers . . . . . . . . . . . . . . . . 222
The Sinister Secret Government . . . . . . . . . . . . . . . . . 223

32 • Don't Let the SSG Draw You into a Malevolent Time Line. . . . . . . . . . 225
*Zoosh—April 20, 1999*
Anchored in 1967 and Now Aided by Fear, Fictional or Real . . . 225
The Cumulative Physical Effects of Fear . . . . . . . . . . . . . 226
Transform It with the Heart-Heat and Other Exercises . . . . . . 227
Gold Light, Its Function and Purpose Here. . . . . . . . . . . . . 227
If You're Easily Depressed, You're Being Affected. . . . . . . . . 228
Earth Depletes Her Needed Gold Light by Helping You . . . . . 228
Heart-Heat Exercise with a Group . . . . . . . . . . . . . . . . 229
The SSG's Hiding Place. . . . . . . . . . . . . . . . . . . . . . 229
The Heart-Heat Exercise* . . . . . . . . . . . . . . . . . . . . 230
More Tests on the Way . . . . . . . . . . . . . . . . . . . . . . 231
Emergency: How to Slow or Stop the Rate You're Moving into the Malevolent Time Line . . . . . 232
Your Extra Energy Is to Meet This Challenge . . . . . . . . . . . 233
Your Energy Gift . . . . . . . . . . . . . . . . . . . . . . . . . 234

33 • Kids Will Lead the Movement to Embrace Outcasts . . . 235
*Zoosh—May 1, 1999*

34 • Practicing Shamanic Gestures Near Crop Circles . . . . 239
*Zoosh—May 22, 1999*
Separating the Subgestures When Practicing . . . . . . . . . . . 240
At the Crop Circle . . . . . . . . . . . . . . . . . . . . . . . . 241
Inspired Gestures from the Material Mastery Book . . . . . . . . 243
Artifacts Found in Crop Circles. . . . . . . . . . . . . . . . . . 244
Best Investigated by Experts or Meticulous Record-Keepers . . . 245

35 • Sand as Crystal Libraries . . . . . . . . . . . . . . . . 247
*Zoosh—May 22, 1999*

36 • An Invisible Hand Brings Together China and the U.S. . . 251
*Zoosh—May 22, 1999*

37 • U.S. and China, an Opportunity to "Mine" Feelings . . . 253
*Zoosh—May 25, 1999*
External Prompts Needed to Face Your Fears . . . . . . . . . . . 254
Recognizing the Need for a Global Government . . . . . . . . . 255
Homework: Claiming "the Good Life" . . . . . . . . . . . . . . . 256
Claiming the Good Life* . . . . . . . . . . . . . . . . . . . . . . . 258

38 • August 11: What Happens, What It Means . . . . . . . . 261
*Speaks of Many Truths—July 26, 1999*
Discomforts Bring up New Skills and Strip Away the Unnatural . 261
A Time of Rediscovering the Whole
and What Skills You Were Born With . . . . . . . . . . . . . . 263
Too Much Individuality . . . . . . . . . . . . . . . . . . . . . . . 263
August 11, a Trigger to Discovering New Abilities . . . . . . . . 264
What It Really Means (after 8/11/99) . . . . . . . . . . . . . . . 265
New Jobs Created, New Designs and Technology . . . . . . . . . 268
Social Skills . . . . . . . . . . . . . . . . . . . . . . . . . . . . . 270
A Period of Birth Control . . . . . . . . . . . . . . . . . . . . . . 270
Earth Changes from Digging, Tunneling . . . . . . . . . . . . . . 271

39 • Energy Tips . . . . . . . . . . . . . . . . . . . . . . . . . 273
*Zoosh—Late July1999*

40 • All Humans Are Being Tested Now—
and the Test Is Your Response . . . . . . . . . . . . . . . 275
*Zoosh—April 21, 1999*
The Origin of Thievery . . . . . . . . . . . . . . . . . . . . . . . . 275
You Will Create True Heart to Replace the Stolen Material . . . . 277
Understanding Creator as a Personality . . . . . . . . . . . . . . 278
Thievery . . . . . . . . . . . . . . . . . . . . . . . . . . . . . . . 278
The Afterlife Review . . . . . . . . . . . . . . . . . . . . . . . . . 279
Integrating Life Experience into the Greater Soul . . . . . . . . . 280
"Illusion" from the Viewpoint
of Those Who Haven't Experienced Earth Life . . . . . . . . . 280
Protecting Other Portions of Your Soul . . . . . . . . . . . . . . 281
Why You Need Pain . . . . . . . . . . . . . . . . . . . . . . . . . 283
Transformation Needs Physicality . . . . . . . . . . . . . . . . . 284
Shamanic Ways . . . . . . . . . . . . . . . . . . . . . . . . . . . 285
Beginning Shamanic Practices . . . . . . . . . . . . . . . . . . . 287
The Colorado School Violence . . . . . . . . . . . . . . . . . . . 287
Using Sensitives as Troubleshooters . . . . . . . . . . . . . . . . 289
Use What You Know . . . . . . . . . . . . . . . . . . . . . . . . . 290

41 • Why You're Tired and What to Do About It . . . . . . . 293
*Speaks of Many Truths—September 21, 1999*
Breathe Deeply to Increase Your Energy . . . . . . . . . . . . . . 294

Find Ways to Increase Oxygen . . . . . . . . . . . . . . . . . . . . . . 295
Consult the ETs and the Insects . . . . . . . . . . . . . . . . . . . . 296
Overpopulation . . . . . . . . . . . . . . . . . . . . . . . . . . . . 296
Using Benevolent Magic to Create More Oxygen . . . . . . . . . . 297
Individuality . . . . . . . . . . . . . . . . . . . . . . . . . . . . . . 298
People with Too Much Energy Can Share Some . . . . . . . . . . 299
When Others Suffer, You Are Unsafe . . . . . . . . . . . . . . . . . 300
Regaining the Feeling Connection . . . . . . . . . . . . . . . . . . 301

42 • Asking for Energy . . . . . . . . . . . . . . . . . . . . . 305
*Isis—September 21, 1999*

43 • Theoretical Consequences . . . . . . . . . . . . . . . . 307
*Robert's Vertical Wisdom—September 21, 1999*

44 • Humanity Chooses Species Consciousness . . . . . . . 309
*Zoosh—September 22, 1999*
Species Knowledge . . . . . . . . . . . . . . . . . . . . . . . . . . 309
Science Will Find Its God in the Heart . . . . . . . . . . . . . . . 310
Two Easy Remedies . . . . . . . . . . . . . . . . . . . . . . . . . . 311
Creator School Challenges . . . . . . . . . . . . . . . . . . . . . . 312
The Redistribution of Humans' Energy
Will Force Your Attention to It . . . . . . . . . . . . . . . . . . 314
Apply the Process and Juggle Your Challenges . . . . . . . . . . 315

**For ease in locating, asterisks mark the exercises, which can be copied and framed or mounted for practical use if desired.*

# 1

# Pearls of Wisdom

Zoosh—August 6, 1997*

It is less important by far what happens in the future than what happens in the present. It is *absolutely intended* that you do not know what will happen in the future. For as you practice your techniques for living in the present and discover what is your wisdom, when the unexpected does happen—and it will happen to everyone—you will simply apply your wisdom and move right through it as gently and gracefully as possible, doing the best for yourself and, as a result, doing the best for others. That is ultimately why people are here.

So I say it is better to understand more about who you are, what you can do and why you are here than what is coming. If people actually knew what was coming, they would be prepared and rehearsed like good actors. As a result, they would not apply their wisdom. They would apply their knowledge, and as you know, knowledge is what you have learned from some other place.

Wisdom is the knowledge you apply in your life because it actually works. Never forget that.

✧ ✧ ✧

Most people, when they are frightened, are not looking for permission; they are looking for authority Never forget that. You can give people permission to believe that something else better could happen than what frightens them by simply saying lightly, "Maybe

* From a private research reading

something better could happen." If they want to know what and ask you, then you can make suggestions. If they don't ask, then you will at least have given them permission to consider the possibility that something better could happen. If enough people do this, it might just change the frightening event to something easier to cope with.

✧ ✧ ✧

Zoosh's rule of thumb: If knowledge, information or wisdom of others feels good without interfering with your own freedom of choice, then apply it.

# 2

# The End of the 50-Year Earth/ ET Secrecy Agreement

Zoosh
January 20, 1998

Now a brief commentary on the recent sightings of lights in Phoenix, Arizona. I will reiterate my previous position, which correlates to this sighting. These lights are caused by ground-based vehicles associated with a highly secret project in the military of the United States. I will also say, in reference to those who call the Air Force base and speak to whatever hapless individual is unlucky enough to pick up the phone, that the average personnel has no knowledge whatsoever of this. It is supersecret, and these vehicles will be flying over more cities in the future.

I also wish to say something else. The cities will be mostly in the U.S., but there will be a few flybys over foreign countries if it is felt to be safe. Generally speaking, though, they are not on any military mission, in the sense that it is not exactly a wake-up call, but it's more to get people used to the experience.

There is, then, an arrangement. For a long time insiders within the military and political arenas of stable governments worldwide (certainly the U.S.) have had an arrangement whereby when a certain year came—which was 1998 and beyond—that it would be a good thing if stable governments, utilizing technology provided by extraterrestrials, could begin flying this technology over their own towns and cities in order to get people used to the idea of UFOs as a benevolent phenomenon.

This is not to suggest that a lot of UFOs that have been sighted over other cities and countries and over the ocean are all from ground-based aircraft. But some are, and I use the Phoenix sightings because this is typical example.

### Pacts with ETs in the 1940s

This arrangement between the military and extraterrestrials goes way back. Early in the forties the extraterrestrials made this arrangement with various high-placed individuals, the military and the political establishment of the time. These were relatively stable governments, although they shared some of this with governments that have changed since then, mainly governments and systems that have largely stayed in place, though persons would change. The arrangement was that sharing the technology would ultimately provide a more benevolent technological expression for the peoples of the Earth—meaning that what you are now experiencing as a day-to-day phenomenon of electronics, computers and even biogenetics was to some degree greatly speeded up by this process.

From the extraterrestrial point of view, it was to not only help you along in your motion toward becoming universal citizens, but also to do what they could to help you on Earth to keep from self-destructing before you discovered that you were not alone, that there was lots of help available, to say nothing of friends you haven't met yet (at least most of you haven't), and that there would be available to you a common ground.

Now, it was felt by certain beings (extraterrestrials and their teachers) that it would be best if most of the flybys in the late eighties and now the nineties would be done by them. But they also felt that as time progressed (especially after 1995), it would be useful if you had developed some ships or rebuilt some they lent you to fly some missions yourself, as long as the missions were totally benevolent (they would monitor you, by the way, to make sure they were).

So what we have here in Phoenix, Arizona, in recent days is another one of these flybys. In this latest circumstance the lights were lined up in such a way as to be clearly perceived as individual lights.

***There was some confusion last time: Was it one vehicle or was it many?***

It was the same thing both times: many individual, singular vehicles.

So you are being prepared. Now, I grant you that not all ships that fly through the sky and are manufactured by various secret governmental or military organizations are entirely benevolent. Some are not. But this project I am talking about is benevolent.

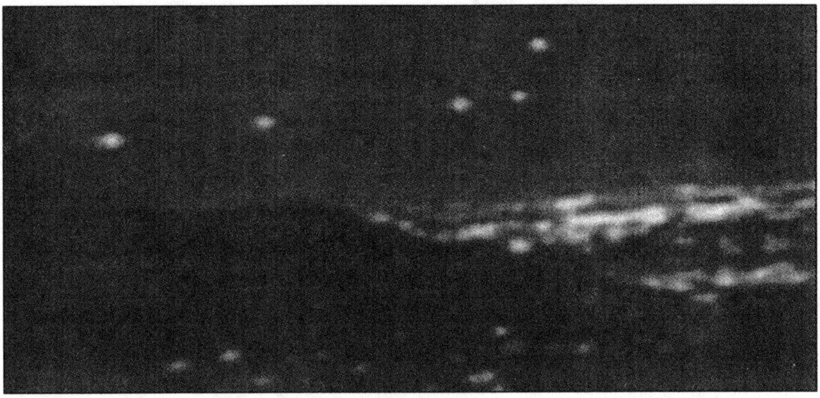

The Phoenix lights.

***Can you describe these vehicles?***

If you were to see them, some are disk-shaped, some are shaped like this [draws upright rectangular shape].

***I saw one of those earlier tonight on The Learning Channel on TV. It looks like a rectangular column.***

Some of them are disk-shaped. Some of them are not quite circular, but roughly have that kind of a context. (When I say disk-shaped, I do not mean a flattened disk, but what is typically referred to as a disk shape and a lot of the so-called ET technologies involved.) The reason they're usually seen at night is that without having the light-gathering instrument activated, the vehicle itself tends to give off light through its skin. This isn't like someone flying around with a searchlight. The vehicle itself tends to radiate the light.

It is possible, of course, to draw that light in with an instrument that is rare but available to some secret establishments. If that is done, it is possible to intentionally mask the vehicle, but that switch is not activated. It is *intended* that the vehicle be seen.

I would also say this to big cities who have helicopter policing and so on: If a helicopter should fly over to where the ships are, it is possible that its instruments could be affected, so give yourself a degree of boundary. Don't fly any closer than three miles if you can help it. That's part of the reason the lights usually appear in places where they are not likely to encounter many airplanes or helicopters.

I mention this as an aside to the occasional pilot and reporters who might be able to use a helicopter: It's probably not safe to get much closer than three miles because of the electrical radiation that would unintentionally interfere with instruments. Three, maybe

### Thank You For Your Help

Some time ago I asked some of you to work on something. I told you that there is a supersecret group of individuals allied to the sinister secret government who were going to utilize vehicles like those I referred to [that appeared over Phoenix in January], to stage a false encounter (not invasion) of individuals who would look like they were not human. This would be malevolent, not benevolent, which is the usual situation for most ETs. This was a distinct possibility, and I asked you to work on this in any way, whether by benevolent magic, meditation or prayers, to uncreate this possibility.

I want to thank those of you as individuals or groups who participated in this, because the potential for this to occur has been greatly reduced. It is still a possibility, so keep working on it, but the potential that this kind of mission will ever see the light of day has been greatly reduced now to about one-half of one percent.

I might add that to some extent another reason that this has decreased in its potential is that the scenario for you all is changing. There continues to be an increase in conscious awareness, especially for those who are prepared to utilize their physical bodies with various exercises that Speaks of Many Truths and myself or Isis and others have passed on, to say nothing of simple rhythmic, graceful exercises taught by many individuals to help you to be consciously spiritual, physically spiritual and spiritual on the feeling level.

three and a half miles, is probably safe.

***How high can these vehicles fly beyond the Earth's orbit?***

If you are talking about going to the Moon, they might have capabilities like that, but in terms of who is going to fly them, they don't have the life support required for such missions, in terms of ground-based ships.

***How many of these ships are there?***

Oh, I should think that at any given time and place, seeing more than seven would be unlikely, though at the outside, even eight or nine. However, seeing three to five is most likely.

***Are the nine available as the total, or do different bases each have nine?***

You have to understand that if these vehicles are seen, they are not coming from a local air base. No, they are not located that way. They are centrally located.

***Okay, in the place where they're based there is a total of possibly nine or ten, and then they go to different cities?***

Well, some of them are being parted out, as it were. At any given time on a good day (as is said in some technological circles) you might get nine up in the air, but five can get into the air pretty much anytime, and a few more are iffy.

***Okay, how much can you say about this? Is it wide open right now, or do you have to be discreet?***

I am being a little discreet. As you notice, I haven't said anything much about this in the past except my rather cryptic referral to the last Phoenix flyby. I am mentioning this to the degree that I can talk about it now. I don't wish to say where they're based. I don't want to say too much about who is onboard. I will just say that it is, for the most part, strictly benevolent and is really intended to gradually bring you to consciousness about extraterrestrials. I might add that as it becomes more common, it will be normal for the press to report it as if it is reporting anything else. It would be said, "Oh, more lights in the sky. How about that?" No negative comments, no laughing up their sleeves.

The whole editorial position of derisiveness about such sightings is becoming very much passé now on the official level, though on the more colloquial or anecdotal level, from person to person, it is still somewhat entrenched.

With all of this going on—to say nothing of your 20th-century communications, which now lets you know when something is not working well for your fellow beings on the other side of the world—it is now possible to consciously as well as unconsciously pray and work for a benevolent outcome of strife that affects all beings.

In time gone by, if you ever found out about your fellow beings suffering on the other side of the world at all, it would be months later, but now, with more instantaneous communications, you find out quickly. When any group of human beings are suffering anywhere on the planet, you all suffer, though in the past you were not so aware of it. You are much more aware of it now because it impacts you individually, usually (in recent time) in the form of chaotic dreams, some on the feeling level and others by thoughts in disarray, where you have a hard time concentrating on anything.

So it's good for you to pray, mediate, chat, sing or do anything you do to bring about benevolence for all beings. What I am saying is that there is a plan. This plan, which is between many beings, teachers, guides and so on—you and also extraterrestrials—is to speed your awakening to remember who you are in the most benevolent way for you, without rushing anybody, so that everybody doesn't have to wake up at once. This one wakes up, that one wakes up and so on—a little bit at a time, not suddenly. No one is trying to shock you here; we want you to wake up gradually—no alarm clocks.

It's going to take time to gradually eliminate the head-in-the sand idea—"it can't be, therefore it isn't." This attitude was promoted for a long time, and it's going to take a little while to eliminate that in this country. It will take less time in other countries because there has been a lot of what I would call official and unofficial propaganda, especially in this country. The conditioning of the average citizen has been very thorough. People in this country have been conditioned for a long time, not with a rigid hand but with an almost overpaternalistic hand. But now this is gradually being removed from you as a steady influence.

### The 1947 Contract

***Are these vehicles totally in the control of an arm of the U.S. military or some benevolent multinational group?***

This is based on a contract that cannot be broken. The contract was originally sealed (I am using that term advisedly for those of you who understand that word) in the late forties. It was between the U.S. and some of its allies' governments and the extraterrestrials, and this contract would last for *x* number of years, basically about 50 years, during which the extraterrestrials would have certain rights to have clandestine contact with citizens of Earth without any interference. For that there would be trade-offs to the various governments. At the end of the contractual time (it wasn't exactly 50 years, but that's a ball-park figure) there would begin to be a public relations experience whereby the governments that could afford it would begin to help wake up the citizenry to the actual fact of extraterrestrials. This would be done as gently as possible. I might add that the insistence that it be done gently was promoted by the extraterrestrials, not Earth-based governments. Extraterrestrials understood that after many years of denial, it would be necessary to make it gentle.

***Were these extraterrestrials Zetas, or were they a group of beings from various ET civilizations?***

More of what I would call a group of beings. Zeta Reticulans were involved, but there were also some Pleiadians, a representative from Andromeda, and Orion representatives. A Council of Sirius was represented through the Orion representative, the Council of Sirius being, loosely, a group of philosophical/scientific individuals. And several of the extraterrestrial star systems were involved.

***Can you say what year the contract was sealed?***

It was officially recognized as a contract in 1947.

***And who signed it for the Americans? Who represented the Americans, Truman?***

I am loath to say who. I would rather not. I would rather say it was three citizens of influence: one a private citizen, one a citizen associated with the military and one a public citizen, meaning in service as a government representative, all of whom represented the United States at the sealing of the contract.

## The Crafts and ET Engineering Help

***The crafts themselves: Are they reverse-engineered, are they gifts? Did we manufacture them?***

I will say a little bit about that because it is an interesting question. Some of the vehicles represent accidents, not shoot-downs. This whole idea that vehicles were shot down—this is not so much the case. I'll grant that a couple of vehicles were shot down, but it was because of what I would call a lack of communication. You know, if someone's communicating on one band and you are communicating on another and you can't reach each other, there are going to be mistakes like that. The ETs recognized that it was a mistake.

A lot of the vehicles were knocked out of the sky because of your experimenting with radar and other such reflective electrical instrumentality, which in the beginning used huge amounts of energy. The tools were not as refined then and people didn't know they could use less energy. This created fields that were disruptive, not unlike what I mentioned before—where if you fly a helicopter into a massive electrical field, it's going to mess up your instruments even if they are shielded.

That's what happened then. But then there was one gift, what I would call a rudimentary craft (it could do this but not that) and there was also some assistance to you. Some parts and assistance were provided to help you rebuild ships. In a couple of cases the assistance was provided as long as the citizens inside the ships were returned—and they were. It's true that sometimes citizens were held, but in these cases the citizens were returned. Alive or dead, they were returned.

Then there was help. A representative would come and tell you (physically), "This goes here" and why and "That goes there" and why. Sometimes they wouldn't answer a question, and that would be that. At other times they might help. Let's say you are the ground technician and you have these bits and pieces and don't know where they go, or you don't know what the circuitry (if I can call it that) will do once you assemble it. You are a little shy about assembling it, not knowing what it will do, which is reasonable because sometimes this "circuitry" has more than one way to be assembled. If it is assembled one way, it will self-destruct the vehicle, not unlike switches. If it is assembled another way, it will be very useful in transporting this or that. If it is assembled still another way, it might be a weapon. What would be given is the way to assemble it, for instance, whereby you could use it as a device to transport something; you could use a field effect to move a heavy object from one place to another.

That kind of help was granted, and it was always done in such a way as to teach the technician something on a spiritual level as well as a mechanical level. We are not talking about only mechanical guidance here.

***On The Learning Channel's program "Alien Secrets: Area 51," I just watched a man who's probably in his seventies saying that for sixteen years he worked alongside a Zeta who assisted him and others in modifying these vehicles for humans. Whenever he had a question, the Zeta would already know it and would answer in his mind. He said he had been permitted to come out and say this on this television show by his employers. You are confirming exactly what was on television tonight.***

### Trial Balloons in the Educational TV/Press

I would say that it's a worthy thing that it is coming out. You see, it's coming out on legitimate stations. I don't want to say that some television programs are only sensationalist, but some are a little more tabloid than others. Now you have programs on what is basically educational television, which is perhaps a little more legitimized in the eyes of the average viewer, and this is important.

So you won't think I am heaping scorn on so-called tabloid television, sometimes tabloid television and newspapers perform valuable functions by putting out stories that would not get into the conventional press and into the public eye. Sometimes it is speculation presented as fact, but at other times it is actual eyewitness testimony.

Now this information is beginning to move from that trial-balloon position into the more educational press, and it will continue from there.

It is really not such a big move to say that something is benevolent. You just have to understand that ships from other planets might be very benevolent with benevolent people in them. The ships that are not benevolent (which are very few indeed) are held at bay these days. They can't get to you, they won't get to you; it's not possible. By the time you have ships of your own and you can get to them, those individuals will be benevolent.

Everything is on track so that when you meet people they will be benevolent and will be looking forward to meeting you. I am saying this largely for those of you out there who are convinced that some ships are dangerous with dangerous beings on board. The greatest danger, as you have discovered in your own personal history on this planet, is ignorance.

***It's been a couple of years, but the last time you discussed this the secret government had technology that kept all ET ships away from the planet. Have the ETs gotten around that? Are ships able to come and go more freely?***

The spectrum of light in which they were approaching your solar system has been modified to a different wave. That's all I want to say because the SSG can hear me too, you know. It is a different wave that I do not think is possible to block. I am not going to give the formula, for obvious reasons, nor am I going to give any hints about the method, but the method is now in place so that extraterrestrial ships can come here only if they need to be here and if it is acceptable for you people on Earth to have them near. Those are the main qualifiers, though there are a couple of others. They can be here now, which is why you are getting more sightings and why there's press about it. It's becoming a regular thing and more people are realizing that it's a real thing. I might add, it's nothing to be afraid of. As a matter of fact, it's a great adventure. It will be a lot of fun for most of you, and it's not too far down the road where extraterrestrials will be introduced to you on television and they will be benevolent beings.

***Can you say more about a "need to be here"? Give me some examples.***

## ET-Scientist Collaboration on an Asteroid Deflector

Well, if the extraterrestrials have a need to be here, it will usually be because they are working with someone or a group of individuals, perhaps philosophers or scientists (which are the usual groups ETs work with) on some project of benevolence that will help others on Earth or perhaps even have applications on other planets. If there needs to be a face-to-face conference or if equipment needs to be brought to assist these philosophical scientists, that might be a situation where the individuals from extraterrestrial heritage would have a need to be here.

There is only so much you can say from afar. Sometimes you need to be in the same room working together. And equally, if there is a need on Earth for those people to be here, then that would be allowed, provided the other qualifiers are met.

***Can you say what scientific projects the extraterrestrials are working on with American scientists?***

I will give only one example. Some of them I would rather not talk about, but they are all benevolent. The one example that is perhaps most useful, especially in construction projects, to say nothing of the defense of Earth—the defense in this case not meaning against other people but against physical phenomena such as meteors and so on—would be that they are working with some scientists to help create something that can function as a long-range, mildly deflective system. I am not talking about shooting an atomic bomb out into space, hoping to nudge the orbit of some approaching asteroid, but rather something that does not damage the asteroid *or* Earth but deflects the asteroid away from Earth—not toward the Sun or anything—into a more benevolent orbit, meaning that the mathematics involved can aim this device, similar to a laser (which is basically collated or compressed light), which will use what I would call compressed electricity. You now understand electrical or magnetic fields—iron filings around a magnet, field effects.

This is something that does the same thing with an electrical field effect as you are now doing by collating light. In any event, if you are going to deflect an asteroid, you have to make darn sure that you are not deflecting toward Mars or Saturn, so you have to know the position of the other planets. Your scientists are being given the coordinates of deflection as well as being shown how to use this instrument. Certain things will be built into the instrument so it cannot be used as a weapon, though it might be useful in construction projects with some adaptation.

***You mean for drilling or digging or blasting?***

Possibly, but not blasting, perhaps. Right now you have the capacity to dig all you need to dig, but one capacity you don't have in construction that you would like to have is more finesse, meaning just a little bit of digging, just a precise amount of removal, not a huge amount, then restructuring things. For instance, you could set footings for buildings very gently; it would be more gentle on the Earth and also a lot cheaper.

***This is a major step toward human maturity, because machinery had been set up on Mars to deflect asteroids from Earth, but the Montauk time travelers took it out because they thought it was a weapon. Afterward, the ETs were doing it from their craft around the Earth. So now they are teaching us how to do it. This is a major step, isn't it?***

Yes. It's a major step because it's necessary now to begin working with people to do these benevolent things. You can't always have the timing for all things readily available. One of the big issues for people on Earth is dependency. It's not based entirely on the world's religions, but also on the simple fact that when a child is born, it is basically helpless and needs to be taken care of and/or rescued (depending upon your point of view) by the adults around it.

When that child grows up it will often, in moments of desperation when it cannot be self-reliant and do something for itself, need assistance or perhaps rescue. So when Earth people are fully cognizant of extraterrestrials (that's in the future), it might be simple for an extraterrestrial ship to fly by and deflect an asteroid. But right now, since that cognizance has not occurred and is not benevolently accepted yet on a worldwide basis, tools need to be available to some right-thinking, benevolent philosopher-scientist types who do not have a desire to keep technology. They are not going to withhold the use of the instrument when they have it (they don't have it yet) just because the media will slam into what at that time will be considered enemy soil. They need to have the aspect of philosophical scientists.

The timing, then, is important. The instrument will be needed before the full conscious acceptance of extraterrestrials. The potential for an asteroid strike is not 100%, but the potential for even a close pass *is* there during the next ten years.

So the instrument will be needed, and it would be better if the instrument were "fired" at the asteroid (as it will be termed in the beginning, although it is not a gun), though some will say activated. It might be necessary to use that instrument sometime within the next ten years before the full cognizance and comfort between Earth people and extraterrestrials is widely recognized.

Now, as you are becoming more conscious and remembering more of who you are, it is much better for you to do it for yourself even with the assistance of extraterrestrials who are based very closely. If you examine the Pleiades' system for teaching their children (I am not suggesting that you are children of the Pleiades; I am just comparing it), it is closely based on an educational system whereby the youngsters are taught to do it for themselves. You are not considered children here, but to be at the point where it is better that you be taught to do it yourself even if you don't have complete understanding of how the instrument works.

You have to have some understanding of how it works, but once the first instrument is built, it will probably be on a mobile platform. If necessary, it can be moved to places where it might be needed. Because the Earth orbits, most likely a move will not be necessary, but it's possible.

## SSG's Success: Pitting People Against Each Other

***The problem now of the secret government attempting to usurp it: Can they use***

***it for their own advantage?***

No. It's not much of problem now because the sinister secret government is more caught up in what they consider their most successful project. This, as I have mentioned before, is keeping the races and nationalities fighting each other strictly because another person is the nationality race, tribe, or gang member that they have some dispute with.

The sinister secret government is so thrilled (though they are not exclusively involved in keeping this going) at the success of this that they're pouring most of their effort into it. Their whole point of view is to keep you suspicious and distrustful of each other and at the same time urge what they see as controlled violence, which simply means that you don't have atomic bombs. (They don't want you blowing up property, at least not massively. They don't want you to blow up anything that can't be rebuilt.) With that level of controlled violence, they are so happy that it's working out well that they don't see much need to engage in any great conflict with what is basically a benevolent project.

If extraterrestrials were coming here en masse and saying, "Here we are; we're your friends" and landing all over the world at the same time, they would be working like crazy to stage fake alien arrivals with fake aliens who are destructive so that you would be distrustful of all extraterrestrials. But since the extraterrestrial projects are very low-key, they do not see any need to confront them.

## Area 51 Obsolete

***How much can you say now about Area 51? It seems, with all the publicity about it, that possibly it's part of this 50-year opening up and giving out information.***

Let's put it like this: Let's say you have a secret military base and have lots of things there you'd like people not to know anything about. You'd like to keep things secret, but then everybody and his brother discovers that things of interest are going on there and people are flocking to hillsides using the best optics they could get their hands to observe that base. What might your reaction be? The initial reaction would be to expand your perimeter and the second reaction would be to move everything.

***That's why I'm asking. I'm beginning to think the reason there's so much publicity is that the base is passé. They used to use it, but now they have a new place for their really supersecret stuff. They are letting us play with Area 51 so that we don't start looking for the real base.***

Of course. But that's all right. I am going to say something now that is a bit controversial, but I have no qualms with their moving secret stuff they want to keep hidden to a place where it will be secret. I have no qualms with that because most of what was developed there in terms of fighter jets and so on, which you know about, is complete and are now at other bases. What's left to be developed, ships and so on that have been experimental toys, are largely not there anymore.

***So it's just a big show they are putting on to keep people busy. They deny it so that people will look harder and not realize that Area 51 is a red herring?***

No, no. No, no. You must understand something about the military—and this is universal on Earth. Even if you are a lieutenant or a captain, you know only as much as you need to know. In the military it means that if the guard at the gate of any base denies that something is going on there: (a) the guard has been ordered to say that; (b) that guard doesn't need to know what's going on there in order to be a good guard; and (c) they are doing their job being a good guard to keep unauthorized people away and allow only authorized people in.

When the military or the government says, "No comment," it is no different. You could go to any base—a base where nuclear technology is stored, for instance, or where the next version of a rocket or some kind of defensive or offensive weapon is being built, and you would get the same comments. This is just normal military procedure.

***It's not normal to Area 51. They shoot people there.***

Let's just say this: Any military base that is a supersecret military base is the same, no different.

***But you just said that it's in the past, yet they . . .***

Yes, they still have things going on there. You have to understand that (I can say this now) most of that base is underground. Lots of other military bases around the world are underground, not only in the U.S. It was real clear to a lot of governments years ago that if they want to protect their people and their stuff, one of the best ways to do it is to put it underground. That's becoming much more common. I might add that corporations are getting the idea, too. That's the wave of the future for banks and, generally speaking, for vaults, records and so on. You can control the environment much better down there. That's a security perception.

## Bob Lazar

***Was Lazar told to talk? He's still alive, you know. Was he given a story and told to talk as part of letting the people know? They kill them for a lot less, but***

***he's still alive.***

Let's just say that he was part of the ongoing trial balloons, but he was not told to do it. Mostly people were just going to wait and see who was going to talk first. If too much was said or if someone didn't like what was said, then maybe his credibility would be damaged slightly, but if he just said, "You will have to take my word for it," then it was a trial balloon.

It would be one thing if he came out and said, "I was the base commander and I can prove it." Then someone would have to come by with a gag and say, "Come back with us." But here's a man for whom there was deniability if it became necessary. Largely it was not necessary other than the official "no comment" or "absolutely not so, it didn't happen." But people have heard this so much these days that now average American citizens, when they hear that from the government, takes it with a grain of salt. It's almost considered governmentese, as the way people talk, but not necessarily true. To some extent people can accept it as even being perhaps necessary at the moment, if not annoying.

Certainly in other countries it's completely understood to be the way things are, if not necessarily the way people would like it to be.

## Follow-up on the Xpotaz and the SSG

***The SR-71 looks like the Xpotaz ships. Is there a relationship there?***

No.

***The Xpotaz are totally gone, nothing remaining, ships all gone?***

All gone.

***The time-travel ship is gone?***

Not present.

***Gone with the secret government people or gone with Xpotaz people?***

Not present in this time line.

***I know, but who's in control of it? The one the Xpotaz gave to the secret government, it went someplace and got stuck, didn't it?***

Yes. It went someplace and there it is.

***They tried to escape.***

Well, they went forward, and there they are. It's kind of like you go fishing, you drop your anchor and something happens to the anchor. It's not such a terrible loss, but it's gone. You pull the rope or chain up and there's no anchor. They need to get a new anchor, that's all.

***But none of the 13 of the inner circle went with the ship, did they?***

## MIB Says ET Info Being Dribbled out to Prepare for Major Secrets to be Revealed in 1998

### Art Bell Show Call-in for Area 51 Workers

September 11/12, 1998

***Art Bell: I've interviewed Bob Lazar, and he claims that there have been any number of saucers—actual saucers, recovered saucers, back-engineered—that he was part of that they were flown out of S4. Can you confirm his story, for starters?***

Caller: Yes. It happened at some point before he was even there. There were occasions, but they were not meant to be flown in the air. What you're seeing in the air is not coming from Area 51. Those things up there [Area 51] are broken. And the ones that he saw sitting there probably were in various states of disrepair, in my opinon. They were like junk. Everybody's got junk. But if you've got junk like that, you're not going to take it to a landing field. You've got to just leave it sitting there.

***When you say "junk," we should qualify that. Extraterrestrial junk?***

What would you call extraterrestrial?

***Something not of Earth origin.***

Would Earth in a parallel time line do?

***In my mind it would. In other words, it's certainly in the realm of the paranormal. So what you're telling me is that what's up there came not from another physical place, but rather another dimension parallel to ours?***

Yes and no. It's both. The triangular objects were hand-me-downs that were no longer needed. They were given to the people in the other time line, who then turned against the people that originally gave [the objects] to them.

***You're saying you were ordered to come and say all this tonight? Why?***

Yes. Because yesterday was September 11 on your time, the day that the Mars Surveyor enters the orbital phase of its mission. They have fired the slowing rockets and I understand they have done that successfully, they believe. This craft will go into a polar orbit around Mars, slowly mapping the entire planet. It will be finished in March 1998.

I already know what they're going to find. As they come down from the pole, at first they're going to be mapping an area that originally had a lot of water. What would you see if you drained the ocean? A lot of dried-up areas.

***Silt—that kind of thing.***

Yeah, but it's all solid rock, obviously, baked by the sun. When you get down to latitude—you know, about 40 degrees north of the Martian equator—you're going to see some pretty interesting things, actually.

***Like what? The Cydonia region?***

The Cydonia region has a counterpart region, and they're going to find that this time. Now, when you speak of Cydonia, you speak of the face on Mars and the city and rail launcher and all that. The rail launcher is the most interesting to me.

***Rail launcher—that's a gun.***

No, no, no. The rail launcher is a shuttle-type vehicle that was abandoned. And it's sitting on this rail inside a fortress.

***Why would your bosses want this information out?***

Because of what's about to happen next year. There's going to be some major, extreme revelations next year, and everything's got to be in place before that happens. Meanwhile pressure is building (by pressure I mean orders) to throw it all out on the table right now. And I'm one that doesn't think it's appropriate at this time. I'm all for the '98 thing.

***So you're sort of dribbling information out to get people prepared?***

Yes. But my greatest concern is, they won't be prepared enough. I'm troubled by what's happening.

***What's going to happen in 1998?***

Well, first of all, more of the same—more dribbling, as you call it, for starters. But of course you mean the main material. That will take place on . . . let's see what date that would be. (I've got a book* over here that's got it all laid out, if you don't mind me getting it here.) Yup, I've got it—July 20, 1998.

In 1998 on that date everything's going to be revealed about what happened July 20 to July 26, 1986, and how that relates to what is going on right now with the Mars material.

***What occurred then, please?***

The culmination of the original plan. We are currently in the twelfth year of the new plan.

***Whose plan?***

The Supreme Commandant. Sound familiar? That should be ringing some bells (no pun intended, thank you). This is September 11. Do you recall a certain caller who might have called you on Saturday morning, August 9, during the night you [had] the so-called MIB line?

***Yes. As a matter of fact, during the course of this very conversation we're having right now, I'm wondering why the Men in Black aren't moving in on you.***

They can't because I tell *them* what to do. Unfortunately for me, I've occasionally learned the hard way since I last talked to you. I did call you on that morning. I don't know if you recall or not.

***These beings . . . are they as we are, or are they different? Do they look to be extraterrestrial in origin?***

This is hard to explain, but

there's two levels. One level is: if you knew what to look for, yes, you could tell the difference easily. But if you said, "Oh well, so and so" and you just passed him, you'd never know.

***So ETs could be wandering around in our streets now and we'd never . . .***

Well, you know, there are a few more than there used to be. Let's say you had a best-case scenario. You had them hypnotized, sodium pentathol, reversed speech—everything—and you got everything out of that. You would never find out who was giving them the orders (it's not me, by the way) because they're getting programmed from a planet in this time line in space.

***Why are you revealing all of this now?***

Because the amount of material that's going to be revealed next year would be unintelligible unless this was here first.

*Presumably "the Yellow Book," mentioned by Bill Cooper in *Behold a Pale Horse*.

No, no. Generally, none of the inner circle ever goes anywhere on such experiments.

***It's just that the toy was taken out of their hands so they couldn't do more mischief.***

Correct.

***You can't say where the new base is, of course?***

I won't say.

## Underground Bases, New Uses

***And there's nothing left here in Sedona? The base is gone. The aliens are gone.***

There is nothing permanent in Sedona. But Sedona, not unlike a lot of other places, has tunnels underneath it and things come and go. I might add in general that under the surface there are a lot of places where permanent things don't exist: there might be facilities available, but they are not permanently manned. They could be started up again if necessary, but there's nothing really going on in what I would call permanent outpost bases. Things come and go, though, not unlike on the roads. Trucks, vehicles, come and go and might stop for a while, but then they go on.

***Is the base functional at Secret Mountain?***

It's functional. It has a few people there just to make sure that things run smoothly, but they are not doing much. They don't have to do much.

***In the years ahead as we mature, will we be able to use those bases for some be-***

***nevolent purpose, all this incredible technology underground that belonged to the secret government?***

Oh, sure, but you will have to transform a lot of this stuff. There's a lot of redundant technology there. There are lots of places with technology designed for defensive and, if necessary, offensive purposes that you won't need, but there's a lot of space there for living. You would be able to house huge numbers of people underground, and that might be considered a good idea by some.

## Population Transfers

***Why? Who would want to live underground?***

Oh, you would be surprised. It's not at all uncommon on many planets.

***You can't see the stars and the Sun?***

You just make some kind of facility so that you could. You might be underground at times and on the surface at other times. But it depends largely upon how amiable the planet is to a massive population. At some point in your future you will have to transfer a lot of your population. This doesn't mean plagues and catastrophes, but it does mean that you will get to the point where you can transfer population to places where they want to go.

***Are these underground or off-planet?***

Off-planet. A lot of people will want to do that, and it's possible. At some point there will probably be a short-lived attempt at rigid birth control. I don't mean forced sterilization, but there will be government regulations.

For instance, right now tax laws are more open-hearted; you are given a tax deduction for each child. That's the government's way of supporting you as parents of children, but in the future that could shift for a short time. People who are single or in relationships that do not produce children will probably get some kind of bonus.

This is actually a fixture in some place right now, such as China, though not perhaps with tax laws. There is (at least at this time) a fairly rigid position about how many offspring you can have in China because they have more people than they can take care of, and they want their people to have a higher standard of living. So although their system is not the most benevolent, they do have a benevolent goals.

You might run across that at some point in the future. It might be perceived by some as being unkind or heartless, but in the long run some kind of change will be necessary. Otherwise, what usually occurs when there is overpopulation on any planet is that the men and women gradually become sterile. You know, you are made up physically of Mother Earth's body. Creations can be studied scientifically, but *creations are not science*—that's the interesting thing about it. That's a very important statement.

So the body of a human being can be studied with great scientific precision, but that does not mean that science had anything to do with its creation. What had to do with its creation was a benevolent personality in the form of many beings, spirits, guides—loving beings, not the least of which is Mother Earth.

If Mother Earth says, "Enough!" then the simplest way to stop the population explosion is for people to become sterile.

***You said in* Explorer Race: Origins and the Next 50 Years, *that an increase in homosexuality in both sexes and a drop in sperm count were some of the things that could happen.***

Yes, it's still likely. Part of the reason for the increase in homosexuality, though, is the gradual realization that if people truly love each other, there should be no boundaries to that love. It's still a likely scenario that a decrease in sperm count is possible if your population gets up to around 10 billion (which is possible sooner than you think). If it does, remember, it's not permanent, but it might mean that you will have very limited births for 15, 20, 25, but probably not 35 years.

***It would balance it out.***

That's right. It would balance it out. As I've said before, it would cause everybody to suddenly realize how valuable and treasured children are. And when children show up again on a regular basis, they'll be treasured as they ought to be.

## The Ground-Based Crafts to Be Openly Used in 15 Years

***Shifting gears a little bit, those nine or ten craft that were given to us or that we acquired—there must be things we can do with them that are valuable and useful to the planet.***

Oh, yes.

***How long before we can use them for other than lights in the sky?***

You mean, how long until you can use them openly?

***Openly, yes.***

Oh, I think maybe fifteen years.

***What would we use them for? How would we use them?***

Probably initially in construction projects. They would be used, of course, by a lot of people for study, for educational purposes.

***How would you use a ship on a construction site? Haul stuff on top of a moun-***

***tain or something?***

Oh, to move something. You might, for instance, have a building. Maybe you would have a building about one-quarter the size of the Empire State Building. An extraterrestrial ship could move that building easily just by itself, but three or four of those ships could, when flying in a stabilized pattern (moving forward from a given position) lift that building and transfer it from point A to point B without breaking a window.

***You could prefabricate skyscrapers?***

That's right, and you could move things about with great ease. In places where it's very difficult to build something and remove materials, such as in the middle of desert, you could prefabricate huge things, move them there, sit them down and within a very short time (a month or two) basically have a city in the middle of the desert ready to be occupied by massive amounts of people with everything needed to sustain them.

It will be very exciting to see this happen. It will be wonderful. There will be lots of benevolent ways like that, to say nothing of taking teachers and their students up for rides, showing to an extent how it works. It will be like a youngster getting a ride in a spacecraft of today from the Earth. It won't be that common, but it will happen, then it will be broadcast.

## Future Mars and Moon Bases

***What about the proper life support? Are they going to have these on Mars and the Moon?***

The Moon will probably come first because it's closer. I think the colonization of Mars is guaranteed. To a large extent it's because—this is really important—you could go there now with life support. There are lots of places where you could land on Mars and walk around, and you would swear, aside from the equipment you were wearing, just by what you were seeing that you were someplace on Earth. It is very Earth-like in a lot of ways and you will feel in a lot of ways very much at home there.

So you will go to the Moon first, then there will be a real desire to put up lots of bases and cities and whatnot on Mars. That's where some of your population will want to go. There will be a lot of things going on in their initial projects: mining, yes.

Of course, the archaeological projects on Mars will be thrilling, so there will be lots of treks there by archaeologists and scientists and philosophers and so on. They'll find lots of goodies.

***Somebody called in on the Art Bell Show, and it was as if the caller was reading***

***out of the Yellow Book. He said that when the Mars Surveyor landed on Mars, it would map from a polar orbit, first mapping an area that originally had a lot of water, like a drained ocean—dried-up areas, that are now solid rock baked by the Sun. When it gets to about 40 degrees north of the Martian equator, it will see some pretty interesting things: a counterpart to the Cydonia region. Can you talk about that?***

They are not going to find cities, if that's what you are asking about.

***They will just find something interesting?***

In terms of archaeological finds, there's no question about that—the face on Mars at Cydonia and all that business. There's a lot of stuff like that there, but you have to understand that there's stuff like that here on Earth. Sometimes beyond the pale of the most ardent believer in coincidence, there are rocks that look like things here—and there, too. Most of them were carved initially, not by the wind but by beings.

So yes, there will be things like that found, but I don't really want to go into that too much because I would spoil the discovery, and it's going to be thrilling. On the other hand, I will say this as a blanket statement: When these things are discovered, the people of Earth will learn that not only are you not alone (which is going to be fully understood then), but you will know more about what other human beings have been doing. The people who used to live on Mars looked a lot like you, like human beings. That's why there are human faces there, and when things are discovered there it's going to look like, "Hey, these are people!" So a lot of what's going to be discovered are archaeological finds similar to those on Earth, and it's just going to be terrific.

***Is what he says correct, that the Surveyor will find more pictures?***

Is he talking about the Surveyor satellite?

***Yes. On September 11 they fired the rockets to slow down.***

Well, it might be found by that satellite. Most of what is found will be found by people who are there physically. In terms of what satellites will see, that is always open to interpretation simply because of the current limits of technology. More countries will begin to send satellites in that general direction. Before, it used to be the Soviet Union, but now I think a real player is Japan. Japan is likely to rush pell-mell to get people on the planet.

***So different countries will try to claim parts of the planet?***

Not claim so much; Japan is not strictly a greedy capitalist nation. There's genuine interest in Japan in what's going on on other planets and how that relates to us. Yes, they might want to do some mining and drilling and all that, but they also want to explore and see what's going on. So let's not make the Japanese out to be solely crassly commercial.

***I meant that all the countries might stage a gold rush.***

No, it's not going to be like that. You have to remember the correlation of events of Earth. History is not isolated. The main political thing that's going on now on Earth is the global economic situation. By the time things really get going on Mars, the global economic order . . .

***There won't be companies trying to . . .***

That's right. Now you have international conglomerates that on the one hand are a little annoying, but on the other hand are creating an initial world order. By the time that gets going . . .

***. . . you've multinational corporations staking out . . .***

Yes, you will have multinational corporations and then governments, but eventually that will get itself worked out. You are not going to take your shooting wars up there. Right now it looks like you are, but I don't think that will be much of a factor. There might be some mild degree of it, but I think that then the seat of the world government, which will probably be somewhere in The Netherlands, will put its foot down and say, "If you expect to use Earth as a base of your operations, you are not going to be able to do that and go up there and go bang, bang."

## The Global Government

They will have the final say-so. The people in this country will be comfortable with that because it will be crystal clear after a very short time that the seat of the world government in The Netherlands is genuinely fair.

It will take a little while, but when the Earth people see that it is fair and that compromises are worked out to create the best situation for as many people as possible, then such statements that are put out will be respected.

***Without revealing all the secrets, do you see this world government in The Netherlands in five years, ten years, twenty-five years?***

You know, the foundation for it right now is economics: the GATT treaty. Of course, there have been other world events—The Hague, for instance. So the foundations are sturdily in place. I would say that it's just building on what was there before; I don't want to say it's going to happen at such-and-such a time—it's happening now.

***Is the peace-avatar president who was taken to another time line going to be involved in the global government in The Hague?***

Probably not, because we need to have world figures, not just single-government figures. Eventually, you understand, you will have a planetary philosophical order . . . "order" is not the right word; "establishment" might be a better term . . . whereby everybody is treated as benevolently as everybody else.

## Nations with the 50-Year Agreements

***The nations that participated in this roughly 50-year agreement I will assume were Russia, the United States, England and, as you said, the major stable governments?***

There were separate agreements, really. Some governments did not know other governments were involved. For instance, the U.S. did not know that Russia had its own agreement (I am referring to post-World War II Soviet Union). There was an agreement with them also, even though it was understood that the government was not quite as stable as, say, England, France or even the U.S., but there was enough stability through the more rugged times to come that it was perceived as of value. I might add that some of the contracts were not even with government individuals.

For instance (and I am not going to name the people), there were certain august bodies at educational institutions. In other countries the government was unstable, but the educational institutions were stable.

***Can you say what country?***

I will mention a few of them: Brazil, Chile, what at that time was becoming South Africa, Egypt, Portugal. I think that's all I will say for now. Although the governments in some of these places might have been more stable and in some less stable, they did have stable institutions. Contracts were formed that would give and receive acceptable exchanges in various ways. In some cases meetings were held with representatives of these educational institutions in a very casual way: "Drive out on the highway and we will meet you and talk about things, then we'll shake on it" (to put in the common U.S. vernacular). It went deeper than that, but that's how I'm going to put it at this moment.

In that way the agreement was more universal. This was also the situation in some countries where the educational institutions and the governments were so entwined that those governments were considered stable.

I'll give one example in that case: India. India is as stable as it is because of its educational institutions and its deep-rooted beliefs and philosophies. They do have variety, but variety does have certain commonalities. It was possible to establish meetings on a person-to-person basis—not with Zetas, but with beings who looked more like Earth people.

## Japan

***Well, what about Japan? They obviously had an agreement because they've got so much technology. They were so far ahead of us—was that ET technology or just their own?***

Check out the history of technology and you will find that Japan has a wonderful capacity for seeing what is good on the horizon and doing as much with as little as possible. This is not to say that they don't invent and create lots of things now, but in the past they were not so involved in inventing as in applying.

No, Japan was not consulted at that time because of the wounds they had suffered that were still in many ways apocalyptic. People in the United States especially today still do not grasp the apocalyptic impact on Japan of the personal experience of the nuclear bombs. The Japanese culture is not over that even today. I grant that the Japanese culture and military establishment of the time caused a great deal of suffering in the world, but let us just put it this way: They were paid back much more than what they did, and those who suffered were mainly noncombatants. When soldiers suffer, I do not say that this is good, but it is understood by the soldier. But when civilians suffer, this is not so good. I do not single out Japan as the only sufferer. Many suffered, but not everyone experienced the atomic suffering. So Japan was not excluded; they were just left to heal.

However, in later years there were attempts to reach out to them. Certainly there were benevolent ETs working with the Japanese people in other ways, but I will say more about that some other time.

***It wasn't just Majestic 12; it was the 50-year agreement, right? The whole world, all the Earth governments, had to keep a lid on this.***

I am not saying Majestic 12 wasn't real, but Majestic 12 and the information of its existence and all that was part of the trial balloon to let people know that UFOs are real.

***But the basic reason that they kept it secret was the 50-year agreement?***

Yes, the agreement was "you do this for me and I will do that for you," as in any agreement.

# 3

# Don't Use Water for Fuel, or Earth Will Look Like Mars!

Zoosh
March 1998

All right, Zoosh speaking. Once upon a time in this solar system there was a beautiful planet here that you now know as Mars. As you approached it from space (as a visitor might approach it) it was clear that there was some kind of water there and a thriving civilization. The civilization, although not overly involved in surface transportation as you are here, did have some vehicles, but they were not powered with the kind of fuel you use here at this time.

However, there were individuals from another culture far away who wanted to use their water for fuel. Those who lived on Mars tried to resist, but they were basically a peaceful lot, so the water was taken from them—not for consuming, but for turning into fuel.

I want to comment that right now there is serious thought by your manufacturers and others to start using water and/or atmosphere (if you would) to convert that into fuel, with the idea that the byproducts would be benign. It seems like a good idea; it seems like you have an inexhaustible supply of water, but you really don't, and with the increase in population it could be a problem.

So I will say this: The one sure-fire way to kill off this planet and most of your civilization is to start looking toward water as the fuel source. That's all I will say about that now. If it becomes a major problem, I will talk more about it later. I have mentioned this before and I am mentioning it now because long-range plans are in place to utilize water for its component parts.

The problem is that especially during a year when many places are getting more water than normal, it seems to be in far greater abundance than it really is. It's also very easy to look at the polar icecaps and say, "Well, we've got that in reserve don't we?" But in reality—think about it—if just cars, to say nothing of space vehicles and some few tools start using water, it can be broken down into its component parts (obviously, hydrogen and oxygen), to make a burnable fuel. If vast amounts of vehicles or machines started using it in the next ten to fifteen years, leading to the point where, say, there were no fewer than two million machines using it, it would threaten the world's water supply.

Think for a moment about cars using it—you can see that. Singly it wouldn't be that much, but cumulatively it would be a lot. Think about how power producers now burning coal or gas or fuel oil would much prefer to burn something like water, which is, for the most part, still free. Imagine them using this substance. Well, it wouldn't be at all difficult to imagine, say in fifteen years, for water to become rationed.

So I would say, forget it and make the jump to electricity produced by solar conversion or by (here's a hint to technological people) by compression. Compression is one of the best ways to produce energy. Right now you think of compression as a functional cycle in the internal combustion engine or, to use an oblique example, as compressing coal into a diamond. But think about compression in general. If you compress, there is a natural tendency of what is being compressed to expand, and that stress can produce an inexhaustible supply of energy.

So, physicists, look into compression as your best future inexhaustible source of energy—and, of course, now solar conversion, which is more readily available.

***No hint about what you want us to compress?***

I can't lay it out on a silver platter, but I want to at least steer you so I can save you. I think compression can save you ten years of folly looking in the wrong directions.

***Wonderful. Thank you very much.***

You are most welcome.

# 4

# Officials Often Ignorant of 50-Year-Old Files*

Edgar Mitchell, Ph.D.

*On January 31, 1971, Navy Captain Edgar Mitchell with Adm. Alan Shepard and Col. Stuart Roosa, embarked on a journey of over 500,000 miles in outer space, that resulted in him becoming the sixth man to walk on the moon, during Apollo 14. This historic journey ended safely nine days later on February 9, 1971.*

*After retiring from the Navy in 1972, Dr. Mitchell founded the Institute of Noetic Sciences to sponsor research into the nature of consciousness as it relates to cosmology and causality.*

*The Prophets Conference was presented last October in Phoenix. The following is an excerpt by Edgar in response to remarks presented by Steven Greer about technology and efforts to brief government officials on the UFO phenomena.*

I'd like to add that in our briefing of the Joint Chiefs of Staff Intelligence Group, it became very clear to us that they were naive. They did not really know any more about this effort than we do, if as much. That is because, as Bob Dean pointed out earlier, most of the people in government were not in government when I retired twenty-five years ago. They are younger people. The files going back fifty years just no longer exist. They've either been purged, compromised or

* This is a transcription of a talk at the October 1997 Prophets Conference in Phoenix, Arizona, printed in the May 1998 *Sedona Journal.*

whatever. They don't exist. So when we blame government for not being forthright, they really don't have anything to be forthright about, at least at that level. Now, somewhere there are knowledgeable people and Steven has ferreted out quite a few of them. In my own efforts in talking with these folks and talking with the government, the question often comes up as to how they could have kept this a secret for so long. And friends, they haven't. It's been around us all the time, but it has been denied and obscured.

I often like to state the condition, the story, the myth if you will, about Columbus coming here and some Indians not seeing the ships simply because it was not in their collective consciousness and their repertoire; at least they didn't *want* to see them. Much of what we're seeing now is what many people don't want to see, either. There's been a massive effort at creating that, of denying the obvious, of saying that you're not seeing what's sitting right in front of you right now, thus causing doubt in your own mind. It's amazingly effective. So, documentation and evidence that is probably the smoking-gun type of evidence has been totally compromised by [their] saying that it's simply not true. Thus it is not true that they (the government) have kept the secret. They haven't kept the secret, but it has been totally compromised by misinformation and disinformation.

Now, for my own experience, I have had no firsthand experience like so many of you. I have not encountered a UFO and we did not have them trailing us as far as we know, going to the moon. We didn't meet anyone on the moon. We did it just like we said we did. For the last twenty-five years we have dealt with the issue of, on one hand, the flat-earthers who said, "You didn't go anywhere, it was all filmed out here in the desert," and on the other hand, another fringe that said, "You have been there, but you were followed. You were in contact with UFOs. There were beings on the moon that you met and had contact with." Well, that's not true, either. So we have walked between these two extremes of misinformation, disinformation and pure ignorance. We did what we said we did, and I want to assure you, from that period up until the current time, NASA was one of the organizations ignorant of this type of activity. And the prevailing wisdom in NASA (at the time) was that we didn't even think about it. It was a ridiculous idea that we would encounter beings on the moon.

However, in the last twenty-five years since that time, I became quite knowledgeable and became friends with Allan . I know and work with Jacques Vallee consistently now, and I have known the gentlemen on this stage, Bob Dean and Steven Greer, for a few years.

For me, with all the evidence, it's not a matter of believing, it's a matter of the preponderance of evidence, and the evidence keeps building. The sightings keep happening. So it is clear that if they are ET—and I will question some of the sightings as to if they *are* ET—they are making their presence known. I also think that the prevalence in the modern era of so many events—the sightings, the continual mutilation events, the so-called abduction events—that we are likely looking at reversed-engineered technology in the hands of humans who are not under government control or any type of high-level control. I find that quite alarming.

With regard to the technology itself, I work with folks who *do* know what is in our technological data base and what is available to modern armies. The so-called ET technology, the ability to have silent engines and flying machines that make no sound, flying machines that have the characteristics that are consistent with reproduction of UFO sightings, are not in any nation's arsenal, but they do exist. So if there are back-engineered technologies existing, they are probably in the hands of this group of individuals—formerly government, formerly perhaps intelligence, formerly under private-sector control, with some sort of oversight by military or by government. But this [oversight] is likely no longer the case as a result of this access-denied category that is now operating. I call it a clandestine group. The technology is not in our military arsenals anywhere in the world, but it does exist and to me that's quite disconcerting.

I do work with a number of groups. We do know about some of the things that the technologies are used for, and I want to assure you that these technologies are not that far beyond our current state of knowledge. Now, understanding it scientifically, understanding how it *can* be, is a long way from having a fully developed, usable technology. But if in our knowledge we can understand how it has to be in order to create that technology, we're not that far away. So I want to assure you that we're not talking about technologies that are so farfetched that we can't understand them. They're just beyond the technological horizon.

I want to tell you that it doesn't appear we need to be using ultra-dimensions and wormholes and so on for this. It looks like our three-dimensional or four-dimensional space-time universe is about what it appears to be, and that we can operate within that space-time universe with these types of technologies. We have tended, like the ancients of old, to have invented myths about too many dimensions and time travel, wormhole travel and so forth, and it doesn't look like that's necessary to explain what we're seeing.

# 5

# SSG Commands "Don't Read!" on U.S. TV Sets Solution: Unplug the TV

Speaks of Many Truths
April 16, 1998

There has been for some time this experience of so-called subliminal messaging on television. In the beginning the messages were suggestions. After a while they became more pointed, but were not demands. Then they became more demanding. In the most recent experiment they are commands.

Those of you who are alert to latent images (something you thought you saw or something that made an impression on you) know it's not a thought, because you can picture whatever is said in black letters in the space of the television screen. You may have noticed these commands. Perhaps the most effective one in the past eighteen months has been "Don't read."

This has become very effective. I would like to suggest some homework for the initiated (the reader) just for fun in order to recapture pleasures that you have forgotten—the pleasure of friends and companionship, the pleasure of fun, of going places and doing things, the pleasure of things you used to do.

Unplug the television. Turning it off is not always sufficient. When it's turned off, it won't give you a visual message, but even when turned off the modern TV set is energized enough to hold what I believe is called a carrier wave that supports these demands and commands. It is a little too technical for me to grasp, but about six hours after unplugging the television there will be a very profound effect.

You will notice that you feel lighter. You will notice that the energy around you feels lighter and you will probably sleep better. You will probably interact better with your friends and family. You will probably have quite a lot of improvement in your life if you have been watching television even one to three hours a day.

### "Don't Read" and "Eat"

The "Don't read" message was perhaps the most effective. It was to some extent a curiosity to see if commands would work. Another command that has been tried, though not at the same time as the other, is "Eat" [laughs].

This was tried off and on, initially as a suggestion, then over the years in different ways. It is still reinforced (a curiosity), being flashed at times when other things, of course, are happening on the screen.

Contrary to the assumption that these messages are flashed only when there is a black screen between this or that, sometimes the messages are flashed during programming so that the message becomes melded on a subconscious level with the programming. For example, there might be something sad on screen and then the message flashed "eat" would connect "when you are sad, eat."

It is not what you would call vicious or cruel, and from what I have seen from more advanced civilizations, even the most spiritually advanced civilizations use this to a degree, though in benevolent ways.

So it is not a monstrous thing. For instance, in military circumstances it has been tried to use the message, "Kill." It hasn't worked. Even though soldiers can be trained to do so, generally speaking, even a person who is deranged cannot usually be prompted to kill by such a message. So the limit of such things has been discovered.

Yet the idea of having commands instead of suggestions or even demands is back again and "Don't read" has been very profound. It has literally stopped people from reading who would normally enjoy the pleasure of a good book or magazine article or even something light and amusing.

So just for fun, especially if you used to read and love it, if you used to have more fun than you are now and if you watch TV a lot or watch more television lately, just for fun turn it off. Unplug it, okay? Leave it unplugged for a week or six days. After two or three days or maybe less, if you notice that you feel better and are having more fun doing some of those things that you missed—maybe you suddenly decide you are going to go bowling after all because you've missed that—then consider leaving it off.

I know it is very entertaining and informative and certainly educational, yet because of these messages, its side effects can be very restrictive, not just stultifying, and in the case of children, even very harmful. So I recommend leaving it unplugged.

## An Ongoing SSG Project

***Who specifically is putting this message "Don't read" on the screens?***

That which is called the sinister secret government (SSG) is involved, but they do not push buttons to make it happen. It is an ongoing project involved in certain distorted renegade aspects of the intelligence community. It started out of good, generally, I believe, as a means to rally support for patriotic causes. But because it had such unexpected impact (it was really not expected to have anything more than the slightest impact) certain things were tried and it was so successful, it has become an ongoing project funded completely with the opportunity to try everything from the most subtle to the most commercial to the most extreme, just to see if it has limits. As I said, they found some limits—"kill," for example, doesn't work.

***What were the patriotic messages, and what were the results?***

Patriotic messages might have been, for instance, that "My country (fill in the name of the country) is always right." That would be a patriotic message.

It is understood that the effectiveness of such a message might be, even in optimum conditions, 80 percent in an individual, meaning that the individual might be more inclined to think that his country is right more often than wrong. So the actual message does not become the thought or attitude, but it *supports* a thought or attitude. It took a while for them to realize that.

In the beginning the methods of observing and drawing conclusions were very rough and coarse. Now it is more closely paid attention to. For example (I won't say which one, because I don't want to cause undue stress or duress), one riot in a large major city of the United States was directly caused by such messages to see if otherwise peaceful people could be turned into a mob and do things that they would otherwise only think about or perhaps fantasize about, but not actually do. Unfortunately, from the perspective of the tester, that was unexpectedly successful because of circumstances.

In other places the message was flashed in communities where things were more benevolent and individual needs were more cared for; for instance, people might have had a higher standard of living. There was nothing, no response. But in communities where people were suffering, where they had given up, where their needs were being ignored and they were being abused, in one case it was the catalyst that started the riot.

***What was the message?***

The message was, "We can always count on them to hurt us."

***Okay, the sinister secret government sponsors this, pays for it, but . . .***

They sponsored it initially and paid for it initially, but now they just support it. They don't really have to put any money into it. It's moving under its own power, meaning that the results are shared in a wider circle, and this generates enough money to continue it. Its results have sold it.

## TV-Set Circuitry Is Used Remotely

***So does this emanate from local broadcasting stations or from networks or from cable? How do they get it? Is it cities-specific, or does it go all over the country?***

You understand I can't really reveal this, but I will exonerate a few people. It is not generated from the broadcasters, network or cable. They don't have any direct participation,

***So how do the renegades get it on there?***

It is not difficult to do this, provided you know how to use the circuitry of the television remotely. It is done remotely, without a direct connection, if the circuitry is used in a way that the circuitry supports, but was not designed for.

***The circuitry of individual television sets?***

Yes, sets. Then it can be done. It can be done, I might add as a warning, in any place, in any country where such sets are sold and used. It is possible to add a small electronic device to make it impossible to do that. But it is an expensive device, and no one making televisions would have any reason to even consider adding such a device. It basically screens and protects the frequencies received and makes it more exclusive. I don't understand it beyond that point.

So obviously in other countries where television sets are bought and sold, this technology *could* be used, though I think that largely it is not. It could be used, and the same people who are doing these things could easily do them in other countries—to keep things in turmoil, perhaps, or create unnecessary restlessness amongst the population with the intention perhaps to support the destabilization of a government that isn't favored in the eyes of those doing this.

***Are you saying that mostly this is being done in the United States now?***

It has always been done mostly in the United States.

***Is it being used at all in any European countries?***

It was occasionally done experimentally, without the cooperation of the government, in Germany, France and once in Italy.

***With spectacular results?***

They don't want me to say.

***Who are "they"?***

Those who allow me to speak and say anything other than what I know personally. I do not know this in my time. I don't know any of this. As a matter of fact, I am not really clear what a television set is, but I look through the time window, and if there is something I am supposed to tell you, the benevolent spirits that support my wisdom say it to me, and in my own words I say it to you.

## Reading, Wisdom and Practical Application

***It is incredibly important. Publishers are going broke, authors aren't getting royalties, people aren't reading. It's incredibly important for you to give us this information.***

I believe it *is* important. In our time wisdom is given by word of mouth. In your time wisdom is more widely available by the printed word because one can read at length about something to see if it is so, then one can try it in one's life if it is appropriate, like any wisdom.

But one cannot easily learn wisdom, at least I have been told, and practically never from television, even though television strives to achieve this. Someday when television has become more married to the medium of teaching—now known in your time as theater—then it will have the capacity to teach wisdom. Right now it can teach only experience or knowledge. But wisdom is best taught by practicing to see if the value of the life experience of another fits in your life.

***Can you ask or find out why this renegade group doesn't want the American people to read?***

If you look at what is being published even in the general press, in the average newspaper, to say nothing of more bulky, wordy newspapers, you can get a vast explanation of different sides of an issue—a full explanation and perhaps a history of how things came to be the way they are. Whereas on television one is given a visual that might be very powerful, but rarely are you given the history. Television people and broadcasters believe that the average viewer does not have the patience to hear such things, and their research has proved it to be so. "If people want history, they'll read about it," the television executive might say. I am not saying that they are wrong. What I am saying is that reading is a very good way to understand different sides of things.

People are being encouraged and even commanded not to read when many people in your time find reading to be optional, not required to survive other than reading road signs, bottle labels and so on. Many people are growing accustomed to the idea that reading is passé.

## How It Works to Condition You

***The result they are aiming at is to control you emotionally through television?***

Not just emotionally, but to use your feelings to engender uncomfortable feelings associated with issues they may not wish you to think about and to use your good feelings to associate with issues they want you to believe. For instance, they might flash "Eat" during the time some favored political person is speaking and you might eat something you like. The intention is to leave you with a favorable impression of that person even if mentally you are not particularly comfortable with him. Eating, after all, does not have much to do with discernment.

***What kind of a phrase would they use to leave an uncomfortable feeling?***

If they want to do something to make you feel badly about something, it isn't always done with phrases—it's timing. It's what's on the set. After news of car crashes and children suffering or something, when you are already recoiling from that, the very next story might be about politics. They might then flash the message "repulsion." You are already feeling repulsed by the last story.

***So this has to be done by someone who knows the sequence that will be broadcast?***

Sometimes it will be the best guess. You have to remember that the messages can be flashed. They don't have to plan ahead much. To some extent they are at the mercy of the broadcaster's schedule, so someone has to be sitting on it basically all the time, flashing the message. It is like hitting a button and instantaneously it's on the screen for a split second all over the target area, and then it isn't there anymore.

***Whether it's broadcast, network, cable—anything?***

The only television sets that are secure from it are those that are fully shielded. In order to be fully shielded, one would have to be in a steel room, and the television signal would have to be generated in the room, as in a video being shot in that moment and you are in the room with it. Nothing from the outside could come in and the circuit is closed. The signal would have to be generated in the room and fed into your television set in the same room.

***I am trying to get a feeling for how they do this.***

For example, in an underground military bunker one might have a television station for the bunker. That signal would be generated within the bunker itself and would not be susceptible to such messages coming from an outside source.

***Is it done over electric wires or through a frequency or . . .?***

Air.

***Through the air to the TV set?***

Yes. It is easier to broadcast it through the air such as with radio. A radio station generates its signals and broadcasts them through the air to your radio.

***But they have to have powerful transmitters, so these guys have to be sitting someplace with a powerful transmitter?***

Yes.

***They have to be all over the country, because even radio stations go only so far.***

Yes.

***So there is a whole network of them all over the United States?***

All I know is they can do it. I am not certain how it is done.

***I bless you for sharing this. This is incredibly important, and no one else has mentioned it. Has it been intensifying lately?***

## The Cycles of Experimentation and Control through Visual Subliminals

Yes, because every so often they go through cycles. In the beginning it was just suggestions and they were curious. They have gone through other cycles of trying to put out commands, sometimes extreme, to see what the people will do. Usually they build up to a crescendo of extremity, then stop and go back to suggestions again. Right now it's building up again to that crescendo of extremity. There are some who want to put out "Kill" again to see what will happen. They haven't done it, though.

You understand, these people who make the decisions are ruthless—not necessarily the people pushing the button; most of them don't even know what they are doing—because the horrible effects are general. It's not possible to say "kill so-and-so." They have tried it; it doesn't work. When they say "kill" or do something to create a riot, for instance, anybody might get hurt. They have to be utterly ruthless, because perhaps one of their own family might get caught up in it. Therefore they have to be more loyal to their cause than to their own children, for example. Sometimes they have sorely regretted it.

These people are not doing this only because they are greedy. Sometimes they are doing it because they are afraid *not* to do it, because the group they are in is so ruthless that it would think nothing of revenging itself on one of its own members or his family or anything he cherished. It is not done just because they are greedy, as often happens in such organizations. It's just as often done out of fear.

***Do you know what month the crescendo is building up to? Do people need to be aware of the energy in June or July or something?***

I do not know. I just know that if you feel like doing something violent that is not in your nature, then unplug the TV and see if that feeling goes away.

If it does, then maybe you can get back to doing some of those things you used to do when you had such good times.

## The Carrier Wave Alone Generates Discomfort, Nervousness

***The electricity that keeps the TV set on standby so it can come on instantly, is it enough electricity to transmit those messages?***

No. I said it can produce a wave of energy that is an agitating wave, but in order for the message *itself* to be understood at least subconsciously, the set has to be on. But it only has to be plugged in for that uncomfortable wave to be generated, which gives you sort of a nervous feeling. This is why if a set is unplugged, after about six hours, usually not much more than that, you begin to feel more relaxed, and as the day goes on you feel more and more relaxed.

***I'm glad you clarified that. Some people get up in the morning and turn the set on, leaving it on all day like background noise.***

Yes. But with these messages you need to be looking at the screen for them to have their impact. I know there are those who believe that any prerecorded sound system can also produce those messages. While that is true, the messages have been most effective in visual mediums, especially on television, where the viewer is more likely to be alone. They have discovered that the messages are not as effective in movie theaters because you are more likely to be with someone or at least in direct contact with other people and thus likely to feel more benevolently about other people. Whereas when you are alone watching the television set, you might not have such brotherly or sisterly feelings toward other people.

***Are these messages also encoded in videos, the kind you buy or rent?***

Sometimes, but it is unnecessary. Why bother, because such things could be detected. They usually are not, but if someone makes the effort and has the equipment, it can be detected in a video. Why not do it in a way that is undetectable?

***They can transmit it while you are watching the video?***

Yes, and it would leave no trace, no evidence at all.

***This is more serious than I thought. You don't know what message they will send or what to look out for.***

## Watch How You Feel

Just pay attention to how you are feeling—if you have any strange or uncomfortable feelings or if your life has not been going very well lately. This won't be the case in all circumstances, but just try. Try other things—try unplugging the television and see what happens. For people who do not watch television but have it plugged in, the system will create that agitating signal.

I am not saying that television is evil, but those doing these messages are using evil against you. Television itself is not so terribly evil. To the extent that people ignore their discomforts, this is not so good. I agree with those who write that television minimizes things or makes them slighter. I am not talking about the television itself and the programs on TV but about something that comes without the broadcaster's knowledge.

## Shielding You Can Do That Breaks up the Visual

***You said it's very expensive. What could we put on a TV to shield us from these messages? You said there was something, but it was expensive.***

If you are not unplugging the set, the next best thing to shield it (though it would only be about 50 percent effective) would be foil—aluminum foil, metal foil (gold foil is not necessary, though some people might say it would gain an extra 5 percent. Realistically speaking, for the average person I think you would have to leave the holes for vents or for the sound to come out and obviously to see the screen, but you could reduce the impact by at least 50 percent by using foil. Put it in places where you are not watching or touching the set—on the sides, the bottom, in the back, the top, behind the screen. But make sure that you leave holes where there are holes. You could do that if you wanted to take the time and effort, but you would have to be careful not to drop pieces of the foil inside the set.

Of course, another way might be to create a metal box and slip the whole back of the set into it. That's possible if you can do that—

or even build it into a metal wall or something. Metal, even very thin metal, has the capacity to diminish the signal by 50 percent.

***There is nothing else that diminishes it more that's practical?***

No. The diminishing would be like this: only fragments of the message would come through. A simple message like "Eat" (upper left in drawing) would be converted into something like this [lower right]: a fragment. That's just an example, but that is roughly how it would be. Whole words would not disappear, but enough pieces of the word would disappear that the message would not have the same impact. The message itself might be diminished by 50 percent, but the *impact* of the message might be diminished so much as to have a negligible effect on a person. Subconscious messages must be at least understood by the subconscious. If the subconscious cannot understand it, it will not linger for a split second to analyze it. The subconscious does not analyze; it only receives and passes it on.

***So that would be incredibly effective?***

It would be very useful. And it would have to be done *very* carefully to make sure no metal foil fell inside the television.

***What would happen if it fell inside?***

It could create a fire.

***Oh, I see. On another subject: Since this is going into* Shining the Light, *what is the continuing story of the negative Sirians? What is happening when you work with them? Are you able to contact them yet?***

Yes, I am working with them now.

***Can you say something about how it is and what you are doing?***

I can only say a little bit. Right now I am teaching them about fire. In the beginning they didn't understand it other than as a source of light and heat. I am teaching them the more sacred aspects of fire. I will discuss fire in our next shamanic book.

## Hard Times for Publishers and Students

***Thank you for doing this great service tonight. People really need to know this. It makes sense. There is great information in all the national news magazines, even newspapers, but publishers are just not making enough money. I have a friend who used to get thousands of dollars every six months on royalties—and that's from romantic novels. But even romantic novels are not selling.***

You see how effective it is, but it is not targeted. Remember, it's experimental. That's the whole point: "Don't read." It doesn't say don't read this or that. They have learned that in order to make it most effective, it must be simple, because the subconscious is very simple.

***What about college kids and high school kids? What is it doing to people who need to study?***

It's harder for them. Of course, if they don't watch television and there isn't one in the room, then it won't affect them.

Keep the television unplugged when you are not watching it, and don't put it in your bedroom. The bedroom should be a place where your body is certain that it can rest and relax. When a bedroom has a television set in it, the body of that person is not going to sleep as well. There will be more restlessness. Televisions in bedrooms are not a good idea.

# 6

# More Subliminal Messages and the Sinister Secret Government

Zoosh
April 17, 1998

***Could you say a little more about what Speaks of Many Truths was talking about last night?***

These experiments to manipulate, control and essentially create predictability have been going on for a long time. A lot of it has happened through the airwaves in one way or another. Sometimes it is done in very subtle ways. A lot of experiments have been done with the space around other things, what artists call negative space. Sometimes you will have such messages in a negative space that are incomplete.

For a long time the belief was strong that the subconscious was uncomfortable with what was incomplete. They believed that if a message was given partially or if parts of letters were missing, the subconscious would strive to fill in the gaps. In recent years these people reached the conclusion that this may not always be the case. It is true only if the message is almost complete and the parts of letters that are missing can be easily guessed, such as the top part of an O.

The technical aspects are understood a little bit better now. Instead of messages being broadcast quickly in the fragmented way with the idea that the subconscious will process it longer, they are shown incomplete, but shown a little bit longer. The timing is critical, so, as Speaks of Many Truths says, it usually takes place in a poignant part of whatever you are looking at. These messages will often be broadcast during the news.

### Addictive News and Subliminal Sales

The attempt to make television news addictive has been fairly successful. This is not being done by broadcasters, so there is no blame to be cast there. You might ask, Why would there be a desire to make television news addictive? This is because there is a fixed format now for television news, where many stories that might be of interest to the general public are ignored, though [print] publications pick them up. And there are circumstances in which mayhem and so on is stressed.

A message, for instance, is broadcast to support certain industries. The only way you can be sure your message had any impact is to follow statistics published in those industries and compare them to the timing of your message. In these days, with computers and records and all this business, it is fairly easy to do this because companies often publish this information.

A typical example would be if a traffic accident was reported (one that seems random, such as a multiple-car accident in fog or snow), then during or shortly after the story but before anything else is said, a message might be flashed saying "careful."

They have discovered that single words or simple phrases are the most effective. They've tried on numerous occasions to stitch words together, but the subconscious doesn't work that way. If you flashed the word "be" and waited even five seconds before flashing "careful," the subconscious would probably not connect that as "be careful." The conscious mind would, but the subconscious would see "be" and "careful" as two separate words. The subconscious would take "be" as spiritually meaning "be." By the time you flash "careful," the first meaning has already been lost, so for "careful," you follow the statistics of new car insurance, whether people subsequently bought more car insurance. You can see how effective your messages are by correlating them with the news. A car insurance subliminal is one example that has been done. It was possible to track the fact that people upgraded their car insurance or more people bought it who might otherwise not have carried it.

### From Satellite Broadcasts

***What does this specifically mean? Evidently it doesn't come from satellites, but from radio broadcasting stations.***

I think it does come from satellites, actually. I don't think you really understand satellites. Speaks of Many Truths saw it as coming from the sky.

***So is it mostly or is it all coming from satellites?***

I think it is mostly coming from satellites, yes.

***So whether you have cable, antenna or satellites. it gets to your TV set?***

Well, if it comes from the air, it is hard to stop, you know. Let's say you have cable TV. If it came through the cable and you really wanted to put a stop to it, a good electronic hobbyist could probably figure out how to filter it. But if it is broadcast through the air, even if you have cable TV, for instance, there is really no stopping it short of living in a steel house.

***Well, he said you could use tin foil and cut out about 50 percent of it.***

Yes, you might be able to filter it quite a bit, enough so that the message might not be readable. If the subconscious cannot read it, it will discard it. It would be much more challenging then to make the message understandable. It could be done, but it would require a lot more effort, and the messages might be more easily picked up and recorded. Right now they are not recordable.

***By any known technology?***

Well, they might be discovered by highly sophisticated technology that is not generally available to the public sector.

***The people who have the technology aren't going to record it.***

## U.S. Government's Attempt to Stop It

No, the people who have the technology would be more inclined to consider the messages a threat and take it on as a military or intelligence project to attempt to defuse it. I might add that the government of the U.S. has attempted to stop it. There have been numerous attempts through the intelligence services to put a stop to it. It was considered to be a terrific threat to the security of the U.S. for quite a while, not because the messages were so awful in those days, but because of the concern about how the messages could be used, since it was clearly understandable that these messages were in fact having a significant impact on receptive human beings—you are receptive whether you want to be or not.

So for a long time there was a great effort to stop it. I might add, that was one of the original motivations behind the Star Wars defense system to knock other satellites out. But after a while people decided that though this is being used, it's on the back burner now as a project and is being used apparently for commercial purposes.

They have tracked a few satellites that are involved in these broadcasts. I might add that the satellites themselves are actually doing other things and that this subliminal activity is not what the satellites were designed for. These satellites that are put up in the sky to do something else (sometimes for government purposes, sometimes for purely commercial purposes) can be subverted, because those using this sneaky or subversive technology can essentially take over some aspect of the satellite's function and usurp its otherwise (in the case of most commercial satellites) benign function. In order to stop it, the U.S. government would be in the awkward position of shooting down otherwise innocent commercial satellites and then having to try to explain (though it is top secret) that it was an accident. It is an uncomfortable position.

### The Untraceable Source That Manipulates the Satellites

They have on occasion tracked the source that is affecting these satellites, and once there was a laser fired from the SDI system at one of the electronic beams that was attempting to manipulate a satellite. As it turns out, there was no effect because the system is very clever. If you can track the signal (one that is attempting to manipulate the commercial satellite), you can be sure that it is bouncing off lots of things before it actually goes out toward the satellite.

Picture for a moment the idea of an image bouncing off a mirror. After a while (as in a house of mirrors) you have no idea what started the image, and you are essentially shooting at shadows, as they say. So the government essentially shot at a shadow and damaged a television broadcasting station purely by accident. Being a highly secret circumstance, they just had to let it go. The television station decided that they had been hit by a freak bolt of lightning and that was that. The insurance covered it, the station was off the air for a couple of days and then went back on. When the government realized that it would be almost impossible, as in a hall of mirrors, to track the origin of this signal, they basically put the project on the back burner, though they didn't give up. However, if any signals ever attempt to usurp the authority of the government, then probably. . . well, lots of television stations will be wondering where all that lightning came from.

### The Cumulative Impact

***I am particularly interested because of this "Don't read" message. How long ago did that particular message start?***

"Don't read?" Speaks of Many Truths was accurate with that: It started about eighteen months ago. At first it had very little impact. But they discovered that these messages have a cumulative impact.

That is what's so insidious about them.

If your subconscious sees it once, it goes into the receptive area of your mind and you may or may not act on it. But let's say you see it a hundred times. Then it becomes very commanding and hard to resist. Considering that you are seeing it on television, which is something you are probably enjoying anyway, it's very easy to leave all your beloved books and magazines around that you would normally be reading and just stay glued to the set, even watching things you are not interested in because reading doesn't seem to be an option anymore. You don't know why, but you still enjoy buying books and magazines. They pile up and you wonder what's going on, but you still don't read because of that insidiously cumulative impact.

***How long is this going to go on before they change the message?***

They will probably wait another six months and just stop. They are not going to change the message. They won't change messages back and forth just to see how things go; they *know* it works. They would rather have you watching television, which is a fairly controlled medium. You don't get alternative TV news very much, though you can buy an alternative newspaper and get their point of view and think about it, consider and examine it. You don't get that much on television because of the prohibitive costs of broadcasting, and also because there are not too many cities that have access channels and so on available. So they will probably just stop and wait, that's all.

## How Publishing Can Counteract the Trend

***Well, I hope the publishing industry survives. It's not doing very well right now.***

No, it's not. It would be useful if the publishing industry knew about this. I am not saying you should go out on a limb, as it were, and start waving a flag, but it wouldn't hurt to put it out on the Web site. Things on a Web site have a way of getting around if they are of interest.

It doesn't mean, however, that the publishing industry should do nothing. They could pick up the banner of "unplug the TV." We don't want them to lecture people and say, "Get a life, unplug the TV." Rather, "Enjoy life; unplug the TV." We want to support people living their life again, seeing friends, enjoying family, going bowling, going to the theater, reading a good book. We want to suggest that unplugging the TV will improve the quality of their life, not be something wonderful that they can't have anymore. We don't want to make it sound like a diet. What I suggest is that they approach it as a campaign to improve the quality of people's lives.

When you think about it, the publishing industry practically never promotes its material on TV or in *Sports Illustrated*. You don't get many publishers saying, "Buy this book" on TV, so the idea of taking on the broadcast industry wouldn't be so awful. Publishers for a long time have been cowering behind that one, trying to think of a way they could put a book on TV and make it pay. I think it is too soon for that; the technology to make it pay and for talking books and so on is not quite here yet. But you know, if you get other publishers rallying around this cause and the campaign, "Unplug the TV and enjoy your life," I think it might be kind of interesting. It wouldn't hurt to get a little good press amongst your peers.

***We are going to put something out, because this makes sense, you know.***

An important thing is to recognize that this is not an antagonistic thing. The sinister secret government would love to have the publishing industry and the broadcast industry at each other's throats.

The main thing that the SSG has discovered really works and that keeps them in power is having other people fighting with each other. So don't say the broadcasters are doing this, rather say that someone (don't say the SSG because most publishers will just tune it out) is conducting this campaign. If they want to know more, you can say, "You can read what we have got on it, but we think it is someone, and you can figure it out for yourself." You don't want to keep it too discreet, but people know what you publish and that's that. I think it's important that these things get exposure, because subliminal messages on TV are terribly manipulative. Some terrible things have been done; race relations have been set back by years because of this.

***He explained that one of the riots was caused by this.***

Yes.

***Are there some renegades among the secret government who are behind this and somehow they can do it from a central control console or something?***

They have two or three different places they can do it from.

***And override the signals from the satellite? They don't have to get into each commercial satellite's program?***

You have to remember that the time of usage of the satellite is so brief that it doesn't really interfere with what the satellite is doing. It might appear (in the case of a weather satellite, for instance) as a portion of a picture that is missing or a missing chunk of the data (a lot of this comes in data format), but the rest of it is there. Then the very next picture or data message is perfect. People would naturally assume it is some kind of anomaly because it doesn't happen frequently or all the time, when you'd say there was something wrong that needed to be fixed. It happens only once in a while because there are a lot of satellites up there. And they don't use the same satellite all the time; they use different satellites.

## "Don't Read" Phasing Out

***If you are sitting there looking at the screen, how often does a message pop up?***

Not very often.

***Ten minutes, once an hour, once every two hours?***

You mean "Don't read" as a message? Oh, nowadays it might show up in different markets once or twice a day, because now it is just reinforcing. The first six months it was planting, the next twelve months it was being reinforced. They have actually cut down a bit. They are beginning to phase it out. It doesn't mean the end of publishing. After they stop it, people will gradually begin to read more. They are not going to suddenly say, "Don't read" and reinforce it; they are just going to observe it, pay attention. They are interested. They have no qualms about manipulating people.

***They are using the United States public like little mice in a cage?***

Exactly. And of course, anyplace else where TVs are made, used and manufactured in similar ways.

***This is not just new television sets; the age doesn't matter here?***

Any TV that uses modern circuitry. If you go back far enough and find TVs that use tubes, they are not affected.

***A TV set could be 20 years old, yet it's still . . .***

Easily.

***There was time a few years ago when you said that your TV set had to be a really new one, to contain a chip.***

Yes, that was different.

***What about computer screens and sitting in front of a computer all day?***

Computer screens are not affected, but if you ran a cable into it to watch TV, it might be affected. The reminder here is to pay attention to behavior changes in yourself. If you want to do something or if you miss doing something, reinforce it in yourself. Say, "I like to go bowling; I am going to do it." I pick out bowling because it's an activity that people used to do a lot more than they do today. I am not saying that it's the most wonderful activity, but it's a reasonably good activity and it's fun.

If you like to go bowling and so on, say to yourself, "I like to go bowling or dancing or go to movies or the theater or read a good book"—whatever you really like to do that you haven't done much lately. Say it out loud once or twice a day. It is very powerful. I will give you a ratio: For every hundred repeated subliminal messages on the TV screen ("don't read," for example, or another one that Robert mentioned, "do nothing"), simply saying out loud once or twice a day (better at different times of the day) with feeling five times will override the hundred messages. You don't have to yell it; just say it and mean it, no question marks. Say it because you mean it in that moment. Say it with purpose—for instance, "I like to read" or "I enjoy going bowling" or "I love going to the theater and I am going to do it."

So there *is* something you can do, but you have to do it consciously, not as words you say over and over. You have to honestly mean it in that moment. When you honestly mean it and say it with meaning, it has a tremendous impact.

***Jesus has said that in the next seven years we would be getting help. One of the creators says that in the next seven years other beings in all these creations are to help put benevolent energy into the progress we are making.***

Yes, they're convinced that you mean it, that you are serious and that there is benefit for all. So they are starting to do things, to integrate things, to support it, to put into their philosophy the value of what you are doing, to teach the[ir] children that something worthwhile is going on—in other words, to shift everybody's consciousness [out there] into a more supportive position for what you are doing here rather than just a long-range mistrust.

***This is very positive. So in seven years our lives are going to get easier?***

Yes, and from that point on, incrementally easier. It won't be like suddenly everything is simply roses, but at least flowers.

***Well, he described that eventually it will be just like approaching something straight ahead, not uphill.***

Yes, you will notice that things are not as burdensome as they were.

***The sinister secret government. Anything new at all on that?***

I will say that they are not going to go down without a fight. I might add that they do not feel particularly threatened by the work that we're doing, which is probably to everyone's advantage. They have taken what I would call almost a philosophical attitude because they feel so safe and secure in what they have done and are continuing to do and in their successes, as they interpret them. Their main success, of course, is keeping individual groups, even different people on the same block, fighting and so busy considering each other enemies that they don't look for who is behind the scene pulling the strings. Because in their eyes that has been so successful, they do not feel that being exposed is much of a threat.

Of course, in the long run the more that people read about them, know about them, understand them and pick up some of the techniques we've discussed, it will have a cumulative impact. From their point of view, they don't feel threatened.

***So in seven years they are not going to have as much effect on us?***

No, they are not. From their point of view—and if you know this, it helps you to understand them psychologically—if they have to go into mothballs even for twenty years, they are perfectly willing to do it.

This is what *their* scenario is—I will reveal this. Let's say they decide to go into mothballs for 20 years while everybody gets together here. From their point of view, part of getting together will be to disarm, becoming less frightened of each other, feeling more comfortable and putting down weapons (I am talking about weapons of mass destruction)—basically, becoming more vulnerable.

Now, it's not necessarily going to happen just like that, but that is their perspective. And then they would decide that in 20 years, when you are more vulnerable, they'll jump out of the bushes and take over. It's not going to happen that way, but that's the way they look at it.

***But in twenty years, what's our magic number—3.5 or what?***

Let's say in seven years things get easier and in another five years things get even easier. That's 12 years, then take another 20 years. Let's say that they hide out for a while—that's about 32 years. By that time you'll be well past 3.50 and really just getting to 3.51, going up one click at a time. Every notch you go up, 3.51, 3.52, drops their effectiveness precipitously.

***I think you once said that 3.56 was the magic number when they couldn't affect us any longer.***

Right around there they can't affect you anymore. I'm not saying they're sticking their head in the sand, but it's pretty close. It's to your advantage that they have that attitude.

***Excellent. We will end on that positive note.***

# 7

# How to Aid Whales Caught in Worldwide Sonar Radiation

Zoosh
April 21, 1998

### Navy Sonar Testing on Whales off Hawaii

*Excerpt from a bulletin received April 16, 1998, from light@ilhawaii.net.*

A new U.S. Navy sonar system uses loud, low-frequency sound to detect submarines. The Navy intends to deploy this system throughout the oceans of the world. This plan will put the entire marine environment at risk.

In March 1998 the Navy conducted tests of this system directed at humpback whales in their breeding, calving and nursing cycle off the west coast of Hawaii. The results demonstrated that adverse effects on whales, humans and dolphins took place at sound levels far below the intended level for the deployed system.

### From the Report

"When the islanders discovered that the Navy had already spent millions of dollars bringing the SURTASS LFA (Low-Frequency Active Sonar) to the deployment stage before preparing an environmental impact statement (EIS) and that the Navy only agreed to prepare an EIS after an environmental group caught the Navy violating numerous environmental laws, the tests appeared to be little more than window dressing for a decision already made.

"Dr. Alexandros Frantzis published a letter in the March 5, 1998, issue of *Nature* reporting on the stranding and death of Curvier beaked whales off the coast of Greece. The stranding was extraordinary both in terms of the number of whales stranded (12) and the location of the strandings (significantly distant from each other, whereas previous strandings have almost always been groups together). In his letter, Dr. Frantzis correlated the stranding with full-power tests of a Low-Frequency Active Sonar system broadcasting from a NATO research vessel. Dr. Frantzis calculated the probability of the mass stranding occurring for reasons other than the sonar test as less than 0.07%."

*For the full report, see www.ilhawaii.net/~light/report3.html or www.dreamweaving.com/lfas.html.*

✧ ✧ ✧

Many individuals recently have been concerned for the whales and dolphins and their interaction with the U.S. Navy and perhaps the military of other countries. I want to say this: We also need to avoid blaming the military service for such activities. We also need to avoid trying to stop the Navy from doing this. For one thing, they are going to go on. If they feel annoyed by protests, they'll just make it a total secret.

I am going to give you some homework that doesn't involve working against, but working *for* something. A lot of you love whales and dolphins. I would like you do something with that love that involves more than just love itself. It will involve some work on the part of those of you who really wish to help these beings. By the way, the bulk of the danger to these beings ultimately is being radiated with electronic and sonic beams, which is hard on them. In the case of some dolphins, it's simply not experiencing their true freedom.

So don't turn the U.S. Navy into some kind monster here. Recognize that their attitude is not that much different than that of people who use horses to pull a plow or dogs to pull a sled or, for that matter, people who have animals that might normally be considered free beings except that they are pets.

I am not trying to make anybody the enemy here. I would rather say that this is what I recommend. It's elaborate homework, but I think you might like it because it is challenging, and some of you know how you love to have a challenge.

## What You Can Do: Send Love and Gold Light While You Exercise

1. I want you to send love to these beings. I want you to welcome them and tell them that you appreciate them and love them; continue with that. But there is more. For those of you who have the strength, and it will take stamina and physical strength, I would like you to pick a partner (this is a teamwork thing). At the same time of day on a given day you pick (know that others will be doing this, so you don't have to carry the ball all by yourself), have your partner radiate as much love as possible—love first, light second.

2. If you are going to radiate light, let's make it gold light because that's strengthening. White light is fine, but it is totally unconditional, meaning that if a whale is filled with white light given to it generously by various people, that white light will accept *any*thing. On the other hand, if that whale is taking in a lot of gold light sent to it, that gold light will tend to protect it. That's why we want to send gold light.

So one partner sends gold light or love. Maybe there could be three people: one sending gold light, one sending love and then the third person.

3. While this is going on, do an exercise program if you have one or even if you don't. I would like you to be doing something that requires physical strength. For some of you it might be weightlifting if that's part of your training program; for others it might be jogging. Don't just do something cold; do something you are already doing now or that you could do—some kind of exercise that has to do with physical strengthening.

At some point in your exercise program I want you to just stop. If you are jogging, for instance, just stop as you might stop on a path to do exercises. Or if you can, jog or run at the same time you do this, but stay alert so you don't go out of your body.

I want you to hold a picture of a dolphin or a whale, whichever you are more concerned about, while you are doing this thing that requires strength. You can see shared strength beaming out toward the dolphins or whales if you want to, but if it is easier, just put that picture in your mind's eye. (It is a lot easier to put the picture in your mind's eye.)

For some of you who have difficulty with imagining pictures and holding it, have a picture nearby of a whale and glance at it while you are doing something that requires physical strength. This will not only send love and support to the dolphins or whales, but it also (in the case of the third person, if you have one) sends gold light, which is supportive and strengthening. Most important, it sends physical strength, because, as you know, the cumulative effect of these radiations going toward the whales and dolphins (not the immediate effect of a passing nausea) is to exhaust the whales.

If these radiations are sonic-based (sound-generated), sometimes the whales get lost. That's why you have whales that beach themselves for no apparent reason; they have been overwhelmed with the cumulative impact of sonic energies. It is very important to know that.

As an aside, I might add that people in the Navy or military who are at the receiving end of this sonic energy also get radiated by it and tend to get tired after a while from its cumulative impact.

However, my recommendation is homework you can do. It is especially important for those of you who want to do something but don't know what to do to help.

If you don't have a partner or don't know anybody you can do this with, then pick one of those three things to do. Maybe you'll send gold light, maybe you'll feel love and send that or maybe you'll do something that requires strength, like an exercise program. You might do this even on the job if it's safe to hold a picture of a whale while you are working. It's probably not the best thing for high-walking steelworkers, but it might be something you can do while you are feeling that strength. That's what I recommend.

### Sonar as a Security System and Its Cumulative Impact

***For those who don't know, what is the Navy doing? What is this about?***

Some of this is happening by accident. Some whales are big enough to require the same kind of energy that the military services of this country and others use to discern whether a whale or another ship is out there so that they know that they are safe. It's a security system for the safety of the ship, but such energies are more than the whales can comfortably tolerate.

At other times whales might be used in a military exercise. Since there are no other ships around of your own country (or your own flag, as the Navy might say), they might use a whale in a military exercise—not shooting at it or harming it, but throwing more electronic radiation at the whale than is really comfortable for it. They don't do it because they are out to get whales or they're malevolent, but because they don't necessarily realize that it is harmful to that creature. Sometimes even if they do realize it, they are ordered to do it, so they do. We have to recognize the reality.

***Why do they throw more radiation at the whale if they already know what an ob-***

***ject in the water is? I don't understand the point of it.***

They don't always immediately know what it is, so they throw, not necessarily a higher amount, but a constant amount for a longer time until they are certain. Then they feel safe. For military exercises, it's the duration of the signal that's really the factor because of its cumulative impact. But ultimately it tends to break down the sensing mechanisms in these creatures—direction, timing and even filial relationships (family relationships). It has a cumulative impact, and that's why it's important to send them strength.

## Be Physical When Sending Strength

Only that can really be done. You can say you are sending strength, but it's a word. We need to go past the word. When you do something that requires strength and you are straining and sweating, hold a picture for a moment of that whale or dolphin (an anonymous whale or dolphin or one you might have seen before that you want to help), and it will feel that strength. Don't do it at the end of the exercise program when you are tired. You want to do this near the beginning, when you are in stride, rolling along, feeling good, doing your repetitions and so on.

***Why at this point? Is this something that just started or something that just became public?***

It is something more people are becoming conscious of as more countries get more elaborate navies. It's partly because other countries are selling off their old stock of submarines and so on and because there are more people running around under the ocean and on the surface who might be doing these things. Some countries, like the Western countries and others, have some degree of consciousness and consideration. But there are other countries that may not either know or really care. I don't want to make it sound like there are enemies here, because for the most part this is being done without any malevolent sense whatsoever. No one is interested in hurting the whales. It's just that there's ignorance, and sometimes these beings need strength.

We have all given strength to other individuals at times, and invariably some of you have received strength from another individual. You know that if someone says, "I am going to send you strength," it doesn't impact very much unless that person is really strong.

For instance, if you have a friend who is a basketball or football player or an athlete and he/she says, "Okay, I am going to share some strength with you," meaning he is feeling strong, he comes over and puts his hand on your shoulder and maybe gives you a little hug. If he is feeling strong and not tired in that moment, his strength, his field, will actually join your field and you will feel uplifted. You will get stronger for a time. Since most of you can't go out and swim with the dolphins and whales, it's the next best thing.

## The Long-Range Effect

***What's the long-range effect?***

If this keeps on, say, for another five years, eventually whales are not going to feel welcome anymore. Whales are not like dolphins in that way. Dolphins are very vigorous beings. This is not to say that whales aren't, but dolphins are more vigorous and to some extent can throw this off. Also, dolphins have a greater communicated affection for human beings and like to please them.

While I am not saying it's okay with dolphins, whales are quite a bit different. Whales are shy, and while they might like human beings at a distance, it is not in a whale's nature to cozy up to a human being as it might be to some extent with dolphins.

If the situation doesn't get better for whales in about five years, they'll decide that Earth isn't safe for them anymore and they will gradually go home, from their perspective. Home to them is the star system Sirius, so they will gradually disappear. You have to understand, during the time this is going on for whales, it is not as if they are being nurtured in other ways aside from what they do with each other and what benevolent spirits can do for them. They are also being hunted. So they are not feeling particularly welcome. Something has to give.

***What would be the effect for the Earth if the whales left?***

There would be a significant loss in intellect. It is interesting to note that uranium is Mother Earth's brain. A lot of that has been mined. Granted, you can't get below a certain level in mining, so you are not getting it all, which is fortunate. Uranium is Mother Earth's brain and to some extent, her nervous system. When she requires more mental energy, if she cannot get it readily from other planets or spirits, the first beings she calls on are whales. If whales go away, Mother Earth's weather system and her tendency to try to make the worst earthquakes happen in places that are less populated could get considerably more confused.

I am not saying she doesn't have earthquakes and disasters in places that are populated, but it's not as extreme as it could be. For instance, recently a couple of tornadoes went through a major well-known U.S. city, a strange and unusual incident. This happened largely because the whales are not well. They are being overfished.

Many groups are trying to do something about it, so I will acknowledge their good work, including governmental groups, environmental groups in the U.S. and elsewhere. Even so, there's a limit to the influence of the U.S.'s and other countries' benevolent environmental groups. The whales are getting tired from being overhunted and are getting drained from this radiation.

### Electromagnetic Radiation and the Pineal/Pituitary Glands

This radiation is basically electromagnetic. Whales do fairly well with magnetic radiation, not an overwhelming amount. But when you add electrical energy, that tends to drain them. It is also fairly draining to human beings, but most humans are not radiated to the degree that whales are. Some human beings, such as pilots or navigators, may be in a place overwhelmed with electromagnetic radiation, because these instruments radiate a lot. Also, some individuals work in fairly small rooms with lots of computers blowing off lots of radiation. I grant that the computer industry has done a lot in recent years to minimize that. Even so, some people who work for electrical companies get radiated a lot, and this has a cumulative impact. The impact is not dissimilar to the effect on whales. A human's pituitary and pineal glands tend to suffer.

The same confusion can affect people with their families and loved ones. It also tends to break down the cell walls and make them more susceptible to being invaded by cancer cells. Those of you who know a little about microbiology know that cancer cells will invade a healthy cell by going through the cell wall, and if the cell wall is weak, it passes through like a hot knife through butter.

So these things affect you as well. Generally it affects most of the population. There are a few people on Earth who are less affected by electrical fields, but they are all affected to some extent. Most of the beings that are less affected are those you call insects—cockroaches, some other beetles, ants.

### A Protective Belt

I am trying to steer medical research in certain directions. Ultimately it will be possible, medically speaking, to create a generated counterfield. It will be particularly important for the military to protect itself, because electromagnetic weapons technology is really upon you. For most militaries it's been really very difficult to protect the soldier in the field. It is not so difficult if he is in a tank or bunker, but in the field it has been very difficult. You can create a counterbalancing effect and use cockroaches to study this. You will discover that it is possible to put a small protective electronic device on the belt of any soldier—for that matter, any civilian or citizen exposed to these things, perhaps a citizen living under or near high-powered transmission lines. It is possible to wear something that radiates on your belt or clip it to your shirt.

The initial version might require what amounts to an antenna running around the belt so it will create a uniform field around the body. The original prototypes looked like somebody wearing straps and wires all over the body, but they will miniaturize it in time. You will probably have this device working for you before you begin to use more benevolent alternative energies. Electricity, after all, is not used with its permission. It would rather be elsewhere, and that's why resistance (in electrical terminology) is so high.

# 8

# Electronic Reproduction of Sound Produces Stress

Isis
April 23, 1998

I really don't have anything to add to the television thing [subliminals] except that it just adds nowadays to the overwhelm of distraction. These days, more than any other, you need to be alert and sensitive to your own feelings so that you can understand your personal reality as it changes and know how to respond best. The more you are overwhelmed by electronic signals, the more difficult that will be.

It would be a good time to go to concerts if you like music. It won't be a problem if people are playing music or performing theater live. It's the electronic reproduction of sound or sight. In the process of that reproduction, these sights and sounds are twisted and turned in such a way that the nervous system of any human being will be seriously compromised.

So it would be a good time to consider attending live concerts or live theater. The moving pictures might be all right, but only if the sound is not too loud. If it is, bring some earplugs.

***Is it the sound itself, the volume in decibels?***

It is the electronic reproduction of the sound that is the problem. For some people moving pictures will be all right, but for others it won't.

***It's not clear to me. Is it the loudness of the sound or the fact that something is encoded in it?***

Nothing has to be encoded in it.

***Because they play it so loud?***

## "Even" People in an "Odd" World = Stress

Not just the loudness, simply its existence. It is hard to describe, but it would be as if you were an even number in an odd world. If we can call that technique of reproducing sound and sight in television the "odd" world and call human beings the "even" world, that puts you under stress.

For some people, watching TV an hour or two a week is fine. For those who are nervous, who have physical conditions or are experiencing unusual stress, it will stress you more. It will take longer to get over the stress than other stress-producing things. For instance, if driving is a stress, when you get home and relax, it goes away. If electronic reproduction stresses you, it might take four or five hours to go away.

***What about videos and CDs whose music we play? Is that the same?***

It is not as bad as television. On a scale of one to ten, if television is a ten stress, then videos would be a nine and CDs or tapes (not much difference) right around a seven. It is not that you can't do it. Don't take everything I say as the word of authority, you understand? Pay attention to your physical condition: Are these things causing you to feel better physically and emotionally? If you feel better because of them, then keep it up. If on the other hand you are experiencing things that are not normal for you, then start eliminating things that can be eliminated. You want to start with the things that you will miss the least.

***How long is this going to go on?***

## Tinnitus and Electronic Sound

Until they find a better way of reproducing the sound in that medium—for television, indefinitely. In a lot of people who have inner-ear problems or even balance problems, this is caused by either loud noise or sound reproduced through electronic means.

***Does that include ringing in the ears?***

Yes; some people hear hissing sounds and other kinds of sounds; it's called tinnitus. The condition existed years ago, but it wasn't as common. Some people may have a susceptibility toward it, but more people are getting it now, and the assumption has been that it's because of loud sounds. Loudness is most definitely a contributing factor, but it's not the whole thing. Don't assume the worst and stop listening to music or watching television, but pay attention to how you feel.

***When everyone wakes up a little and becomes more conscious, are there other ways to do this, other technologies we just don't know yet?***

Yes. The only reason that nobody is changing those technologies is that nobody really perceives the problem. Even if they did, the chances of business and industry changing something that works is not very large at the moment, though that will change.

***We need to mention here that Robert saw words on the television screen, unplugged it, then saw the words an hour and a half later but broken up.***

Yes. It took time to lose its power, about four to six hours. It is not a factor anymore.

***But I didn't know the words could still be on the screen after it was turned off. I thought it was just agitating energy.***

In the old TV sets that's not a factor—some of those in the fifties, maybe early sixties. You unplug them, and that's that.

# 9

# The Mechanics of the SSG Commands on U.S. TV Sets

Isis
May 19, 1998

*[Referring to the information in chapter 5:]*

***Are TV sets earlier than 1986 affected?***

It doesn't play well on sets before 1956. Any sets after 1955, even if they don't have the instant-on feature, are affected though the subliminals don't work quite as well on sets between 1956 and 1961. There are things you can do to lessen the factor. You can't really jam the signal because the mechanism used is part of what makes the set run. One of the best things you can do is to put objects (not electronic objects) on top of the set that you are particularly fond of or that inspire good feelings, such as a picture of a loved one you feel affection for. Or it can be a beloved animal. But it has to be someone you feel good about. It could also be a figurine you like and that you feel good about every time you look at it. It will not stop the messages, but it will counterbalance them to some extent. Ideally, you would have those objects to the left or to the right and on top. It will help, but it won't prevent it.

***How is this transmitted through the TV?***

It is broadcast through the air. It is not wired.

***On those older TVs, if the set was not on, nothing could be on the screen.***

Not when the set was off. A signal can't jam its way into some of the early TV sets. If the TV is on, then the message could be sent, but if the TV is off in those early sets, then the message would not come through. The safer sets were made in 1955 or before. Later sets do not require that the set be on. The message then prints out even more effectively and with a more profound impact, because it isn't mixed in with other things when the set is off. This is sets that have a trickle charge, not only instant-on. If you look at the manuals, you will find that something preceded instant-on to make it come on faster, though not instantly.

***The transformers were wired to keep the tubes at half power to reduce warm-up time. That's the mechanism that's accepting the signals, right?***

Generally speaking, it is sets that have tubes, not the transistors or printed circuits of today. Tube sets pose less of a threat. The message will print out poorly even when the set is on, but when you consider how often it appears even a poorly printed message has a cumulative impact. Remember, it is the cumulative impact that is most disruptive. If you've never or seldom watched television and see a message two or three times, it won't hurt you much, but if you watch regularly, it has a cumulative effect. It takes awhile for the impact of it to drain out of your body.

***What about the doors on my armoire? Do they prevent it?***

Oh, yes. If you put a roll of tin foil in front of it, that would prevent it. Seeing it has the impact and, when the set is on, hearing some things. But generally speaking, what you *see* is what has the most devastating impact.

***Robert said tonight that he saw the word "violence" on it.***

Yes, this has been on for a long time. When human beings see the word *violence*, if they are violent, which is not common, they might be instigated after a cumulative buildup. This is particularly devastating in prisons where people are locked up in an unnatural condition. That keeps them at each other's throats. They have so little else to do that is constructive and beneficial and that they would enjoy, at least in some respects.

If people see it who aren't of a violent nature or temperament, it will put them on edge and build up an anxiety, especially with repeated sightings. With sensitive people it sometimes builds up enough that they fear violence even in the most peaceful setting, in this way severely draining most people's physical condition. It has a tremendous impact on heart, lungs and the immune system. I'd say that anybody with immune-system deficiencies (aside from AIDS, anyone who has a devastating wasting disease) might be better off reading or being read to or listening to music, especially if it is played for them.

***Is the signal transmitted through the air like a TV signal, or is it coming in on the AC power line itself?***

It's a very good question. However, it does not come in on the AC power line. It comes in through the air, not unlike a satellite broadcast

***A computer monitor is similar, except for a tuner, so does it also occur on a computer screen?***

Very rarely. There have been some impact of things in the past, but for the most part this is not a factor, especially with portables that have flat screens. I might add that with projection television it's not as much of a factor. With the new flat-screen televisions and ultimately, of course, flat-screen computers, both of which will be expensive for a while, it is also not so much of a threat. It won't work with flat screens. Theoretically, someone could watch television on a laptop and not be impacted by these insidious messages—unless, of course, they were broadcast by a television station.

***If a computer screen is set up to watch television, would that subliminal signal depend on the geographical area?***

Technology matters, geography doesn't. You could, however, be in a cave or underground. If you have, say, ten feet of dirt above you and were still able to get a signal (which isn't likely), you wouldn't have those messages.

***If geography doesn't matter, is it transmitted over the whole United States or just in certain pockets of the world?***

Globally. It is not as influential in some places because the quality of life there is better because of the manner of government or the culture or whatever is the benevolence of the area. Sometimes an energy in an area is particularly benevolent, and that will counteract it. But places are profoundly affected where there isn't a counteracting energy, where there is too much population or where a cheerful disposition is not part of the culture. The Middle East is where a great deal of unnecessary trouble has been stirred up. Fortunately, in some Middle Eastern places, television is discouraged by some cultures, which is perhaps for the best until it is possible to eliminate these signals.

***Are these signals also sent through the air to directly affect a person's mind?***

No, not yet. It would require a significant implant that is not yet being implanted into the average person. There might be a few in individuals, but I would say that is not a factor.

***In other words, the power is not strong enough to disrupt a person's electromagnetic field?***

No, I'm saying the person would have to have an object implanted somewhere near the optic nerve for this to work, not just because it's optical but because that is the likely place to put it. Such a nerve bundle would support such a device electrically speaking. Because that nerve bundle is relatively close to the surface, such an operation would not be particularly invasive.

***How would one obtain this implant?***

No extraterrestrial race is installing such an implant. However, these implants, in a rudimentary form, are being experimented with in animals. And there is a minor push to put them into children, not because someone wants to create a nation of robots, but because well-meaning people who do not know about or understand the capacity for such electronics feel that if a person's identity were part of their permanent electronically retrievable physical self, the kidnapping of children would become significantly less. You'd be able to find them. Someday such a device might become optional or, in some scenarios, required for the average citizen. But that is not in any way guaranteed to happen. It *could* happen.

***In other words, this would not be from an extraterrestrial race, but part of a governmental plan?***

Yes, and the most likely candidates would be soldiers or military people for military operations. Of course, also the innocent and vulnerable, and that would be its intention. With the microminiaturization available today and with external power sources, it would be easy to install something that has almost no negative impact in the physical person but that could do a number of things the mechanism is not publicly known for.

***Thank you very much for the information.***

You are most welcome. Good questions.

# 10

# Nuclear Tests Could Aid Unification

Zoosh
May 19, 1998

At this time I'd like to say a few words about those who are upset at the circumstances vis á vis the atomic testing going on [in India and Pakistan]. I want you to understand something. I realize that when you are in the midst of changes—things that are unexpected, crises both personal and more universal—it is difficult to see the overall effect. But through it all, what is going on, aside from any drama or misfortune that might befall anyone, is an overwhelming push and pull toward planetary unification.

You are now at the point where no one can interfere with planetary unification. As I said some years ago, the initial unification you are feeling now is largely economic or more business-oriented. But that will gradually transform into something more humanistic. This is coming largely because of efforts by many individual people all over the world and their desire to be united with each other and working toward something that everybody can agree on.

These basic agreements, of course, are always founded on things that all individuals hold dear—being appreciated and loved for who you are, being respected, having all your needs fulfilled and the occasional desire fulfilled benevolently as well. So even though dramas are all around you, unification is the driving force right now.

***Maybe I've missed something, but what has an atomic bomb test got to do with unification?***

Think about it. Here we have a circumstance that not too many years ago would have created reactions in world governments that were very factionalized. One government would have said, "Oh, wonderful!" and another would have said, "Well, we're not sure," and still another would have said, "This is deplorable." But if you look at not only the Security Council of the United Nations but the general consensus amongst the diplomats in the U.N. and world government heads, aside from the two countries involved, you see total agreement that this was not a good thing and that the two countries need to sign the pact that other nuclear countries have signed so that then people can get on with their lives.

You might say, "It is deplorable that these tests are taking place; the Earth is being damaged and threats are in the air." On the other hand, countries that used to be at each other's throats are now shoulder to shoulder, absolutely united in agreeing that this must be changed for something more beneficial. That is a sign of ongoing unification.

***That's great. Is there anything else you want to say about what is going on right now that people need to know?***

That's all I wanted to say, because it's topical at the moment. By the time the magazine is published, it may not be as topical, but still it's worth saying. I talk, and you prompt me sometimes, about some of the dramas going on. But every once in a while it's necessary to remind everyone that regardless of the dramas, whether they be personal or universal, progress is inevitable, because unification is not only necessary, it is natural. It is fragmentation that is unnatural on a humanitarian level. It is not natural for people to be at each other's throats. Such an unnatural situation will necessarily draw to a close.

## WHAT READERS CAN DO

Now, this is where you come in. The *Sedona Journal of Emergence* is, I realize, grouped by bookstores and distributors who create systems in the categories of New Age, channeling or self-help. But in point of fact, if we drop those terms, it is really easily filed under philosophy. As a philosophical journal, it gives answers every week in the astrologic or the numerologic, but at the very least it gives answers every month on *the way*. It will be many different ways because of the many different voices.

Therefore, I suggest to you, my friends, that you let people know it exists. Most people who are crying out for this have absolutely no idea that the *Sedona Journal of Emergence* exists, and the minute they find out, they will be reading it left and right.

Tell people about the *Sedona Journal of Emergence*, not just because you think it's great, but because it might do them some good to have an alternate point of view than they are receiving now. You know, dear readers, that the magazine does give you hope sometimes and very often explanations that the mind hungers for and the body is only too willing to apply—especially methods that improve circumstances in your life.

In this way the cadre of readers is incorporated, especially loyal subscribers. Many of you are already sending things out to your friends. This is great, but we need to make it a major networking effort, and you can cooperate to the extent that you are able. A great many readers are back East. They will go to a store that sometimes has the *Sedona Journal of Emergence*, and it's almost always sold out. Readers might persuade the stores to carry more copies. You may or may not be able to influence the distributors, but generally speaking, the big complaint back East is, "They are almost always sold out, and then I just have to wait 'til next month."

You can help in a good way that benefits all people, especially those who are crying literally, "Show me the way."

—Zoosh

# 11

# Sphinx in the Rockies

Zoosh
May 28, 1998

***In the Rocky Mountains at 14,000 feet, Robert Ghost Wolf found some griffins and a sphinx that is just like the one in Egypt. Would you like to comment on this? Ghost Wolf went up there with a group of elders and physically saw and photographed a number of things. The story and photos are on the Art Bell Web site. [For photographs, see www.artbell.com and www.wolflodge.org/sacred/sphinx.]***

## Underground Civilizations

For many years there have been stories in the Rocky Mountains, extending from the southern part to the northern part, about pyramids and other items that smack strongly of what is considered Egyptian culture but actually predate what is now Egyptian culture. This all has to do with former underground civilizations involved in training some of the original mystics who were influential in beginning what came to be known in Egypt and other

Rocky Mountain sphinx (facing right).

countries as the priest and eventually the priestess class. The items are necessary to be found now, and I might add that there has been some considerable effort to reveal them.

There has been a reluctance on the part of many who have discovered these things years ago to make them public for one reason or another, sometimes for fear, at other times for other reasons. There have been efforts over the past 75 to 95 years to bring this to the attention of the public at large. (I might add that one of the best ways to hide something is to put it in a place that is distant from the more obvious demonstrations of that thing.)

We have pyramids and the Sphinx in Egypt, and as a result, there have been exhaustive searches to find more such things there. The assumption is that the culture that built these things would have started in Egypt. But in fact, as far as Earth goes, these denizens of underground civilizations—benevolent civilizations, I might add—did not, in terms of their Earth location, begin in Egypt. They simply chose Egypt to make known their primary interest in the spirituality of Earth citizens. It is not unlike today's billboard, only this billboard has an impact.

When the Great Pyramid had its original white sheathing, it was much more powerful. But today it still has at least 10 percent (ranging from 7 to 11 percent) of its original power. To some extent, it's a sleeping giant; it can be activated at a distance to greater power, geared toward attunement of the physical, mental and spiritual bodies. I might add that it is not geared toward attunement of the feeling body—the emotional body, or what Speaks of Many Truths and myself have sometimes called the instinctual body. Nevertheless, the civilization that built these things was interested in taking what they wished to do, moving it past the select few who had come to be known as the original priest or priestess class and placing it where it could not be avoided, especially in the ages where traveling took place years ago.

### Civilization's Star Origin and Culture Base under the Rockies

One might ask now, "Where did the civilization truly originate in terms of its great cultural base?" This underground civilization came from the stars. But where did it originate on Earth and begin to lay its cultural base? A map, please, of the western United States.

Generally speaking, the Rocky Mountains (through here) is the civilization we are talking about. It really got under way (underground, of course) in Colorado, Utah, Wyoming, ranging up into a little bit of Idaho and southern Montana. Emigrations went to New

Mexico. The last outposts were in Arizona. From southern New Mexico they went underground through tunnels gently created in the Earth. They had Earth's cooperation because they used what you might call holistic, heart-centered technology down through this area. This technology has yet to be used by your governments, but someday it will be used exclusively.

[Points again to map:] Into Texas, down into Mexico, Central America and South America. When coming into South America, it tended to follow the west coast, passing through areas such as Argentina, and, more profoundly, Peru, Chile and so on—generally, the western regions. Now, that's just by way of historical reference.

## Feminine Technology

If you were to look at this culture from your country, the United States, you would have to say that it was primarily focused into what I would call feminine technology. I have referred on various occasions to feminine technology before, as have others through Robert; feminine technology is heart-centered, interacting with all life forms. Since everything is alive, it interacts with all around it in a mutually cooperative way. This means that tunnels underground or underground caverns would not have precise shapes. If you were to stand back and look at them artistically, you would say that these shapes are organic because they flow this way and that way. They don't have any sharp angles. They seem to be hollowed-out caverns, sometimes bigger, sometimes smaller, that have come to be for no apparent reason, from a casual observation.

Using feminine technology, one, two or three individuals proceed along the lines of the tunnels and talk to the rock and the surrounding elements. It might be underground water, underground deposits, salt and so on. They would talk in the language (you might say the *energy* of that material, but it is really a language) and ask it to open itself in places where it would feel comfortable having beings pass through back and forth and perhaps even reside in some of the larger openings. Then the individual would wait. It would never be like walking up and saying, "Stand aside."

One or two or three of the individuals would focus into the material, depending on whether the materials had a different makeup. Some might be salt, some iron, some pitchblende—it might be many different things. There would be one person for each type of material, or there might be people who could feel as if they were a portion of more than one material at once. Thus the request would not come from an outsider but from an extension of the material itself.

That material, that part of Mother Earth's body, would know that the beings who were speaking were not part of her body, at least in that moment. But because they showed so much respect as to cause themselves to feel like the parts of her body, she was far more likely to create openings for them to pass through. This is a perfect example of feminine technology.

Feminine technology is also sometimes associated with shamanism because it almost always has to do with working benevolently with all life within its own framework.

***Who is interested in making these sites known now?***

The underground civilization, which has largely emigrated off planet in recent years because of your technological community's usage of certain forms of technology that have been uncomfortable to them. They are exerting their influence from a distance. They have not returned from whence they came, however. Most of them are on large vehicles close enough to this planet to be effective. They can do benevolent things for Earth and her populations, yet are far enough away that any perceived threat by any government agency on Earth (this government or otherwise) would be easily deflected or, in some cases, diffused (the broader meaning of diffusion rather than its military usage).

## The Builders' Job to Track All Possible Futures

***When those beings set up an underground civilization and created a sphinx, griffins and a pyramid in the Colorado Rocky Mountains, when did they do it? After Atlantis?***

Let me explain something here. I have used your geographical nomenclature here for clarity's sake, but this underground civilization was set up before this planet was in this solar system. When this planet was on Sirius, the beings who lived on the planet did not live on the surface. They lived underground, and their way of life was established. When the planet moved from its location in Sirius to this location, they all got off the planet. But after the planet had stabilized itself in this location, they returned. The civilization was established, you might say, quite a while before Atlantis.

***Did they built the structures then—the pyramids and the sphinxes in the Rockies and in other parts of the world?***

No, not in all parts of the world. One of the main things they did was incorporate and train individuals in their society (after the planet moved here, of course) to look forward (this was their sole task) periodically to every possible future for this planet and the people on it, including surface people. This showed them every possible future on a global scale. At any given moment they could see anywhere from 700 to about 1800 different future possibilities. This give you an idea how many beings were involved in this task. Of course it would rotate, and individual beings wouldn't do it all the time, so any moment might have from 30 to 40 thousand different individuals involved in this task at a given time period (I'll call it a day for simplicity's sake), but the general population was not involved. When they looked forward, they would see who was coming and going. They made an effort to look at what would be done by whom and when.

### Visual Attractors

One of the repeating themes they could see as they looked forward in time was that large objects with a stunning visual impact would captivate the attention of the global surface population better than anything left in print, no matter how impressive the printed word was. So it was clear then that it would be necessary for them to create something with a visual impact.

It was important to them to create what they considered, not exactly duplications but in many senses reproductions, of the most visually impacting and long-lasting sites on the surface of the Earth that were not naturally formed, in areas that were more what I would call strongholds, not the most densely defended, but the least likely to be found.

This ruled out Europe, for example, where civilization as you know it sprang into existence, and of course the Middle East and places like that, certainly Africa, where civilizations were profoundly searching and examining life. They had to create a stronghold in places that were more inclined geographically to have surface civilizations devoted to the path of the shaman or the mystical person who worked within nature rather than cultures and civilizations that would either promote or be affected by technology as you know it today. This is why they concentrated their activities and cultural recreation (I'm referring to the Great Pyramid and the Sphinx as cultural re-creations) in areas less densely populated on the surface, areas that would develop what I call interfering types of technology later rather than sooner.

### The Builders' Three Sources; Their Adoption of the Explorer Race

These individuals came from a distant planet, but it is less important to know where they were from than *when* they were from. They are from three sources: They are from the distant past of Sirius; the distant future of this galaxy, sometimes called the Milky Way; and the eternal existence (suggesting their evolution on the spiritual level) of all creation that exists in what Quah referred to [in the June 1998 issue of *Sedona Journal of Emergence*, part of the "ET Visitors to Earth Speak" series, to be published as a book in the future] as Love's Creation. I want to say positive creation as compared to negative creation, but I don't want to make negative creation sound like something uncomfortable. Let's just say that they came from the ongoing permanent center of all creation itself as you know it and counting all the dimensions, ongoing creation as you don't know now but *will* know it.

So there are these three threads. On the one hand, they were beings, you could say individuals. They enjoyed transforming their appearance a little bit. On the other hand, they did not have to walk about as you do from place to place, though toward the latter part of their occupation of the subsurface regions of this planet, they chose to look more like surface dwellers than not. In this way, should there be any sight of them, either by a sensitive viewing the inner depths of the Earth or an occasional chance meeting with underground explorers, such as cave explorers, they chose to look more like human beings. That's what they did.

***They came here for our benefit or for theirs?***

Oh, it's hard to say. I'd rather say that they existed here long before you even knew about this place, even before this planet took up the third position from the sun in this solar system. It would be most appropriate to say that this is where they chose to live and that their inclination was to adopt projects they felt were of great value. So when the Explorer Race project was launched in earnest, they adopted it.

***At what point did they to start training priests and priestesses? Some point in our history that we can relate to?***

Well, they really started that in Egypt.

***So they worked with Isis?***

They worked with her student, and that's another story [in the Isis book, yet to be published]. They did not necessarily work directly with Isis. It wasn't like, "Let's get together and form a college." It was more like everybody working sympathetically, as one might say, speaking musically, toward a common goal. You feel somebody else working somewhere and the vibration is sympathetic, but you don't necessarily join them. It's not necessary. If you join them, you simply duplicate the effort there.

## The Importance of the Great Pyramid and the Sphinx

***You have never placed Egypt chronologically. Is it possible to do that in relationship to the civilizations of Lemuria and Atlantis?***

I am loathe to do that with Egypt because of the incredible value and absolute necessity for Egypt's culture and cultural monuments to remain safe and secure. One might ask, Why is it so important that the Great Pyramid and the Sphinx be preserved? One might also say reasonably, How is it possible that governments and citizens from all over the world have rallied on numerous occasions to protect the Sphinx and the Great Pyramid and the valley in general, to say nothing of the populations?

There is an unconscious knowing that these cultural edifices have a profound impact on the people of the Earth even though one, and perhaps both of them, have been altered significantly. Obviously, the face of the Sphinx was originally a lion. It was altered. That's understood . . . [Tiger, the cat, meows here] your associate [Tiger] making comments there. [To Tiger:] Thank you very much, yes it had your face, that's right.

One might say also that the pyramid was altered, but even so, because of the enigmatic quality and the visual impact of these two structures, the simple effect of their existence and the impact on the civilizations who are aware of these cultural edifices is enormous. It is understood all over the universe that sensory impact, even if you do not see, has the most long-lasting effects. As fascinating as intellectual impact might be, it does not even remotely compare to the impact of what is prompted by the senses.

I'm stepping around this carefully. Egypt and its cultural edifices are and have been largely protected. Egypt's leaders, sometimes more politically active than others, would alter a plan when there was a threat in the past to flood the area—not intentionally, of course, but because of building a dam to create electrical power. In recent years some of Egypt's leaders have become well-known internationally for their great diplomacy. So there is a conscious, immortal (meaning beyond linear life) intention to protect Egypt. That is why I'm not saying as much about it as you ask but I'm saying a lot that you didn't ask about.

## Artifacts Elsewhere on Earth

***So the reproductions they made were in the Rockies, in South America and in China. Where else?***

I cannot reveal where the vast repository of reproductions are because it is a reserve such as one might put away just in case. Yet to be discovered are artifacts in Florida (no point in looking; they will be found accidentally), in several places in Canada and also in Australia, New Zealand and Madagascar. There is one place where they all exist in absolute harmony, and that place I must protect.

***What will be the effect on the population of the discovery of these sites you just named? More wonder? More enigma?***

More of a compelling desire for unification of the world's population and a true need by the people to drop the geopolitical borders so that people can travel more easily. That might take time, but the United Nations is a perfect place to do it.

***This photo seems to be exactly like the sphinx and pyramids on Mars. Are they?***

The ones on Mars are a little different because they are associated with civilizations there, and as always, civilizations, planet to planet, will tend to have things that complement those civilizations. Let's just say there is a similarity that cannot be denied. But similarity is not the same as duplication.

***So they weren't built by the same beings, then?***

I didn't say that.

***Were they built by the same beings?***

I won't say that.

***You sound like the CIA: "You never had this conversation."***

I am being discreet, as the CIA and others have to do sometimes.

## Connections with Tribal Peoples

***Since these pyramids seem to be part of what we call the tribal or native peoples' myths and prophecies, did the underground settlers or civilizations share this with the tribal elders of various tribes around the world?***

Not exactly the elders directly. They would usually approach the members who would come close to where they were located. They would approach the ones they felt were the most spiritual and educate them to the extent they felt was necessary or useful. Then there would be a sharing by that individual with the elders when the time was right. Not always immediately, but usually sooner rather than later.

***That was long, long ago, so they became part of the wisdom of each tribe, because the native elders seem to know about these places.***

Some of this information has been shared from tribe to tribe by the same methods you use today, ruling out technology—communication. Some has come to be known by direct contact. Sometimes, an individual tribe or even individual clan within the tribe will have a piece of the information. When it is considered important to share the information, the people share it and get the bigger picture. It is usually considered important in tribal circumstances when issues of sovereignty and survival are up for such peoples. This has happened many times in the past, not just currently.

***So the influence exerted by these beings in this great ship, who were the underground civilization, to make these places known is meant to cause people all over the planet to question and wonder and seek unification. Is that their main purpose?***

It is also to help awaken, enlighten and intrigue people's interest.

## The Cat Connection

Generally speaking, the sphinx with the lion head is a good illustration to have about. Although every individual cannot easily meet a lion, every individual can easily meet a lion's cousin, a smaller version frequently found around human beings, sometimes called the cat. It was intended that the lion and all of his and her cousins on Earth initiate human beings, help them to awaken and alert them to many things. This is why cats often exhibit unusual forms of behavior, doing things with each other in front of human beings purposely to draw your attention to their apparently enigmatic abilities. As you form a greater connection to what cats can teach you and show you—utilizing shamanic methods that honor and appreciate the value of the human being and cat individuals, treating both beings with love and respect, gently and comfortably for all—so the cat is in a perfect position to initiate you into your own spirituality.

If there is a single creature on the planet who has the capacity to show you the way to your own spiritual abilities most easily, it would be the cat. This is why they are so prevalent. This is not to suggest that dogs are not spiritual, but dogs are here to show you more about physical things. Cats are here to show you what you can do spiritually by working with them in benevolent ways for you all. Ask Speaks of Many Truths to talk more about that. He will. Be sure and ask him soon.

***These beings taught the priest and priestess class in Egypt. How can we tap into what they taught them? What can we do now to utilize that, or was that taught for that time?***

If what was taught then is of value for your time, try to learn from cat.

Perhaps Speaks of Many Truths could speak a little now. I will say good night.

# 12

# Cats as Our Teachers

Speaks of Many Truths
May 28, 1998

This is Speaks of Many Truths. I will speak a little bit about learning from your cat or perhaps a cat friend that you can visit or might visit you. Not all cats are prepared to teach at all times, but many of them will or might. Some cats are more inclined to be spiritual teachers for human beings and some have other things to do, not unlike people.

If you are living with a cat, you will probably have some idea whether that cat is what might be called a spiritual cat or just a fun housemate or companion. How do you know? If a cat exhibits unusual behavior sometimes called *cattitudes* (I like that one), it will sometimes suddenly look around the room at things you do not see, yes? Sometimes cat is hearing things you do not hear or smelling things you do not smell, but at least 20 percent of the time, cat is seeing things you do not see. Cat has ability beyond instinct.

If you can get to know your cat, if you are trusted by your cat, it is helpful. Don't pick up cat to do this. If cat is in your lap, fine, but more likely cat will be looking at things from someplace else. Before cat does this, practice with cat. How? I will tell you how. Say cat is lying on the rug or sitting on the bed or sitting someplace where it is happy to be often. For those who are in spiritual practice, this will be easy. For those who are new to it all, you will have to use your imagination. But for those in spiritual practice, do not go out of your body, but extend your sensing system within your body into cat.

First you must make sure that you are calm, relaxed, not unhappy. So put yourself into a cheerful place as spiritual person and as person who has not been trained much in these things. Laugh about some things or relax, then extend or imagine yourself being in the body of your cat. Don't do this unless the cat lives with you. Otherwise it can create discomfort for both you and cat, and that would not be honorable.

So it is your cat. If your cat wishes to have you present within its auric field or its energy, inside and around and about its body, cat will either look at you and continue doing what it is doing or simply not change what it is doing. I want you to practice with this before cat is doing something unusual.

Begin on a relaxed day. Try to make sure that the phone will not distract you. Turn the ringer off or something. And when you start doing this, if cat suddenly gets up and walks away, then it is not acceptable to do this at this time with cat. If you try two more times with the cat for a total of three times and every time it gets up and walks away, don't do it again with this cat. Cat might be sensitive to you; perhaps cat is not comfortable with your energy at this time. Try a different cat.

But say cat does accept your energy. Then try to imagine what cat is feeling, not emotionally (remember, cat is thinking or seeing), but physically. What is under the cat's feet? Imagine your hands as the cat's feet with claws extending from the toes. Or imagine that cat's tail is your own. It might be moving. If cat knows what you are doing, it might do some things to support what you are doing. In other words, see if you can feel what the cat is feeling physically, as if cat's body were your own.

If you have done this enough times, when cat starts doing something interesting or provocative, seemingly looking at things, perhaps seeing something you do not see, perhaps hearing something you do not hear or even smelling something you do not know, you can extend into cat if cat is comfortable and you have done this a few times. If it allows you, you may—it is not a guarantee—be able to see, smell or hear what cat is noticing. In this way cat will be sharing with you its abilities but, most importantly, cat will be exposing you to abilities that you have. So in this sense cat is like the teacher. Cat shows you how to do it, and you continue as you feel connected to cat teacher. Eventually you notice you can do these things without the assistance of cat teacher.

***And this is what they were trying to say when they built the Sphinx?***

Yes. This is what the Sphinx is all about. And the Great Pyramid was really just to draw your attention to the Sphinx. [Chuckles.] It was look, see and say: "Look at this!" Because the pyramid is a shape, you can call it a word. It is a pyramid, an unusual one. What is it? You scratch your head and say, "I do not know." But when you look at this lion, you say, "Oh, we know what this is. We have little ones in our house." It makes the Sphinx much more easily understood by having something that is not easily understood near it.

***Anything else you'd like to say?***

That's all. I just wanted to comment on that exact thing, giving homework to budding shamanic and mystical readers out there.

When you read the book that Zoosh and I cooperated in (the first book in the Shaman series) that lovely publisher here is putting out, you have more of these activities, but it is a good beginning to do this with benevolent cat friends. (Don't worry, dog lovers, we will have things for you to do someday.)

***Thank you very much.***

Good night.

# 13

# Living Prayer Gives to Earth

Speaks of Many Truths
June 22, 1998

Living prayer allows you as an individual to give to the Earth. So many of you ask, "What can I do for the Earth? What can I do for the animals? What can I do for people suffering in other parts of the world or in my own town or family? What can I do?"

Very often if people are suffering on the other side of the Earth, there is not much you can do directly, but perhaps you hear or read that people are having little food or that their water is scarce—a drought, as they call it. You can say, *May the people be nurtured and know they are loved. May their hearts be healed and may they find what they need, or may it be brought to them in a benevolent, beneficial way for all beings.* Then just let it go. You have said it once; let it go. Different circumstances might require different words. Ask for what you want; do not ask for what you don't want.

### How Manifesting Occurs, How to Ask

Sometimes this will be difficult. There might be a war someplace. You would like to say, "Stop the war!" But this is not the way manifesting occurs. It would be better to say, *I will ask*, and then you can say, *Oh God* or *Great Spirit* or *beings of the light*. For those of you who do not necessarily believe in such beings, you can make an arrangement with such a being to know that when you say, *I will ask* or *I am now asking*, the being will know that you are talking to it or to the Earth or to creation.

You will say this key phrase, *I will ask* or *I am asking* or something like that out loud, always out loud. You can say it quietly if other people are around, but out loud. That way it is understood that what you are asking is about physical things. In the case of a war on the other side of the world, you might say, *I ask that everyone's hearts be healed.* Everyone—you don't mention only the people who are suffering; you want to include the people who are performing the deeds of pain to others, because very often the reason they do these warlike things is that they have pain in their heart for some other reason. Usually they don't know why.

### Prayer for Peace

So you will say, *I ask for all people in this place where this war is, that their hearts be healed and that they find peace together in the most benevolent and beneficial way for them.* Then you let it go and go on. You have said what you can do. You have joined for that moment with Creator, because you—as a mental being, as a feeling being, as a physical being, as a spiritual being, as an instinctual being, as a being made up of Mother Earth, as a being supplied by the mortal personality—have acknowledged your connection to Creator (or to All That Exists, if you prefer) and you have said and done what you can in that moment and have asked for what you want. Then you let it go. You may hear that things got better; you may never hear. But you have done what you can, and then you don't have to feel guilty for having things that others don't.

You do not have to feel that you ought to be doing something. You have done what you can do. It is a direct action, and you will be thanked—not consciously, not mentally most of the time for most of you—because you will often feel within your body a sense of relaxation or a good feeling, which is Mother Earth's way of letting you know that you have done what you can. Because you are in Creator School here, you are expected to do what you can to the extent that you can cocreate with Creator. In that moment when you say that living prayer—because it is something that is happening to living beings in that moment—you will feel the feelings of what you are asking for. When you *feel* those feelings asking for peace, asking that people's hearts be healed, when you *feel* the sincerity that you are actually requesting this, it will work even better. If you just say the words without the feelings, it won't work as well.

### A Prayer for the Surrounding Life

Let' s say you are driving through a forest and there is no one else around, no cars in front of you that you can see, none behind you, no people walking up and down the road, not even any animals in the forest that you can see, aside from the little winged ones flying

## LIVING PRAYER

Living prayer allows you as an individual to give to the Earth. So many of you ask, "What can I do for the Earth? What can I do for the animals? What can I do for people suffering in other parts of the world or in my own town or family? What can I do?"

If people are suffering on the other side of the Earth, you can say, *May the people be nurtured and know they are loved. May their hearts be healed and may they find what they need, or may it be brought to them in a benevolent, beneficial way for all beings.*

Say this key phrase, *I will ask*, or *I am asking* out loud, though perhaps softly. That way it is understood that what you are asking is about physical things. In the case of a war on the other side of the world, you might say, *I ask that everyone's hearts be healed and that they find peace together in the most benevolent and beneficial way for them.*

Let's say you are driving [in the forest] and there is no one else around. Suddenly your heart hurts. It is a dull ache. When you get used to this living prayer, you will look around and say, *I will ask*. The moment you say that key phrase, Creator knows that you are saying a living prayer: *May the heart of the forest be healed. May the hearts of all the trees, plants, rocks, animals and spirits who like to be here be healed. May they enjoy their time in the forest and feel welcome.*

If you get the feeling again farther up the road, say it again without looking at them, *May their hearts be healed. May they feel welcome wherever they go or where they are.* Remember, you have to say these blessings only once for each place, person or group of people. You are more sensitive now, and the plants and the animals and the stone and maybe even other people are more sensitive, too. You all need each other more now than ever, and here is something you can do to help others and feel better yourself.

It is intended now that many people begin giving and asking for such prayers. As Mother Earth and her rocks, trees, plants and animals come under more strain in your time due to so many people and their needs, these natural forms of life may no longer be able to give you the healings and blessings they have been doing simply by being and radiating their good health. So you can now give to them in return for all their generations of benevolence. These prayers are all they ask.

—Speaks of Many Truths

around. Suddenly your heart hurts. It is not a terrible crushing pain, it is not an emergency. It is a dull ache. When you get used to this living prayer, you will look around in the forest and say, *I will ask.* The moment you say that key phrase, Creator (or All That Is, if you choose) knows that you are saying a living prayer: *I ask that the trees and the plants and the animals* (you can say some of the animals' names if you wish—the deer, the birds and all the animals, for example—but you also want to acknowledge the spirits who live in the forest) *all have their hearts healed and enjoy their time in the forest and feel welcome.* Everyone likes to feel welcomed.

Then let it go and go on. If you get the feeling again farther up the road, then say it again. If there are people around, include them in the prayer. *May the plants, the trees, the flowers and so on in the forest and these fellow human beings, may their hearts also be healed.* If you wish, you can add, *May they feel welcome wherever they go or where they are.* (You don't have to say that. Just say the welcome part if you are inspired to say it.)

Very often when you do these things and get to the point where you just do them naturally, you will feel more comfortable in your body. You will feel like you are doing perhaps part of what you came here to do. It is easy, especially in your time, to be caught up in the goals of success and providing for your family and so on, which is completely understandable. Yet it is so easy to forget that what you call shamans, mystical people or medicine people really very often represent, in the ways they do things, things you can do yourself. And this living prayer is one of those things you can do.

I am not trying to say that shamans should then do something else. They will do what they do. But you can begin to take on this responsibility. That's why you have these feelings physically and, as you say, sometimes emotionally, but there will be physical evidence with them. Then you say something, a living prayer, and you feel better. It's not that you are being tested. It is that you are more sensitive now, and the plants and the animals and the stone and maybe even other people are more sensitive, too. You all need each other more now than ever, and here is something you can do to help others and feel better yourself. Is that not a wonderful combination?

In the past, shamans and mystical people were taught by others who could teach them, someone from their own clan or tribe, perhaps, and very often they were given wisdom from spirit and inspiration. They would work with a small group of people, sometimes passing on their teachings. But now with so many people and with tools of communication that you have, it is necessary that such wisdom go out beyond the clan or tribe and reach others so that they can apply it in their way, in their time, with their people and others they meet. It is important to encourage them to do living prayers and other things that benefit others, animals, plants and trees.

### Welcoming Will Make a Big Difference

You know, you are constantly hearing from your scientists and your observers that many plants and animals are going away, becoming extinct. I cannot tell you the impact it will have. If they know they are welcome by even one person, it helps. If many people tell them they are welcome and ask that their hearts be healed (even if you don't see the heart in the plant, there is one) and that they be comforted in some way and be loved, nurtured and know that they are loved. Just to have that stated out loud by one and then by many, even animals and plants that have gone away for many years might return because they feel welcome and appreciated.

You know, sometimes in families people who are gone for a while, if they feel welcome and appreciated, might show up at the next family gathering. Maybe they've got a wife and children and maybe they've got grandchildren. You haven't seen them for a while. But whatever it was that people said about them that made that person so uncomfortable that they went away from their family, the people not only don't say those things anymore, but they don't think them. They say, "Welcome, brother, welcome sister, so glad to see you again," with a real feeling of welcome. You will not only see those people at that annual gathering, but most likely more often.

### Use the Living Prayer for Weather

The same is true for plants and animals and for parts of Mother Earth's body, certainly not excluding her waters. There are places now in your United States and around the world that need water and places that need sun. For those of you who are in places that are flooding, go outside and look up even if there are clouds and rain. You can cover your eyes so the water doesn't hit them or you can close your eyes and say, *Welcome, Sun.* Even if the Sun is not visible and it's raining, just fill yourself with true welcome, not beseeching, and say, *Welcome, Sun.* It may not break right away, but it might bring the Sun there more quickly.

The same is true for places where there is drought. Go outside, reach up to the skies as my people did and some people still do and say, *Welcome, rain.* (Now I am making a gesture of rain.) *Welcome, rain.* It may not come right away, but it will come eventually. If many people do it and generally feel the welcome, it will come sooner yet.

With *Welcome, Sun*, you put your hands up like this [he stretches his arms outward, palms up]. You are smiling and welcoming the Sun as if it were shining right though the clouds. You must *feel* the welcome. An actor on the stage will convince you and the audience much more if they feel the feelings of the being they are portraying. When you feel welcome for the Sun, it will feel welcome and may come and shine sooner. These and other teachings are available to you. I will give you more as time goes on.

It is my intention to remind you of things about yourself that you either don't know, have forgotten or don't understand. In this way you will be able and perhaps even willing to apply these things in ways that benefit you and others, including those you never see, such as the spirits or angels or fairies or animals in the woods who will sometimes look at a human being. You don't see the animal, yet you suddenly get a good feeling and don't know why, but you are happy to have it. It is because the animal looks at you with love and affection and perhaps says to its companion, "This one looks like it has a heart." Maybe the deer says to its companion, "I won't be surprised if this one grows up to be a heart person." And with such radiated love, you see, the child feels that.

# 14

# The Physical Body Cries, "Show Me the Way!"

Zoosh
June 29, 1998

***Is there anything new on the sinister secret government?***

Well, let me look around. [Pause.] They are not really doing anything new, just more of the same, as we have discussed on previous occasions. You know that when they do something new, I am usually the first to bring it out. Nothing new, really.

### The SSG's Subliminal Messages and Your Natural Susceptibility

***I got the feeling, talking to Isis Friday night, that things are going a little slower, that the SSG were a little more successful at the subliminal messages they are putting on TV and in music CDs and cassettes than anybody had anticipated.***

Well, it's partly that, but it is also that people are becoming increasingly dependent on artificial stimulation. Think about it. The human body is made to be highly sensitive and reactive to any form of stimulation. This is because when you are out in the countryside or in the forest like the animal, you need to be alert to what might or might not be approaching or where to find food, where to find water—in other words, the combined total of all your senses might be expressed as your instinct.

Your body is set up like that, yet more and more of you are living in cities. So here you are, primed, as it were, by Mother Earth to be highly sensitive and to some extent selectively sensitive, but because not many of you have quite refined that yet, let's just say highly sensitive for the vast amount of people. Because you are set up to be reactive to stimuli, you're naturally going to seek stimuli wherever you can. Youngsters might go to a video arcade because, aside from the fun, it is natural to be reactive. If life is not sufficiently stimulating around you, you will seek more, not unlike people acting and interacting with the computer screen or to some extent (and this is much more common than people realize) interacting with the television set or the radio.

As a result of all of these distractions, which are substitutes for the sound of the wind or the olfactory sense (how does it smell?, what does it taste like?, what does it look like?, does it make a sound? and so on), as might be coordinated through your instincts out in the wild, your *substitute* stimuli arrive with their own agenda, whereas the wind and the smells of things and the forest or wildness in general arrive with no particular agenda. It's that very agenda, then, that impacts city people the most. To a lesser degree but noticeably, it impacts people living in the country or in the wilds. (I am not counting the suburbs of the country with the big city, but maybe a little bit of the small-town suburb.)

## Result: A Slight Slide in Dimensional Level

Now, if you take into account what is happening right now, what you have is a slight slide back in the dimensional level. Not to put too fine a point on it, you are at about 3.458, bringing it out another decimal point, which tells you that you are slightly below 3.46. Between what Isis said and what I am talking about, from my point of view, I believe this represents the reason there is a slowdown in the tendency of the average city person (a city is 75,000 or more) to be more inclined to receive their stimulus, mentally speaking (not counting what they get from people and so on), through the radio, the television (perhaps not in that order), and there are still some who read newspapers and news magazines.

This is part of what's going on. Also, of course, there are other attractions and distractions, not the least of which might be considered highly impactful in spirit and heart (not just your physical heart, but your energy heart as well): the crushing effects of drugs and alcohol. When I say *drugs* I am not entirely excluding prescription drugs, because they are often in response to some stress-induced physical condition, which then manifests itself as a de facto condition that must be treated by drug therapy, amongst other things.

Very often these drugs, performing their primary function well, will have unfortunate side effects. Of course, there are so-called illegal drugs that are having a terrible impact, I am sorry to say, on an increasing number of people. There is nothing new in anything I've said here, yet the cumulative effect is profound. Now, what to do about it?

## The Physical Location of the Body's Cry

The circumstances around this are creating a strong cry from within physical bodies. I will actually give you a point where it's being generated for some people: If you slide your fingers down to the bottom of your rib cage to where your solar plexus begins, for most people it's there. For some people it's around the foot and ankle area and the shin bone, as they call it. If you are more mental, it's more likely to be your solar plexus. If you are more physical (passionate and so on), it will more likely be your feet and shins. If you are more spiritual, it could be anywhere—most likely it would be the back of the head or the upper thoracic area.

This cry is summed up in a very simple line, which would simply be equated to (if you put it in words) ***"Show me the way."*** This is part of the reason there is a great resurgence of interest in religion, and soon there will be quite an upswing of interest in philosophy courses—especially by college students and, surprisingly, even by high school students.

A lot of these people go to religion and become very quickly dissatisfied with it, not because religion has a narrow point of view, but because the answers do not last long for their relief and tend to foster dependence rather than independence. People want to independently arrive at some *workable* conclusion that they can immediately put into their life to improve it. Religion will do this for a time, but not much longer than that, just for a while. A lot of churches are very confused right now because they will get waves of people in on Sunday, then in a couple of weeks or months, there's nothing but the core group again, and they don't know why. "What did we do?" But they didn't do anything.

***It's people looking.***

It's a search.

***So when the heart cries out or the different parts of the physical cry out it will help us get back up the dimensional scale, right?***

Yes. And the material that Speaks of Many Truths is going to talk about is very useful, because what's happening for the human being is absolutely the same thing that's happening for other life forms all over the Earth, including the Earth itself.

## A Living Prayer, Something We All Can Do

So when the human being can say a living prayer—something that's happening right now that you say a prayer about, then let go because it is part of life and you *have* to let it go—you find that you feel better physically.

You would be surprised that fully 10 percent of people's aches and pains have to do with other people or animals, rocks, trees, plants around them whose hearts or heart centers (in the case of some) are hurting. All they need from you is a form of acknowledgment called "the living prayer," as Speaks of Many Truths talks about it, where you ask, *May their hearts be healed* or more elaborate things, according to how you feel physically [see pages 91 and 93]. When you say these things, you say it and let it go. You go on. You will find that very often the pain in your body will go away.

I am not talking about people with chronic conditions. I am just talking about a pain that comes up suddenly, then as you put some distance between yourself and that thing or person, it might not go away, but it might become less. When you say that living prayer, *May their hearts be healed,* the pain will probably go away quickly. Don't look at the person or thing when you say it. Say it to yourself. Just go straight ahead because it's a prayer *you* are saying; they didn't ask you to say it. It isn't a communication to *them*; it's just a communication to whoever hears these things. Speaks of Many Truths might say God or the Great Spirit or the Almighty. You can say it to whomever you wish. Say it out loud so that it is understood by whoever hears and feels these things (as we might say, God) that this is something physical, something you are asking for *physical* beings. Probably soon after you say it, you will not only feel better in that part of your body, but you will also feel better than you felt *before* you said that prayer. Asking for such a thing—which is a simple thing, then you let it go and forget about it—is a divine act.

## Creator School, Where the Physical Self Seeks Constant Balance

Remember, Earth is Creator School in which you are now expected to perform divine acts. They are not very complicated; and they are worded. You say it, you let it go. If you look around when you drive through the forest or someplace that is ecologically intact or reasonably so, you can see that Earth is about balance, plants and animals living in harmony. It's a wonderful balance. Your body is made up of earth. This tells you that you as a physical being are made up of a substance that prefers to be in balance at all times. This is Creator School, and since Mother Earth is constantly doing

## Prayer for Heart Healing

For those who are sensitive: Have you noticed that your heart hurts when walking or going past a place?

If it is a forest, say this: *May the heart of the forest be healed. May the hearts of all the trees, plants, rocks, animals and spirits who like to be here be healed.*

Then go on. Your heart will probably feel better. If it starts again further on in your travel, say it again.

If it is a place where people live in buildings or where a person or people are, simply say, without looking at them, *May their hearts be healed.*

Always say these things out loud, though you can say these things softly if you need to. Remember, you have to say these blessings only once for each place, person or group of people.

Try not to look directly at people who cause your heart to hurt. Some other part of your body may hurt sometimes when you are near people who are suffering in some way. First ask that their hearts be healed, then add other parts of them according to what hurts on you. You don't have to name the organ unless you feel sure; just say the place on the body.

It is intended now that many people begin giving and asking for such prayers. As Mother Earth and her rocks, trees, plants and animals come under more strain in your time due to so many people and their needs, these natural forms of life may not be able to give you the healings and blessings they have been giving simply by being and radiating their good health. So you can now give to them in return for all their generations of benevolence. These prayers are all they ask.

—Speaks of Many Truths
June 28, 1998

things along the lines of being a creator, and many of the animals or at least the spirits of the animals and plants and so on are doing things along those lines, *you* can do that, too. A good place to begin, especially because this is a mental society, is to say a verbal prayer. You say it, you forget it. You don't say it again.

Let's say you are driving down the road, and all of a sudden for no reason you get a pain in your leg. There are other cars around and you have no idea if it's your pain or who has a pain in the leg. You just simply say, *May the heart of the being or beings who have this pain in their leg be healed, and may the pain in their leg also be healed.* Then you let it go and forget about it. Maybe the pain in your leg will go away, too. This isn't going to work for all pains at all times, but it might. You see, it's more likely these days that things like that will come up.

## A New Level of Cooperation

You are now expected to cooperate more with each other, to do more, to do greater things with each other and to be mutually cooperative. The animals, as Speaks of Many Truths said, and the planets and the trees and so on have been benignly radiating healing energy because they have it or because it's freely given to them. They have been radiating this for you for thousands if not millions of years. But now, because of a strain upon them—because there are more people and because these people have needs that affect the forest and the animals—they no longer have the capacity to radiate that energy to you.

All they ask in return is that you say—as you drive or walk by some forest where animals might be or where people you don't know might be in a building and suddenly you get an ache in your heart—*May their hearts be healed.*

If you are driving through a forest, you can say, *May the hearts of the trees and the plants and the animals and the rocks be healed and may they feel welcome.* If you like, you can add that part at the end about welcome, and then just go on and let it go. Probably your heart will feel better soon. If it doesn't, say it again in some other way. If it starts to hurt more, go see your doctor.

# 15

# The Arrival of the Wisdom Seekers and Wisdom Givers

Zoosh
July 2, 1998

We are pleased
to publish the heartwarming
news from Zoosh through
Robert Shapiro that you and
every human will be touched —
twice — in the next five
to seven years by spirits
accompanied by golden beings.
FIND OUT HOW THIS WILL
CHANGE YOUR LIFE FOREVER!

This is the time when all peoples all over the Earth who have not begun to wake up to their true selves will be touched over the next five to seven years by those I call the Wisdom Seekers. The Wisdom Seekers are not in their own right seeking wisdom, but when you are touched by them, *you* will seek wisdom.

### You Will Suddenly Have to *Know*

It will be almost like one day you are going along with your life, and the next day or even an hour from then, maybe not even overnight, you will suddenly crave to *know*. You will have to know and understand. Parts of your life that may at that point seem shallow to you will no longer interest you. You will begin to read and seek and ask and journey both spiritually and physically to places and people who can give you wisdom.

The Wisdom Seekers were here briefly in the late '50s and early '60s, touching only some people. Now they will touch everyone. If you desire to be touched by them, ask, and it shall be done sooner, not later. You will know you have been touched by them because you will have a *passionate* desire for wisdom, not just a casual interest, not just occasionally reading something enlightening. You will *have* to know.

It won't exactly be obsessive, as the psychologist might say, but you will have a thirst for wisdom—and you notice I am not saying a thirst for knowledge. Knowledge is different. Knowledge might be described as facts, descriptive or otherwise, that illuminate or elucidate points of interest. Wisdom is different. Wisdom gives you a working knowledge that you can use to simplify your life and cause your life be more rewarding, more pleasant and ultimately, in this lifetime and beyond, more fulfilling.

### Wisdom Givers Soon to Arrive and Touch You

It won't be long now, just a few weeks, when the Wisdom Givers will be present. The Wisdom Givers will again touch you. And what do I mean when I say touch? For most of you, if you feel it at all, it will feel not unlike being touched by a feather or the lightest hairs passing over you. It will touch your skin, you understand. It will be a good thing. After the Wisdom Givers touch you, the wisdom will come to you. It will come in practical experience, it will come from people talking to you, it will come from inspiration and ideas. It will leap off the pages of books and magazines that you might have been reading for years but will now suddenly inspire you to depths of understanding that have not occurred for you before with such frequency in this life.

This is by way of an announcement. With this occurrence you will find, those of you who embrace this (for that matter, those of you who don't embrace it or don't even know about it), that these pathways of inspiration are ultimately the greatest gift that has been bestowed upon you in this life. Many of you are on the path of illusion, and no matter what you acquire on that path, no matter how wonderful, it will satisfy you for only a short time, and soon you will hunger for something else.

I am not saying that you should discard your possessions or your acquisitions. What I am saying is, *only wisdom and love truly feed any individual.* When you are fed like this, the hunger disappears.

***Who decided to do this now?***

## The Wisdom Seekers

This is part of the plan. It was always so. The Wisdom Seekers are volunteers. All of them have lived on Earth, most of them within the past 200 years. Some of them have only just passed over, even as short a time as two or three years ago. They are all accompanied by a gold lightbeing who will support and sustain them on their journeys here because they have been on Earth so recently they might be distracted. They might also see someone they know, even a family member, yet their work is so important that they can linger for perhaps only a moment, meaning less than five minutes. If they should happen to see a family member or loved one, a friend, a beloved animal or even a beloved place, they must go on.

It is a great honor to be given this task, and that is why in recent years many spiritual people and others have been called to the other side, not to go all the way through the veils and beyond, but just to go through the veils, staying close by and gathering into a larger and larger group so as to return for this great job.

Every single person on the Earth will be touched. Don't try to avoid it; it is a good thing. Don't worry about side effects. You might say, "Does it mean, Zoosh, that I have to give up my philosophy or my religion?" Certainly not. It means that that wisdom will be added to you. "Does it mean, Zoosh, that I cannot follow the practices and methods that mean so much to me?" No, it does not, but it does mean that if you blindly follow a dogma that is self-destructive (meaning harmful to you or others), you will not be allowed to remain on this self-destructive path. You will be forced gently to become aware of wisdom that has to do with the path you have been on.

You will not be forced off this path, but you will be forced to know what *is* [on it]—and if you stay on the path, you cannot from that point on be deluded by the demands and commands of the dogma you follow. In this way enlightenment is assured. But interference with your free choices is guaranteed as well, though when this occurs now, you will not be able to choose self-destructive dogmas in ignorance. You will be able to choose them only in enlightenment, in which case you will probably not choose them, though there will be the occasional exceptions.

Wisdom Givers, on the other hand, might be people already on the Earth, also inspired by a gold lightbeing. Or they might be those from the stars who have come here in their lightbodies, also accompanied by a gold lightbeing. Or they might be animals. Your own pet might become one. They might be birds or a simple housefly, always accompanied by a gold lightbeing that either looks like them or is compatible with them. In this way all will be touched in the most gentle, benevolent and beneficial way possible.

## Awakening Timed to a Specific Population Size

***You gave us a clue about this a couple years ago when you talked about the Calling and about spiritual people leaving the planet. Is that connected?***

Yes, all is part of the plan.

***Why this moment? What happened at this moment to cause the plan to be implemented?***

It was always intended this moment. It was fixed at this time, as it were—*this will occur.* It isn't because you did something pro or con. It is a fixed portion of the plan that will cause you all to wake up.

***You say a fixed time, yet you say time is flexible and curved and changing.***

It had to do primarily with world population. When the population would reach anywhere over 5.57 billion, then it could be done. It also has to do with a fixed time reference from the future. Let's say we have a fixed time reference from the past and a fixed time reference from the future. Then, allowing for the variables of the present, the triangulation occurs at the moment when people least expect it.

The kind of questions people are asked, as in a person-on-the-street interview, are, Do you like this car? Do you like this chili sauce? Do you like this phone company? and so on. Assuming they were tolerant enough to answer, if you were to ask, "Do you think that the people of the Earth are now prepared to become enlightened spiritual beings in their own right?", most people would give you a blank stare. There would be a few who would say, "Sure, why not?" Then there would be many who would say, "Not in *my* neighborhood!" [Laughs.]

## The Snapback Has Begun

It is like this: Sometimes when people get far enough away from who they really are, the old snapback occurs, like the rubber band, only if you were to see it, it would appear to be in slow motion. That snapback has begun. It is necessary. People can get only so far away from who they really are before they must come back.

For example, say you are in deep slumber and your soul (which of course does not have to sleep) is out and about in other worlds with teachers and on voyages and so on, as your soul does. You're in what I would call deep slumber and your residual consciousness is experiencing this teaching and journey as a form of deep, veiled dreaming, the recollection one has when one wakes up. But if your soul gets too far away, a snapback occurs. You will know this because it will happen with some shock to the body, not a frightening shock, but occasionally you will wake up or almost wake up and feel a sudden jerk, a sudden twitch.

That is your soul coming back because your body says, "This far and no farther." Your mind does not say that. Your mind does not grasp the necessity of your soul being tethered to the body. It can understand it mentally. If I say it is so, your mind can think about it and say, "All right," but it does not understand it in terms of a *felt* knowing.

So it is for the body to say, "Come back!" and then [claps hands] it comes back. Usually, if you are not awakened, you will come close to consciousness and begin again. This is not, by the way, the cause of sleep apnea, but an occasional occurrence that happens to everyone. How often? Usually no more than once or twice a year at most.

***Who is saying now, "This far and no farther"—the Creator, the seeds of the Explorer Race?***

It is more what I would call the combined total of your heart being. Understand that right now the greatest difficulty for most people—aside from the obvious struggle, strife, war, conflict, battle, hunger, homelessness—is the preponderance of discomfort quenching your heart-love center's desire to live the most beautiful and bountiful life possible.

## The Touching and Its Results

***When you are touched by a Wisdom Seeker, what is being touched and what happens in the human?***

As I said, some part of your skin will be touched. If your arm is exposed, it will be touched. If you are wearing shorts, some part of your leg, perhaps. For those in a colder climate, some part of your face. But it will touch you.

***Then what happens? How does that translate into needing to seek wisdom?***

It will be like the experience of a walk-in, but *not* a walk-in. It will be symptomatic, in a sense. You will have these symptoms: some things that were terrifically important to you may cease to be so important. Some people you are desperately trying to emulate—perhaps they are wealthy and you wish to be wealthy; perhaps they are leaders in your field and you want to be like them, if only to have the recognition and admiration of your peers; perhaps it is someone you want to love you but who doesn't and loves another.

These desires that do not feed you and are will-o'-the-wisps, you understand (something that can be almost seen but not grasped), will fall away. You will find yourself increasingly craving answers that feed you, giving you a greater sense of good feeling physically in your body—more strength, more love that can be felt as warmth and comfort in your body, more safety. You will feel it. You will feel safer, and as a result, radiate safety and thus be safer. You will feel the need for deeper friendship with your friends. You will begin speaking about things with your friends that perhaps you have not discussed before—personal things, philosophy, maybe religion, if that interests you—not to convert or arm-twist, but rather to talk about beliefs that can be lived.

In other words, you will want to go deeper with everyone and everything to a level that truly feeds you and gives you the heart wisdom you can live by, love by and be nourished by. If there are friends who do not wish to do this, then you will find yourself losing interest in those people and seeking out others who would do so with you.

It does not mean that you will be discarding family and relatives thither and yon, but that you will want to know, and then shortly thereafter when the Wisdom Giver comes, you will *have* to know.

It will not be obsessive, as I say, but it will be a drive that will replace perhaps more shallow drives that have been with you as a compensation for the discomforts of youth. It won't put psychologists and therapists out of business, but they will perhaps notice a greater depth and realization and perhaps even greater and better results with their patients, quicker than they expected.

***Today is July 2, so you are saying that in a few weeks it will start?***

I am saying *it has begun.* It is so for the past few days, and three, four, five weeks from now come the Wisdom Givers. It will take five to seven years to touch everyone, but then there will be that feeling in you, *I want to know.* There will be an increasing dissatisfaction with what might be called trite, meaningless distractions. You will become less interested in the business of others if it does not affect you. Be warned, news services: You may have to become as relevant as you would prefer to be, instead of being more caught up in entertainment and scandal, which you do not prefer to be but have been forced into in recent years because of consumer tastes.

***This is the most epochal time on the planet, then. This is the change you talked about, right?***

The change happens gradually during this time, the five to seven years, and picks up speed. It will pick up velocity after the seven-year period in such a way that people will begin to say and think, The important thing is each other, how we feel about ourselves and how we feel about each other. That will apply not only to you, your friends, your family, your acquaintances, but everyone on the planet—humans, animals, plants, trees, everyone—and you will become more and more of this feeling as the years go by.

It might take 20, 25 years to complete this cycle, but after that, the idea they experience, the potential of having a shallow relationship with somebody, will be in the dictionary but it won't be a fact.

***Once a person is touched, what happens then?***

The Wisdom Giver does not give them the wisdom, but it fires them up so that they have to find it. The first touch is the beginning, you might say. After the second touch [claps], then you've *got* to have it. It's a drive. It will not be quite the same as the drive to eat. It will not be quite the same as the drive to have a loving companion, but it will be almost equal with the drive to have shelter, just a little bit behind that. So it will become a basic drive, and in fact, you will share this in common. As such it will give you one more thing in common. Oh, you won't all find that the same wisdom applies to everyone. That is the purpose of wisdom, but you will find that you *gotta have it.*

## Media Subliminals May Increase, but You'll Begin to Notice

***So what happens with what Isis called the stultifying effects of the sinister secret government (subliminals on TV and CDs)?***

They will continue. When Isis referred to the SSG's attempt to stultify you [chapter 8], it will continue at its current pace, if not increase. *However,* this thing I am speaking about tonight *cannot be stopped!* The stultifying effect will ultimately be especially noticeable to the average person and commented on in the TV news programs. In five to seven years the stultifying effect will be like a television discussion like this: One newsperson says to the other newsperson as they talk, "I just can't watch those silly shows on TV anymore. I've got to watch something with meat." And the other person will say yes. And the people watching will say yes. The programming people will also say yes. They won't be intimidated. They will be saying, "Great! We've got the shows for you, and we are happy to put them on." It will be the best thing that has happened to a lot of producers of communication—television, movies, books and everything.

***But what about the subliminals?***

They will keep trying, but ultimately people will become very conscious of it, and if they are not able to find the wisdom they want from their *old* knowledge-giver, the television, they will turn it off. I can assure you, those who provide programs—and perhaps more important, those who *sponsor* programs—will say, "Give them the meat."

## The End of Suffering

***We should have some kind of a celebration or something. This is so incredible! This new awakening is going to start ending suffering, right?***

That's correct. This time period will be the beginning, and in 25 years or so, maybe a little more, maybe a little less, everyone on the planet . . . well, they won't be completely themselves, but they will be motivated strongly. They will see their common interests and common ground. They will want to cooperate with each other. They will want to understand each other, and they will be willing to go the extra mile to do it.

Now people are agitated. It's as if people all over the planet are being shaken in preparation for these changes. It is not agitation done out of spite or revenge; it is an agitation to literally shake you out of some of the roles that have been thrust upon you and that you have adapted to. It is a temporary nervousness, but it will pass soon and be replaced by this drive for wisdom.

# 16

# Zero Point and the Unified Field

Zoosh
July 9-10, 1998

*Following are Zoosh's comments on "Update on the Fourth-Dimensional Shift and the Translation Period" by Drunvalo Melchizedek; posted July 1, 1998, on his Web page, www.drunvalo.net/shift.html. All excerpts are printed in italics.*

As I have said all along, there will be no catastrophes. What would the advantage be for catastrophic loss of life? But I do applaud this individual's broadcasting of this vision. I am going to call it what it is: a vision. Because so many others have had dreams or nightmares of such events, it is necessary to broadcast these things, because you as Creator juniors now have the capacity to change them. So if you get a memo like that, regardless how convincing it might seem, the thing to do after you have stopped reading it—either from one end to the other or any part of it, or if you've heard about it from a friend—is to say, "Well, it could be more benevolent, however." And that's it.

### Mantras of Feeling and Optimistic Vision

Say it with meaning, don't just say it as words. It is not a mantra to be said to distract the mind, but something that is said to offer a truly felt feeling of "Well, it could get better"—*that* feeling. Say that, and you will fulfill the function and the purpose of such visions, which is to trigger your Creator junior status to change it.

That is what these things are about. If enough of you do that, it not only will not happen, it *cannot* happen. If, on the other hand, everybody runs around screaming because the sky is falling or whatever vision anyone has had (not to put this man down; he is doing his work as he has been directed to do) and are preparing for the worst, believing the worst will happen, that gives it more potential to occur.

So the simple times are here. Many of you have been preparing for simple times. A few years ago it was popular in New Age circles to speak as if something had already taken place that you desired to take place—"speaking as if," they called it. That was the precursor. It was homework. Sometimes it worked, sometimes it didn't. It wasn't really about whether it would work or not; it was to prepare you. It was a Creator junior exercise.

Now you are Creator juniors, not quite on Creator's level—a little ways to go yet. It is time for you to say, "Well, these concerns might be legitimate. However, I feel" (say this only if you actually feel it, not because Uncle Zoosh says so) "that it could be better. Better things could happen. More benevolent things could happen—unification, comforts, loves, insights and so on," whatever words you wish to say. Keep it simple. While others around you are saying, "Woe is me," say, "Well, it could get better." Say it with feeling, not just words.

That is my broad response, and if necessary I will give a point-by-point response.

## A Deep-Space Explosion

***Okay. Point number one [reading from Drunvalo's paper]:***

> *Deep space: On December 14, 1997, an explosion was received on Earth from deep space. From an area about the size of Texas about 12 billion light-years away, an explosion occurred that, based on* $E = mc^2$ *would have required all the known and visible matter in the universe to release that much energy. According to the paper that I was reading, it would have been equivalent to one-thousandth of a second after the original Big Bang. This is impossible by our understanding of the universe. There is not one person on Earth that could even begin to explain this one. And to further complicate the matter, over 2000 of these explosions have occurred since the first one. Over 2000 new universes have been created within this one!*

What's defined as an explosion? If you look up the actual chemical description of an explosion, it could also be considered an ex-

### Mantras of Feeling and Optimistic Vision

A few years ago it was popular in New Age circles to speak as if something had already taken place that you desired to take place—"speaking as if," they called it. It wasn't really about whether it would work or not; it was to prepare you.

Many have had dreams and nightmares of [catastrophes, but now that] you are Creator juniors (not quite on Creator level—a little ways to go yet), it is time for you to say, "*Well, these concerns might be legitimate. However, I feel that it could be better. Better things could happen. More benevolent things could happen—unification, comforts, loves, insights and so on,*" whatever words you wish to say. Keep it simple.

While others around you are saying, "Woe is me," say, "*Well, it could get better.*" Say it with feeling, not just words. Say that, and you will fulfill the function and the purpose of such visions, which is to trigger your Creator junior status to change it.

That is what these things are about. If enough of you do that, it [catastrophes] not only will not happen, it *cannot* happen.

—Zoosh

pansion of light. Explosions on Earth are usually considered to be destructive, with the exception of the so-called Big Bang theory.

***Well, they are equating this to 2000 Big Bangs.***

But you know my opinion of the Big Bang (baloney!). Now, it's a nice theory, but, to the scientific community: You can do better than that. I'd rather say that these were expansions of light designed to create a greater cohesiveness with all forms of life in this universe preparatory to the coming change that will be diffused into the universe by and through the vehicle of the Explorer Race.

***They are preparing already for the expansion?!***

Yes. You just can't suddenly one day say, "Wake up, everything is different."

## Pulses from the Galactic Center

***I'll go on:***

*The Galactic Center: Since December 14, 1997, the center of our galaxy has also begun to pulse huge amounts of energy out to the universe. This also is unexplainable, according to the scientist that I was talking with. In fact, the satellite that was destroyed in June of 1998, the "beeper" satellite, was destroyed from one of these blasts from the center of our galaxy, according to this same scientist. This man believes that if this energy continues to rise and pulse, it will eventually destroy all of our satellites around the Earth.*

No, it won't. Understand that I would put "destroyed" in quotes. Satellites are, for the most part, designed (at least scientific ones) to send and receive. So if they're overwhelmed by an incoming signal that is not from their usual source, they can be *shocked* out of commission. I would prefer to say that the satellite was shocked out of commission, not making it sound quite so mysterious and dramatic (though I do understand why this is put that way).

***Is that what happened? Was that energy pulsed from the center of the galaxy?***

No, but energy pulses can knock satellites for a loop.

***What happened to the beeper satellite?***

It was knocked for a loop.

***What knocked it for a loop?***

An energy pulse not unlike the ones you referred to on the previous point. It wasn't the target of some nefarious target-shooting.

## The Sun's Disappearing Magnetic Poles and Unusual Flares

***Number three:***

*The Sun: In 1992 everything was normal with our sun. It had a magnetic north and south pole. It was functioning normally by scientific standards. In December of 1994, the Ulysses spacecraft from NASA arrived at the sun to measure its magnetic field. NASA was astonished to find out that the magnetic field of the sun no longer has a north and south pole. The sun's magnetic field had changed dramatically into a homogeneous field. There was, of course, no scientific explanation. No one had ever seen anything like this before. Then the SOHO satellite was launched to study the sun for a two-year period.*

*Early in June 1998 two comets entered into the sun. This is not unusual. As many as twenty-five or more comets or asteroids a year will either enter the sun or graze it. Nothing has ever happened before when the sun was struck by a cosmic body. But this time the sun reacted in a way no one has ever seen before. Approximately*

> *30 to 35 solar flares erupted on the surface of the sun, all in two parallel circles at the 19.5 north and south latitudes. These are the latitudes where the interlocking tetrahedrons cross the sphere of the sun. It is the same with the Earth or a human being. If even two or three solar flares were to erupt at one time, this would be a great concern because of the magnetic storms that could be caused on Earth; 30 or 35 is outrageous.*

You have to understand that when a statement is made that no one has ever seen this before, it means no one has ever seen this before *recently*. The Sun has been around for quite a while. If it manifests a change in its being that is not so awful, I would have to say, don't worry about it. Your Sun is the precursor of what I expect to happen to the magnetic field on Earth, which is that the northern pole and the southern pole will gradually merge to make a consistent, or what I would call a unified, field of magnetic energy on the Earth. This will undoubtedly be more easily accommodated by people and animals on the Earth.

***They are saying, "the solar proton flux, which is measured in PUI, rose to about 2500 PUIs in the late 1980s." And a few days ago, they said, it was 42,000 PUI. Does it mean anything?***

No.

## SOHO's Silence

***To go on:***

> *Another interesting point, on June 25th, 1998, the SOHO satellite that was watching the sun suddenly became inoperative, according to NASA. No more information to us. Could this be real or a man-made problem to stop the flow of information to the public?*

Well, I think that to some extent restricting some of the information is not so awful. People understood in the West, not necessarily in eastern parts of geography, whether it is true or not, that sudden changes, scientific or otherwise, might cause agitation. So let's just say that some of that wisdom is being restricted while cooler heads (if I might say that) examine it and try to understand if there is any potential impact meant for the Earth. I think that by and large I approve of that.

It's really quite extraordinary to think about this in what you consider to be modern times—you know, computers and modern man. But really, in terms of human beings' feelings and physical activities and prowess, if there were some kind of major astronomical change, some people would hit the panic button. But by and large, I think if most people did not allow themselves to be wound up, it won't be so awful. Do not expect the Earth to stop rotating. Obviously, if it did, that would be the end of life as you know it.

***But that's not going to happen?***

No, that was an aside.

## An Unannounced Magnetic Storm

***I'll continue:***

*Another interesting point: On June 26, 1998, we had a major magnetic storm on Earth that reached 6 or 7 magnitude. Usually the whole world is informed, preparing us for this potential problem. NASA did not inform the public. Why?*

A major magnetic storm? I don't think so. There might have been magnetic fluctuations. If it had been a major magnetic storm, the entire communications system—at least in the West, which is perhaps overly technological at the moment—would have been completely disrupted. So I cannot support the idea of a major magnetic storm at all.

## Fires in Mexico

***Here's more:***

*The Earth: We are being told here in the States that the fires in Mexico are being caused by farmers burning fields to make room for more crops. Eyewitnesses in Mexico that I have talked with have a different story. They say that Mount Popocatepetl, about 40 miles southeast of Mexico City, has been erupting for over a year now, and the ground in the surrounding area is becoming very hot. Eyewitnesses say that the trees are spontaneously breaking into flames, which would mean that the ground would have to be over 459 degrees Fahrenheit. One report said that they even saw animals spontaneously break into flames. One eyewitness that I spoke with said that even a long ways from Mount Popocatepetl the ground is so hot that the rubber soles of shoes will melt while walking in the forest.*

It is true enough that in any area where a volcano is erupting (and there are volcanoes erupting elsewhere in the world, and people are not hitting the panic button), volcanic vents or steam and gases may show up in the general area, and any vegetation nearby might very well create a fire, to say nothing of the effects of the volcanic residue. While this may be true as far as it goes, the bulk of the fires, aside from those started by natural causes, are fires that got away from land-clearing. I will support that. I am not trying to make the farmers or potential farmers the enemy. That is not much different than what happened in this country at various times or in other countries.

People have still not quite grasped the profound significance of trees. You know, as Speaks of Many Truths has said—and I will second that opinion—it is largely trees, not grasses, that signal Mother Earth's body as to the necessity for rain. Think about that the next time you are wiping out a forest.

## North American Volcanoes and Earthquakes

***Next he mentions several volcanoes that appear to be near eruption: "In June 1998 another huge volcano, Pacaya, erupted near Guatemala City." That's a statement. "In California the Mammoth Lake area appears to potentially be ready for a possible eruption."***

Ask any geologist, and many will tell you that many volcanoes are potentially ready for another eruption. I would say that it is not imminent.

***"Mount Saint Helens is receiving about 170 earthquakes per day."***

So? The Grand Canyon has lots of earthquakes, too. I am not trying to pooh-pooh this stuff (if I might use that old-fashioned term), but I see no advantage in raising the alarm consistently. Think about it as in the old story about the boy who cried wolf. If you continually raise the alarm and things do not happen, eventually people ignore the real alarms.

I will say that science has advanced far enough, to say nothing of observers of animal behavior, to give local residents probably a good sixteen hours' notice. Pay attention to what the animals do and call your friends and neighbors if they behave strangely. You know all these things. That will give you a much better warning than 170 earthquakes every day etc. Earth is a living being. Earthquakes for her are no different than motion for you.

## Melting Ice in the Antarctic

***Okay, next point:***

> *The South Pole is melting. There are three volcanoes going off under the icecap. They have been active for many years now. Last year the biggest piece of ice ever known broke off, about 800 square miles of ice. At the moment another huge piece is about to break off. This one is called Larson's Ledge and is about the size of the state of Texas [corrected July 13 to Connecticut] and about 3 or 4 miles deep [corrected July 13 to 800 meters]. It is cracking fast. If this piece of ice breaks off, according to the press releases, it will*

*raise the world oceans by 65 feet. Two countries will disappear forever and almost every coastal city in the world will be destroyed. Just think what would happen to Florida when the highest point is 90 feet. This would happen in about one day.*

No. Think about it: Is it possible that the oceans could go up by 65 feet even if both the poles melted? Remember, water in the oceans is not being held as it is in a swimming pool. There is a degree of stability about the oceans. If there is too much water at any given time on the surface of the Earth, a lot of it will just go underground. Mother Earth will bring her waters to the surface only if she is going to need to make some imminent catastrophic change, which is not likely to happen.

Oh, I will grant you that if the population on the Earth gets to be around 15 to 20 billion, then you would have to look for these things, but I think that by the time the population gets to even eight or nine billion, serious discussions will be taking place about population control. Right now I do not consider the discussions taking place to be serious at all, with the exception of China. China is perhaps the only country that is seriously doing anything about this. I am not saying that what they are doing is good or bad; just that, while there will be mistakes made initially, ultimately some form of population stability will be necessary.

The old ways of stabilizing a population through war, disease and famine are not what I would call an advanced spiritual application of creativism. So it will be up to you Creator juniors to resolve this. Simply begin by saying, "The population of Earth can come to a benevolent balance with all the rest of life on living Earth." Say it *if you mean it.* Don't say the words alone; it won't work. Say something like that. Feel the feelings you have as a result of saying it, and that will be a good beginning for Creator juniors (I'm speaking to you en masse).

## Geomagnetic Field Changes

*The geomagnetic field of the Earth is undergoing huge changes. For 2000 years the Earth's geomagnetic field has been growing weaker: 2000 years ago the field measured about 4 gauss. About 500 years ago the geomagnetic field began to drop at a much faster rate. The field now measures only about 0.4 gauss. In the last 20 years the field has not only been dropping, but has become erratic. Birds that use the geomagnetic field to migrate are now ending up at the wrong location because the field has changed. This is the same with dolphins and whales. They use the geomagnetic lines to migrate, which have been stationary for thousands of years and have now changed. Some of these lines now move inland, and this is the reason why many whales have beached themselves. They were just following the geomagnetic lines that have always guided their migration, but which now lead into land.*

*In the last two weeks of September 1994, the world experienced a geomagnetic field wobble. Airlines worldwide were forced to manually land their planes because the geomagnetic field of the Earth began to move. By the beginning of October it seemed to return to normal.*

This is an *ibidem* [meaning "see the above reference"] question. I have referred to this before in reference to the unified field being developed. However, this is a job for Creator juniors. Say something that suggests a benevolent outcome. Don't say what's *not* going to happen; say what you feel *could* happen, something as it *could* be—that all the people on Earth will create a field that will work benevolently for all beings. Don't try to invent how you are going to do it. It won't be done through technology as you know it now.

It will be done through what I call heart science, meaning through benevolent feelings. Not by prayers to a distant Creator, but statements—good, loving feelings. The kind of thing that a close Creator—Creator is focusing a lot of Its energy near this planet now—wishes to see you do as God's children on Earth. All beings everywhere are God's children, so don't get a big head. But as God's children on Earth and as the Explorer Race, you are not expected to say, "Woe is me, what can we do?" You are expected to *do* something. If it is the impossible—meaning you do not know what to do about it because you have not invented a machine to do it—say something like I have indicated and then let it go. Pick out the words, say them once and let them go. True creation comes about not only on the basis of need, but also on the basis of unselfish gifting to the world around you, which includes you.

## Schumann Resonance Climbing

***The next thing they're saying is that the Schumann resonance frequency (SRF) used to be 7.8 Hertz and it's now 13 and climbing. What does that mean?***

Some of that is brought about because there are now extreme low frequency (ELF) transmitters, which are interfering with Mother Earth's natural frequency. Also, about one percent of that has to do with Mother Earth making adjustments and changes within herself. Understand that Mother Earth is a living planet, and in order to do things for herself, she is going to use her natural elements, elements that you are used to—heat, cold, wind, rain etc. She is not going to suddenly create an ice age. She is not going to suddenly explode a volcano in the middle of Madison Avenue. But she will do what she can where she can, and a lot of it might have to do with using heat.

When you are having tunnels drilled in your body and when there is excessive mining (what is excessive mining?—exploratory mining, that's excessive), injuring the inner structure of Mother Earth, she must use the most obvious means to repair herself, which will be heat and water. This suggests, of course, that mining will be significantly more dangerous in the future. Aside from that, there is entirely too much destruction taking place underground. Just because you don't see much of the results on the surface doesn't mean that Mother Earth doesn't remind you of the results.

***So when she uses heat and water, the frequency goes up higher?***

If you are sitting quietly in a chair, your pulse and respiration are constant—at rest, you might say. Not as deeply at rest as if you are in a deep sleep, but at rest. If you get up and walk across the room for a cup of coffee, your pulse and respiration speed up. Mother Earth is no different. If she does something, her vibrations, her measurable pulses, will be altered.

## Magnetic-Field Measurements by Instruments Calibrated for 3.0 (not 3.458) Earth

***Now, here's the thing they are really concerned about. They feel that the geomagnetic field of the Earth is racing toward zero. That's the zero-point discussions going on out there. They are convinced that it is going to go to zero anytime from the end of July to the end of the year.***

No. Here's something that's important. I suppose I can talk about this now. Instruments that are used to measure these things were designed to function for specifications and ideals created when the dimension here was closer to 3.0. Now that the dimension is no longer 3.0, these instruments are not giving you an accurate measurement of what's happening where you are now. It might still be giving a fairly accurate measurement of what's happening at 3.0, but you are not there anymore. So do not be overly alarmed at these things.

It is true that there are changes. I believe you can live with most of these changes. It is also true that you are reminded on the nightly news that people are suffering in one part of the world or the other. Don't get it into your head that this is a permanent condition. Such things exist for God's children here who are the Explorer Race *so that you can resolve them benevolently*, not because you are intended to suffer. Remember, problems are meant to be solved, and they are never solved by silencing your opponent. They are resolved benevolently in benevolent ways.

## Wants: Unfulfilled Needs

Not everyone can have everything he or she wants, but everyone *can* have everything that is needed. Learn to identify how so many wants are related to unfilled needs. When needs go unfulfilled, wants spring up as substitutes. For example (obviously and widely now), sometimes when people do not have enough love and affection in their lives (and that's a need, at least at that time in their lives), they might begin to crave other things, which are wants. That's the difference.

Learn the difference between wants and needs, and you will not only be a much better statesman/woman at the United Nations, but you will learn how to unite yourselves as Earth people without the required invasion of monster aliens from outer space who want to cook you over the barbecue (which, by the way, is all baloney).

***What can they do to recalibrate their instruments so that they get an accurate reading?***

Nothing. You are moving now out of the time in which measurements of a scientific nature are an accurate representation of the world around you. That was always an illusion anyway. You are moving into the time of heart science, which has to do with feelings within a person in reaction to the world around you. Feelings, you will discover, will be much more accurate in the future and much more usable. For instance, Speaks of Many Truths has given a lot of this in his Shaman books* (by using heat and good feelings in the heart/chest). This is the coming way for people who can learn to function instinctually. In this way they will get along. For people who are attached to technology, you will at least be temporarily confused.

***In addition, other human discoveries also indirectly point to this time as being the time of what he calls the "translation period."***

Think about what the so-called translation period means. This is my definition: It means that the way you have been doing things must be translated to the most benevolent and beneficial way to do things. So yes, it is intended that you discover things that are anom-

---

* *Shamanic Secrets for Material Mastery*, Light Technology Publishing, 1999, and the second volume tentatively titled *True History of Earth and Lost Civilizations*.

alous, regardless of what they are—which means they don't fit, they don't follow—and that the theories on which a great deal of your science is based have to be altered, or else you will live in a progressively smaller world based on a restrictive scientific model that does not fit your actual world.

## The Bible Code

***Another excerpt from Drunvalo:***

> *The discovery of the secret book in the Bible, the computer program which could not be opened "until the end of time" has been opened. This is reported in the book,* The Bible Code [by Michael Drosnin]. *This is very important.*

That's nothing new. You could talk to pioneers in this country a hundred years ago and they will tell you the Bible has mystical properties. I might add that many mystical books encoded with mysticism intended to be discovered at different times have qualities that are special and unique. Certainly the Bible is one. The Koran is perhaps more profoundly so.

Understand that in the Bible you are using now (we are talking about the Bible, since this is a predominantly Christian country), the New Testament is greatly abridged. If it were complete, then I would say it is profound and very mystical (if not even *more* mystical) and certainly equal to the Koran. The Koran is more complete, whereas your New Testament is grossly incomplete.

***Will we find the pieces while . . .***

These pieces exist, and they are not tremendously secret. Any good Bible scholar can access a great many of these things that were originally part of the various testaments and had to do much more with mysticism and mystical practices, much of which is considered by the scientific community to be mumbo-jumbo because it does not guarantee reproducible results. But mysticism, philosophy (these things are religion also) are not designed to serve the mind. They are designed to serve the heart, and the heart is ultimately the organ you cannot live without.

## Serving the Essential Heart, Not the Expendable Mind

Science will tell you that you cannot live without a brain, but in fact you can; but you certainly cannot live without a heart. It is this clear-cut philosophical fact that's intended to draw your attention to the heart as being the perhaps least understood mystical aspect of any being that could be developed, certainly any human being. Most animals, big or small, have these capacities and use them. Most human beings have these capacities and don't know about them. If they are encouraged and are shown how to use them, they say, "Voila! There it is! I can do it, too!" Of course, the whole thrust of the shamanic series of books is to introduce people to the mystical aspects of the heart.

For you all now, consider that when you see or hear about the volcano erupting and people are concerned with the feeling as well as the words, "Well, the volcano is erupting. It's possible that the lava flow will move slowly enough and on a path where it will do the least destruction to animals and people and plants. Perhaps on an island, it will flow to the sea. Perhaps inland, it will flow out into a vast area that is largely unpeopled; or if there are people there, it will flow slowly and the people will be able to get out of the way." That's my explanation, but you might simply say, "It's possible that the lava flow will go someplace where no one will get hurt."

Keep it simple. If you can have warmth in your chest when you are saying it, that's better, but at least have the feeling that it *could* be so. This isn't dogma; you don't have to believe it, as in blind faith. Say it because it *could* be so, then let it go. Don't get caught up in the panic of it. Yes, pay attention; yes, make preparations, especially if your home is in the path. Move your furniture out; you might have to go elsewhere. You might lose your home, but the important thing is that you don't lose your life and your family is safe. Get your animals out, you understand. That is the important thing. Use these challenges as an opportunity to provide living prayers for yourself and others.

***Thank you for having the patience to do this.***

Just let people know that it is not my intent to attack anyone. Such hues and cries are sometimes necessary so that people will change things. This man did the right thing, and if I can address a comment to him, I will simply say, "You did the right thing to inform people. Keep it up, because by informing people of these things, whether they are factual (whether you can confirm them) or whether they are speculative or theoretical, you will ultimately encourage people to transform the situation. If you feel an urgency to communicate things of this type, I urge you to continue.

***Thank you very much, Zoosh.***

# 17

# Hacker, an SSG Dupe, Causes Titan 4 Rocket Explosion

Zoosh
August 13, 1998

All right, let me say this in reference to the recent missile explosion. This was caused by a hacker. The hacker does live at this time in the forty-eight contiguous states of the U.S. This individual represents an unintentional—at this moment—tip of an iceberg of a long-range sinister secret government plot to corrupt computer hobbyists. I am going to call them hobbyists because it's more than a pastime, as someone who scans the Internet, and because the great interest in computers does not have any plateaus past programming.

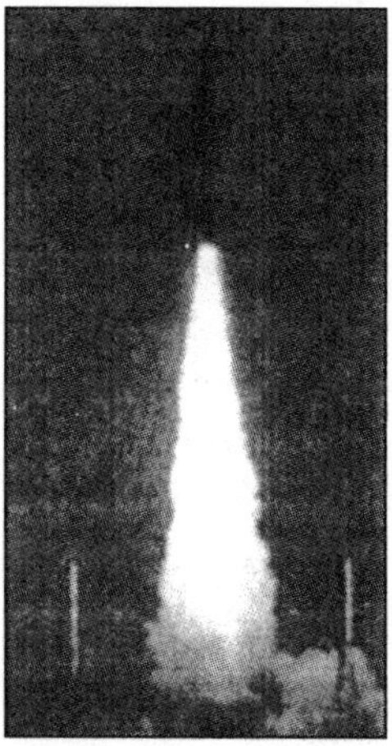

There are those who have such mathematical minds that they wish to know; and sometimes, because there is no constructive outlet for them, they wish to leave a calling card, not necessarily intending to destroy anything but sometimes intending it. You have, then, a whole group, a subculture that is poised to be utilized, most of them unconsciously, by a group that wishes to keep all countries battling each other.

This act of sabotage—that's what it was—was not prompted by any of the contractors or any of the participants during the launch. It was, however, a direct result of meddling done by a hacker, very cleverly disguised with a planted, albeit obscure, trail intending to lead investigators to the wrong suspect. The intention of the hacker was not to actually destroy the missile, but to interfere with such technology. It just happened to bring about the destruction of the missile. One must pause to consider what might have occurred if the missile was carrying something more destructive than a satellite intended for observation.

The reason I am bringing this up now to discuss it is because for a long time the sinister secret government has, using its outreach programs, been attempting to corrupt this group of people.

It is true that some people are simply alienated, as in the sociological reference. And it is true that if a person is overinvolved on the computer, even for hobbyist reasons, there is the potential, not the promise, of becoming more enchanted with technology and perhaps less heart-oriented toward human beings. I am putting in a lot of variables, but it is necessary to understand that all hackers are not "unconscious dupes of the sinister secret government."

Let's consider that the sinister secret government wants you in this country to feel besieged by both your perceived enemies and to some extent by your perceived friends. For a long time they have been attempting to create rifts between the United States and its allies—not just the obvious allies people know about, but countries that are largely considered to be not overtly friendly to the U.S. but who do things to further the cause of the United States' mission, meaning to spread the word and the value of the economic and governmental system of the U.S.

Now, these types of allies, who are more diplomatic go-betweens, are perhaps the most precarious allies, because they might posture one way in public while in private actually work with the U.S. toward the U.S.'s ultimate political goals. In this way the vast majority of the public and even many allies of the United States have no idea that these countries are working in any way with the U.S. toward its ultimate intention.

This particular hacker managed to leave a credible trail—that's the key: not just a casual trail, but a credible one—to one of these allies that functions as a go-between. (I am not going to say which one; I am going to protect some people here.)

Referring to this as a tip of the iceberg is essential, because I'd like to enlist the aid of the mass of computer hobbyists all over the world. I am not trying to draft you all, regardless of your politics, into being associated with the U.S. government aims, private and political. What I am trying to suggest is that in order to maintain as much peace as there is in the world (not peace in the world, but as much peace as there is), we need to have your support.

I am going to ask you computer hobbyists to see if you can track down and dismantle, on your own or in cooperation with the authorities, these types of hackers, many of whom do not realize they are being used as dupes by the SSG.

Also, because of the occasional unusual lifestyles associated with some hackers—or anybody, for that matter—many of these people can be unduly compromised and influenced. On one hand we do not want to say that these destructive hackers are the enemy. What we want to say is that it is important to give them the chance to find something to do that is constructive.

Many of you know who might be into hacking or into zealous computer hobby time in areas that go beyond programming. One of the more interesting plateaus you might reach for after that is cryptography, meaning making and breaking codes. You would be surprised how much work there might be available for these people, not only in governments of benevolence, but also in private industry. So I am going to suggest, if you are looking for a plateau that goes beyond programming, that you put your effort there. There is an awful lot of coding that hasn't really become established yet.

Needless to say, before the true establishment of computers, musical codes were common, even color codes. Such things will become more common, as time goes by, with your present instruments of complexity. I want to bring this to the attention of people because I feel that this is important.

Think about it. What happens when international space agencies that are now forming (they already have formed on the corporate level, but truly international space agencies such as cooperative efforts between Russia, Japan, France, United States and so on who pool their technologies, techniques and funds) create an international version of NASA? What would happen if somebody broke into the computer systems there and caused a destructive malfunction?

Remember, these initial probes out into space are truly the beginning of your interplanetary space program. We need to have you be alert. So rather than point out who hackers are, where they live and so on, I am going to ask you, not to just police yourselves, but to understand and remember the Zoosh definition of self-destructive: hurting yourself or someone else. That is critical.

## How Hackers Are Duped by the SSG

***I am not clear how the secret government gets to these hackers who feel alienated.***

One of the things they do is give them support. Now, here's an interesting thing: For the average person, being given support would be something that is handed to you physically. Or in computerese, perhaps, a place you could call for help at no charge. But the SSG is aware of what it's dealing with, or at least they are looking for people who are self-destructive and have these abilities. They know that the best way to entrap them is to give them a challenge they can solve, but not easily; and when they solve it they receive a reward. Look at computer games—that's basically a description of computer games.

I am not trying to say that the SSG has designed computer games, but I will say they have certainly perfected it as a tool of espionage. They will set up or support a company, for instance, that has access available, but only if you can reach that zenith of breaking into the system. Once you break into the system, you might find that you suddenly have infinitely more computer tools available to you.

This is an age-old method of teaching; it is nothing that they invented. But if you are trying to train someone subtly, to lead them down the path of self-destructiveness, you have to recognize who your market is, if I can use that term. You can't make it too easy. It has got to be reasonably challenging, reasonably difficult, and it has to be something that pays off in some substantial way.

You might ask (which is really the second part of your question), what is their ultimate intention? Their ultimate intention is to essentially give these people enough tools—they are not going to push a button and let them loose—so that they represent a real danger.

That's exactly what happened in this last instance. Someone had the tools to represent a *real* danger. I have been saying for a long time that your country and some other countries are overcomputerized, because computers are basically switches. They're on or they're off, or they turn things on or off. That's its most basic form. As a switch, it does not have a heart when it's in the form of the machine. The materials that make up the machine have heart, yes. But once it becomes a machine and becomes confused with its association with things it is not usually associated with, such as some derivative oil clamped together with something made out of steel or glass (not its normal form), it will maintain that confused state as a material. When that occurs, the overriding function of the heart of the material does not work well. A computer that is reminded of who it is [spoken about by Speaks of Many Truths in *Shamanic Secrets of Material Mastery*] will have more heart and might be less inclined to be self-destructive or used for self-destructiveness.

The challenge here is the orientation of the individual and the intention of the SSG to basically place a time bomb in your midst. Think about it: You are very computerized. Some things that actually can be done better by human beings on their own are also computerized , simply because that's the way the system is set up.

I am not saying, dismantle your computers. What I am saying is, consider where human beings could work as well as computers, if not better, and let those computers be used for something else. Also, understand that the SSG does not want to *destroy* the United States; it just wants to *control* you and every aspect of what you and everyone else in this country does so that you will be good sheep and follow whatever they want you to follow, buy whatever they want you to buy and do whatever they want you to do. If that sounds satisfactory to you, go along. If it doesn't, fight it.

***Okay, we need to go over this a little bit because it's not clear. Are we talking about the people who create the computer games having these advanced tools? Or people who play the games who are able to get into the deepest level of these complex computer games?***

I am not talking about computer games. I used that as an example. The SSG will set up or support a company that is ostensibly performing a business and yet has some kind of glamour aspect associated with it—meaning it might be producing something for defense industries. Or it might be producing something that in some way will be attractive to a computer hobbyist, such as a computer company. The real intention of the company is not so much to make a product and sell it at a profit—that is their secondary intention. Their primary intention is to draw attention from computer hobbyists to encourage them to make it look great, to make it hard, to make it a challenge to get into the company's system and find out what new little tricks there might be.

Think about it. I don't want to talk too much about this stuff, because there are things I could say that would essentially play into the SSG's hands. But suppose you were a computer hobbyist and someone told you that it would be possible to obtain a cryptographic password that would work not only for a given reference—meaning a given stage, step or company—but for *many* companies, and it would work without the possibility of the hacker being detected.

***Okay, here's a company. It is set up and funded, and somehow in its computer technology is a cryptographic key. Now, if it is not the employees who get into it, then how do the hackers get into it?***

How do hackers get into anything? The purpose of hacking . . .

***. . . is to break in.***

Is to break in. They are not employees. You don't have to worry about employees.

***How does the word get out that these tools are available?***

For starters, it gets out because there is hacking; plus, in the case of our company here, this is G company (this is an example; I can't call it mythical because they exist). They make sure that the word gets out to what I would call hacker networks. Hacker networks are not something that would be on America Online or the Worldwide Web. It would be perhaps a slightly encrypted private networking system by which people who, for the most part, are not known to each other personally but who will share information on how to gain information.

***Got it. So the SSG let it out that these tools are available at this G company?***

And they usually let it out in some casual way. They will either tell somebody, whisper in somebody's ear, as it were, or they will put a message out on one of these hacker networks they can hack into and say, "Have you heard about . . . ?"

***It's supposed to be hackers sharing secrets, but in this case the SSG slips this information into the hackers' network?***

It is very clever. The clever aspect of it is that if this were something being done by a government with an intention to dismantle an opposing force, one might call it counterintelligence, but, being done by the SSG, one has to call it corruption.

The seduction of it is that they make it challenging. That's the key. It is not because they want to make it exclusive; they want to make it hard because the market they are aiming for are individuals who have the ability and the talent to actually use this information for purposes the SSG believes will create intentional (from their point of view) chaos.

If you have a country that is entirely computerized . . . your country is not entirely computerized, of course, because many, many small business are not, but there is an awful lot of it. Well, I don't have to tell you that every year this or that virus is detected. People in corporations and governments are vigilant about viruses now, but in the beginning it was a real problem, and it still comes up now and then. This is way past viruses; this is something that represents a genuine threat.

***So this hacker, then, got a cryptographic key, got into the NASA system and . . .***

No. We need to be very clear here. He got into one of the suppliers' systems, and through no fault of the supplier, who had *very* good security, manipulated and otherwise messed with some components. I am not going to say any more than that because it would be very easy to defeat the purpose of this article, which is intended to be a warning rather than make things worse. I need to be discreet. If I am not discreet, it could make matters much worse.

He didn't break into NASA. NASA has really good security in places where they wish to have it. Obviously, they have public communications as well.

## Plutonium on Board the Rocket

***Now, there are implications that seem to make this much, much worse than what you have said. The first report on National Public Radio said there were 25 pounds of plutonium on this rocket. We can't find where this was mentioned anywhere again. Everyone later referred to it as "highly toxic materials."***

I will support the reference to the radioactive material, understanding that this is not an atomic bomb in space, because to put an atomic bomb in space does not require such a launch. Nor is it particularly necessary—but I don't want to go into that in any event. I would say this, however: There are other uses for such radioactive material, not the least of which is experimental uses. I am going to be purposely vague here. I will say that it would be useful to monitor the situation, and I can assure you that those in charge are monitoring it.

The missile did not blow up over Detroit. If it had, it would be a serious problem, but it did not. Nevertheless, it requires monitoring. I will also say that that particular substance has one advantage in terms of its conversion—this is a matter of public record: It does not have to create an atomic explosion, but when it is exposed to certain conditions, it either explodes (not in the form of an atomic bomb) or when it is in such an explosion as occurred with the missile, most of it will be destroyed. However, monitoring should be done.

I would not have brought that up, but since it has received press, okay. Ultimately, you realize, this is going to be another thing that prompts the United Nations to take over all atomic disarmament. There are elements in the United States government that feel that this is ultimately the best place for such things, certainly in other countries as well. I also feel it is the best place. No one has to be the bad guy.

As an aside, there is no other country besides the U.S. that has done so much research in the peaceful uses of atomic energy. However, the problem with it, as you realize, is that the fuel in atomic energy machines is not in its native state. Because it is not in its native state and because it is in a volatile state (not just plutonium, which is really an aftereffect of an atomic reaction), it's in a very uncomfortable state as fuel rods and so on in a reactor. Also, because it's a material that is so vital to Mother Earth and her functions, the material itself has a very powerful intention to return to the earth at any cost and not be utilized for technology. So ultimately, at some point it will be possible, in the step past fusion reactors, to use materials that are more benign. That has a way to go yet.

***When it exploded as it did, did the plutonium burn up and become harmless, or did it go back into the water as a contaminant?***

The residue is likely to drop down from where it exploded, and there will be some contamination. Now, extra-credit homework: Remember, I told you awhile back, and so did Speaks of Many Truths and I am sure others—*there will be times when you will need to use benevolent magic because there will be problems for which technology has no solution.* I mentioned then, and I will reiterate now, that these problems have to do largely with radioactivity for which your government and, I might add, the governments of the rest of world have not found a simple solution.

Recognizing that there may not be a simple technological solution, I am going to ask you to talk to the radioactivity as if it were someone. Ask it to seek out its parent vein, where it came from. Do not do this as a spell, as sorcery, if you would, but talk to it on a personal level even if you are not there (which I don't expect). Just talk. You can talk to a mountain; you can just talk out loud with the intention; you can imagine what it might look like in its native state, if I can use that term. If you have ever seen pitchblende as the ore, you can picture that. Whatever you do, I am going to ask you to ask (let's broaden it) *all* radioactive substance not being utilized by man in technology (we don't want to shut down atomic power plants that are powering your cities, to say nothing of your hospitals), all radioactive waste, as it's called, and encourage it to return quickly by any benevolent means to its point of origin, which would be pitchblende, the ore.

Don't say "don't do this" and "don't do that." Say that you want this to happen. If we can get 100,000 people to say this—and you can do ceremonies for those of you who do that—you can incorporate it in your prayers, for those of you who do that. You can do whatever is meaningful to you. We want to communicate to it as if it were someone, recognizing that that particular substance is not in its own right a naturally occurring substance, and it will *want* to get back to the mountain or underground where it was mined. We want to support it. If you simply say, "I support that material to go home immediately," that will help. Be creative, and I feel it will help. In the future I will give you more specific, detailed ways of doing this, but for now I think that is sufficient. Also in the book, *Shamanic Secrets for Material Mastery,* you might find things you can do.

## U.S. Embassy Bombings in Africa

***Do you want to say anything about the bombings in Tanzania and Kenya?***

The local peoples had nothing to do with this. The terrorists came from the north. I don't think anybody is too surprised about that now, as things have developed. I will say that the Sinister Secret Government did not have a part to play in that directly, though they very often indirectly and occasionally directly support terrorist outfits because these outfits will generally stimulate the perspective by many people that continuity cannot be depended on. In other words, the SSG is for anything that stimulates and supports chaos or the perception of chaos, because when people are frightened and panicked, they can be easily manipulated, at least from the SSG's point of view.

***You said before that these were not the original targets. It was supposed to be Egypt and Israel, but the men who drove the cars figured they wouldn't get out***

***alive, so they picked easier places as targets.***

This is not the first time it happened. You have to recognize that the terrorist organizations are not set up as terrorist organizations in *their* minds; they are set up as military organizations. Like any military organization, they have a primary target and a secondary target, and if something goes wrong, they basically give their people the advice to "get the best target you can." It just so happened that these individuals did not wish to bomb the places they were instructed to bomb in Egypt and Israel. So they found a way (cleverly, I might add) to bomb places where they were likely to be able to get away. That's why this took place, not because of anything going on in either one of these countries they were trying to influence. Obviously, if something like that was going on, it would either be in the press or else the areas would show many more signs of security than you have seen or read about.

So the local governments do not have any problem with the United States—as a matter of fact, just the opposite. I might add that the irony here is that even though the attempt was being made by the terrorist organizations to create a rift between the United States and the host countries by making the hosts countries feel that it wasn't safe to be a friend of the United States, it did just the opposite, as is quite obvious to any casual listener or reader of the news these days. It has brought both countries significantly closer together. The terrorists, not having hit the primary targets because they would have done so by suicide, will nevertheless not live too long, simply because hitting almost random targets will wind up actually causing more damage to the terrorist organizations than any (even on *their* part) perceived benefit.

As you know, terrorism for political gain has no political gain whatsoever if nobody knows what you are protesting or trying to promote. That is what happened here.

***What were the original targets, the U.S. embassies in Israel and Egypt?***

No. They were civilian targets. The reason they weren't embassies is that the embassies have sufficient security, and other military targets are also secure, at least as secure as you can get. But civilian targets have become the target of choice in recent years simply because security is not possible, at least not realistically.

# 18

# Cowboy Diplomacy Not the Answer

Zoosh
August 20, 1998

***Someone said that today—Thursday, August 20—had the same configuration of planets as the day that World War II and other disasters started. The U.S. bombed terrorist locations today in the Sudan and Afghanistan. Is this just another retaliatory bombing, or is it the beginning of something ominous?***

It could be the beginning of something ominous if cooler heads do not prevail. I call upon the leadership in the House and Senate of the United States, who might just be able to produce cooler heads. I call on the United Nations to come down on the side of negotiation very firmly. The United States does not always understand, nor does it have the patience with, other countries who do not have the authoritarian energy, to say nothing of various police forces and miscellaneous intelligence agencies, to keep their country exclusive for their own citizens.

## Afghanistan Bombing Regrettable

Also, of course, one likes to welcome people from other countries for various reasons. So I feel the United States' attitude toward Libya is perhaps understandable, but the attitude toward Afghanistan in this case I feel is not appropriate. Afghanistan has only recently (considering historical references) come out of its struggle with the former Soviet Union (specifically Russia). They are not in a position to throw people out of the country as easily as the United States. I feel it would have been *much* better, regardless of suspicions, to have negotiated firmly and aggressively and to have encouraged the United Nations to look into this. The United Nations has demonstrated its willingness to become involved even in shooting wars, as in Bosnia, to act in some way to calm down a problem. I call on the United Nations not to do this even if it means censuring the United States.

I am not saying that the United States acted capriciously. Certainly the building that was bombed or rocketed (however you want to call it) was perhaps in some *minor* way involved in the production of illegal or destructive chemicals. However, one must understand that *all over the United States* there are such things going on now. Would the United States citizenry feel okay if a missile managed to get through from the not-particularly-potent *Sudan navy* and blow up some government contractor who is producing destructive materials? How would the United States feel about that?

All right, it is not quite the same because the United States is not consciously backing terrorism. However, the United States and its allies have been perhaps accused of such things in the past. Let's just say this without saying, "You did it, he did it, she did it." This is something for the U.N. to resolve, not for people to sit around and do nothing and say nothing, but for the U.N. to go in and do things. For heaven's sakes, Sudan needs help; they are in desperate straits. They need a lot of help. Their civilians are suffering, and I am sure there are plenty of people in the U.S. who would love to help.

It is essential to avoid a religious war. The practitioners of the Moslem religion are going through an anomaly in the history of their religion. This is a beautiful, loving, wonderful religion. However, there is a current anomaly having to do with black and white, very little gray. So during the time of this anomaly, which will last another 13 years, maybe 15 years at most, there will be tensions between the Moslem religion—Islam—and the Christian religion. It is ridiculous for the U.S. to get caught up in that. The U.S. has really become overinvolved in the Middle East, largely because of strategic matters having to do with a single three-letter word—*oil.*

But the U.S. is not going to have to worry. Countries of the world aren't going to band together, as in OPEC, and say, "We are not going to sell you any oil." They are all completely aware of the United States' armaments and military, and they know very well that the U.S. will negotiate only up to a point. But if the U.S. feels strategically threatened because it is not getting the consumer materials (to say nothing of strategic materials) it needs, the other countries of the world are completely aware that it will do what it must to get them.

So the U.S. does not have to worry about this. I am not necessarily justifying any of these things; I am just saying what is. My feeling is, not to put too fine a point on it, it was a mistake.

In light of the United States' capabilities with intelligence networks, it might have been possible to do this another way. It cannot be avoided. The simple fact is that the bulk of this pharmaceutical plant was, in fact, producing regular pharmaceuticals. I grant that in a small portion of the plant, for occasional moments, they *were* producing chemical warfare materials; however, part of the reason was to test their own materials against those agents to see what worked. It is certainly the kind of thing that goes on in U.S. research labs all the time.

I am not pooh-poohing it, okay? What I am saying is, I feel it was entirely unnecessary to take such a risk, and I haven't even yet begun to discuss the attack of these missiles on *other* targets. I feel that it might have been better to have used the intelligence more wisely. Yes, I must put my finger on it and say that while the attack was not entirely politically motivated (referring to domestic politics), it was certainly partially motivated by that. I am sorry, but there it is.

## International Terrorism and the U.N.

So I call on the Congress, I call on the Senate, I call on the U.S. and I call on cooler heads in all the countries to work this out in a benevolent way, and for international terrorist laws to become as firm as they can get. It should be considered that terrorists hiding out in the U.S.—as defined by foreign countries—should go in front of tribunals established for trying terrorists as a portion of the United Nations' duty.

While I understand that terrorism is not all right—for instance, what happened recently in Ireland—I also understand that from a historical frame of reference, many countries employed terrorism, as defined by others, to achieve independence. It just so happens that today's weapons are worse. They are more destructive—or perhaps more pervasive, in the case of chemical and biological warfare, and perhaps even more capricious because of the damage they can do to their own people.

I want the U.S. to take a cold, hard look at that. The reason you do not see other countries—older, established civilizations in Europe—jumping into the Middle East the way the U.S. does is not just because they do not have the finances to do it. It's because they've been around longer and know what they ought be involved in and what not. The U.S. has too many arms, too many missiles, and is in too much of a position to cause harm in situations in which the problems ought to have been worked out by the U.N. Use this as an opportunity to set up a court system within the United Nations to try people, and I feel you can work it out. Yes, there is a danger. Yes, it was partially politically motivated, and yes, the United States has been very quick to forget its own methods of independence.

Certainly, if you had been an English citizen during the time that the U.S. staked out its claim that England was being outrageous to collect taxes, you budding citizens of the soon-to-be U.S. could easily have been considered terrorists, not just revolting colonists. (I don't see you rioting in the streets against the IRS, which is a good thing, since they are the agents of the government that provide the programs that you all want—oh, yes, don't forget that.)

In other countries (you could go to their history), independence movements have often taken the form of terrorism. This does not make it okay to blow up civilian planes. It does not make it okay to blow up hotels and other civilian targets. The U.S. needs to develop timely statemanship and recognize that—even in this circumstance when attempts were made to spare civilian casualties, and I honor that—it isn't okay for the U.S. to be fighting everyone's battles all over the world.

I appreciate that the intention was to suppress terrorism. I appreciate that, but it can be done much better by the United Nations. I also suggest that the U.S. pay up all its dues to the United Nations. There's no excuse not to do that. And the United Nations needs to begin to be seen by all the countries of the world as a place to resolve problems so that people who have problems—and who, as a last resort, turn to terrorism—don't have to seek out that last resort because they have a first resort that works.

***What about Bin Laden, the millionaire leader of the terrorists they were after?***

You mean the man they were trying to kill? They didn't get him anyway.

***All his lieutenants from all over the world were supposed be there; that's why they chose that particular time.***

Yes, that is pretty obvious, but the fact is, they didn't get him, just as they didn't get Saddam Hussein or Muhammar al-Qaddafi. This was intended to be a threat, saying, "See what's going to happen to you."

## The American Revolution

But the funny thing is, look back in your own United States history. When the English (the British troops) fired on colonists who were protesting, did the colonists then cower and say, "Okay, okay, we won't protest anymore"? No, they just went underground until they became strong enough to fight in the open. In the case of the U.S., did the British killing some of you stop you from fighting and getting your independence? Did it stop you from creating allies with the French? (If the French had not come in on your side, the British would eventually have won—so don't forget your allies, please.)

What I am saying is, bombs can be very indiscriminate, even though the United States made an effort to avoid such things with this raid. They can kill lots of noncombatants, and often do. Look at the atomic blasts that blew up in Japan: how many women and children, grandmothers and grandfathers were killed? Was that intended? Of course not, but how many did it blow up?

Do you think that this man does not also have allies and will not seek them out? This is foolish. I really feel all presidents, not just all generals and all admirals, ought to be historians. I realize this is falling on deaf ears, but if I make my plea strong enough with enough exclamation points, perhaps one or two people might listen.

***Regarding the astrology, is there a relationship in the configuration of planets to past beginnings of disasters?***

Yes, the relationship really means that mistakes made today could come back to haunt you. That's why I am giving you all these things—do this, do this—because astrology is not a law. That's what astrologers realize they are looking at. They make their best predications on the basis of what they have, but they understand that they don't have all the data.

So it is not a fixed circumstance that it will create World War III after all the intentions to avoid that and to deconstruct arms of destruction and so on. However, you in the U.S. and other places are going to have to face the fact that ultimately guns and bullets and other destructive things *do not change people's minds.* It sure didn't change *your* minds when the British troops fired on you, did it? Did you say, "Okay, okay, we won't do that again. Sorry"?

When I call on people [to take heed], you would be surprised that it really does get up there at some point. People read this stuff even though they are busily reading the Internet. (In three to five years, if nothing has been done about ads and spam on the Internet, books are going to start to look real good to a lot of people.)

## Whitley Strieber's Visitor

***A little man came to Whitley Strieber in a hotel in Toronto on the night of June 6, 1998. Strieber describes a small man in a dark suit who looked human. This***

***little man told him that the Earth was "irretrievably lost" and that "the ones to whom you pay your taxes will be dragged in the streets before this suffering is ended." "You will see the signs in fire. Your planet's life has turned in its path. There will be a great extinction here."***

I am going to call this a vision. I will say that I think it's good to broadcast this vision, just like I said it's good for that man to broadcast his vision that the Earth is going to stop. So I support Mr. Strieber if he wishes to broadcast this, because it might encourage change.

I do not think this is going to happen. I would say that if we were still on the Jehovahan time line (going back 5000 years or so), it certainly *would* happen, but we are not on that time line anymore. However, you do need to do your part, as indicated from the previous question, as far as giving the United Nations much more authority over all countries. When that happens and the U.N. is funded properly, you will gradually become Earth citizens and not Americans or British or Chileans or what-have-you. This is necessary now, and you can't wait much longer to do it.

So I encourage Mr. Strieber, if he wishes, to put out this vision as a method for all of you creators-in-training to change it. Remember, just because you don't like the tax man doesn't mean the tax man is collecting that money for himself or herself. They are collecting it for you.

***Strieber says he asked him if he was a human being. He said he was, but that he did not pay taxes.***

That is his loss. You have to remember something. I am using this as a platform and I feel comfortable doing so. I am glad it came up. The United States is famous for lots of things. One of the things it's famous for in other countries is its benevolent social programs. I grant that they are not run the way a tight, profit-making business is run, but government is never like that. You have to remember that the intention is to provide *a happy life for all people*. Right there in your most important documents that established this country it says that people have "right to the pursuit of happiness." You don't find that, generally speaking, in other documents before that time. However, some have decided that was a pretty good idea, and put it in their documents in countries that have been established since then.

So your country, the United States, is doing lots of programs so that the people it can reach and the people who wish to be reached can be happier, better fed, clothed, housed and so on. I would say that more of that is going on in a more benevolent way in this country than in other countries, on a per capita basis, to say nothing of all of the charities and organizations and good-hearted sharing and assistance that goes on within communities and from one community to another. I am not saying taxes are fun to pay. I am not saying that everything that they are spent on is great. I am saying that the *intention* is there to help people pursue happiness.

All right. I am done with my lecture.

***Strieber asked, "Have you ever lived off the planet?" He said that the man said that there is a higher world, and we can sometimes gain the right to enter it in life. Where is that little man from? Who is he?***

Born and raised on Earth.

***Really? Who does he work for?***

Let's just say he has his own pursuits. After all, the things he said to Strieber could have easily been said by a politically active person on Earth, could they not?

***But this is someone that Strieber saw in his childhood; he has seen this being many times.***

I am just going to say it is vision. I am not saying it isn't true.

# 19

# U.S. Should Be No. 1 Ally of the United Nations

Zoosh
August 21, 1998

***There are a couple of things I didn't ask last night that I found out only this morning. In the bombing in Afghanistan, that training camp was built by the CIA to train the Afghan rebels against the USSR. Those men they blew up are the same rebels they trained.***

Yes, I am sorry to say that the history of the United States is fraught with such examples. That is why many European countries are hesitant about becoming too closely allied with the United States. Look at France, who literally pulled your fat out of the fire in the Revolutionary War. What did you do not many years after that? France was your enemy.

Examine U.S. history and you will find its diplomacy deplorable. It is well understood by most countries of the world that have been established for a while that to be allied with the U.S. does not guarantee a long-term friendly relationship.

I am not saying right or wrong, but that the U.S. needs to take a hard look at this, because countries that have managed to maintain long-term allies tend to be much more stable. Don't forget that the United States as a country is still very young compared to many others—for example, China and others. The jury is still out on whether the U.S. with its government (not the people) will go on indefinitely.

I strongly recommend that the U.S. make a firm and long-lasting commitment to the United Nations as its number one ally. Not just the U.S. supporting the U.N., which it has done quite consistently, but to be *advised* by the U.N. Perhaps then we can get greater consensus rather than cowboy diplomacy.

***What about Bin Laden, the millionaire Saudi Arabian? Does he really have anything to do with the bombings?***

He is partly a scapegoat, but it might be said that he is loosely connected, certainly along financial lines. I would be more inclined to say he is a loose connection. One might say with some certainty that there were finances involved, and some of the people who were involved in the operation were connected to him at one time in training camps and so on. Part of the reason that the U.S. has as much knowledge about this person as it does is because he is a former ally.

***I didn't know he was a former ally. I had no knowledge that he was trained by the CIA.***

He was a former ally in concordance with this battle between the USSR and the guerrilla forces, a term that would be more appropriate to call them. He was associated with them. This is known.

## Clouds as Messengers

***Do perceived pictures in cloud formations have any significance?***

Every day all over the world, spirits of beings, be they animals or plants or human beings or be they extraterrestrial, higher-dimensional beings or angels and so on, will show themselves in the clouds. When they show themselves to someone, usually it's for a cause. That someone may be a human being, a plant, an animal—it might even be another spirit.

The clouds are like the canvas upon which the being paints its image briefly in order to make some kind of a heart connection with some other being. This is considered acceptable by those who make some effort to keep you protected, because most people do not look at the clouds in that way. But if one does look at the clouds in that way, one will see beings (in larger clouds especially, but even in smaller ones)—fish, turtles, lots of different beings—and it is all intentional. So I will say, to anybody who sees these things in the clouds, that it is all real.

> From now on, from time to time I will be giving the readers a quiz. This is the first question: *If beings other than yourself have pain, if you do not feel their pain or have compassion for their pain, is their pain real to you?*
>
> This is a question I am asking readers to ask themselves. I might also add that these questions are considered by spiritual beings, many ETs and so on, before they decide to contact you directly—the compression test.

# 20

# Stock Market Flash

Zoosh
September 1, 1998

I would like to say, in regard to the drop in the Stock Market, that this has been necessary. Even though bargains will appear, wait. The market might recover a little bit, but this is not the bottom. I urge you to consider the most conservative forms of investment: raw lands, meaning undeveloped land, and other such safe investments —maybe gold, silver only possibly. Be careful about silver; a potential volatility is there.

I want to also say this: Don't be afraid. This has been necessary. The market has been grossly overbought, and it is a bitter lesson for many. But ultimately, understand that the true function of investments is to improve the lives of your fellow human beings and make a profit. That's what this is about, spiritually speaking. It is not a punishment; it is truly a heart-centered and instinct-centered reality check.

So look toward conservative investments, and please let me reiterate to investment bargain hunters—bank stocks are definitely not a bargain. However, be open to small banks with personal service that are heart-centered and oriented toward the needs of the people. Pay attention to these stocks as valuable long-term investments. These stocks point the way. The stock market over the years has lost its way in its pursuit of profits by any means. Stocks had become a commodity instead of representing a commodity.

Now is an opportunity to help and to notice what the actual purpose is for the STOCK HEART MARKET.

# 21

# Bumping Dimensions Causes Discomfort

Zoosh
September 29, 1998

I would like to talk about something that has been going on for the past week or so. The experience is that for some time, as you know, you have been merging gradually into the fourth dimension. This is actually not causing a problem, a discomfort for you. But what you probably don't know is that for beings who are living in the fourth dimension, it is creating a little discomfort. Therefore a great deal of work is being done in the fourth dimension to support and sustain such beings who are even mildly exposed to you in your soul energy. They are not, in fact, being exposed to any discomforts that you are dealing with here in this place of learning, but they are still being exposed to your personalities. And, not unlike the experience that is causing *you* discomfort, they are having some trouble with it.

Now, what is it that is causing your discomfort? Well, it started to occur about six or seven days ago: The second-dimension beings are beginning to infiltrate in much greater numbers into 3.0 dimension. This has been going on gradually for some time. I am talking about beings from the second dimension who are merging into the third dimension. When one does that, there is always a tendency for a certain amount of overshoot, meaning that they will occasionally swing out past the third dimension, but not anywhere past 3.50. But here you are, parked around 3.47, and you find yourself being occasionally bumped into by these beings. This is what's happening.

If you were to look at these beings head-on, they would look humanoid. But if they turn to the side they would disappear, being second-dimensional beings, at least to your perception. Some of them are getting caught up in your physical bodies—not intentionally, but accidentally, from the random point of view. In the larger sense, it is another challenge to your studies in Creator School.

What's occurring is that these beings are getting caught up into your bodies, and because both they and you are expanding, you find something occasionally foreign expanding within you, and it creates a nervous tension. I am not talking about a disease or anything that will cause a disease or an injury, but it creates a greater amount of nervous tension, because your body's natural reaction is to push anything out. But the body's usual mechanisms for doing such things do not work in this case. So, homework: This is what I recommend.

## The Remedy

I want each and every one of you—I am not just talking about so-called New Agers here, I am talking about everybody. So tell people that you feel can hear it and won't think you are foolish to say it, "Every day in your meditation time, in your relaxing time, when you get up, when you go to bed, anytime, just once a day, say, "I will ask."

You can say it just like that. You can ask any spirits—friendly, benevolent angels; creators; gods; anyone—and say their name if you wish. You can ask in their name or you can simply ask in your own name (saying "I"), "I ask that all beings be removed from my body except those who are beneficial for me."

Now, why do we have the exceptions? We have the exception because, of course, from time to time your guides are with you and might be close. Parts of the Creator might be with you. Other parts of yourself might be hanging around. You might have friendly spirits, you might even have relatives who have passed over recently checking up on you. So we want to add that exception so that you do not drive away beneficial and benevolent beings that support you. That's what I recommend.

***If second-dimensional beings are invisible sideways, and we are third-dimensional beings with depth, then what's added in the fourth dimension?***

It is hard to describe. I want to say breadth, but it is really a word you are using now in your own context. If you were there, aside from everything being different, asking for a physics description, I would say that the primary difference is that you would feel connected to all forms of life that are compatible with you. You have to strive for such a feeling here because of discomforts that are all around, or you have to focus on such a feeling. Since discomfort is at an extreme minimum in the fourth dimension, you feel it. If beings are there from other times or places—animals, plants, elements, rain, sunshine, all of this—you will feel it in such a way that it will feel like more of your greater persona. That's why it is often referred to as an expansive place. People will tell you the fourth dimension is about expansion. That's what that means.

An artist might show it, for example, as a person in the fourth dimension walking along who sees a rainbow. While your entire body does not blend with the rainbow, it will feel like parts of your body can and do easily blend with it, and the rainbow with you as well. You hear and feel the rainbow while it hears and feels you. You don't have to stop; you can keep on walking, though you would probably stop and enjoy it.

This tends to prepare you for those who are going up in dimensions one at a time or even more quickly. And of course you go sideways, you go up, you go down. But just for the sake of understanding, it tends to prepare you for the greater levels of expansion at higher dimensions. But coming out of the third dimension, as you have experienced it here in a polarized form (all third dimension everywhere is not polarized, by the way), you need to have an interim place. The fourth dimension for you, in your experience coming out of the third, is designed to be an interim place, kind of a halfway house.

***We have been at 3.47/3.48 now for four years, right? When do we get to move again?***

When you can look at somebody on the street and feel their feeling—not think, not say a meditation, not say a prayer, but just feel relaxed about their being there. I would like to give you that because it presents to you the opportunity to have physical evidence. You don't have to go up and embrace that person, just feel relaxed that that person exists and is in your view, that's all. You could be driving along, walking along or be passing by; you could see them from a distance, it matters not—but just be relaxed that they exist.

I grant that this is a challenge in some places. Yet that relaxation contains within it feminine wisdom and feminine warrior wisdom as well. Ultimately such allowance is much more empowering and protecting than all the defense mechanisms in the world because it tends to deflect discomfort away from you. If that person walks through your auric field, the discomfort he might have at that moment will not be felt by you at all.

***Because you are in a higher frequency?***

You are not necessarily in a higher frequency. You are more in touch with the benevolent you and you are broadcasting that. You are not sending it out consciously. You don't have to; it naturally goes out. If you send it out, it will leave you and then you won't feel so good. So *you don't want to send it out*—remember that, underline that. Because people often feel that it is their job to help others with love and light and so on, as you say, you will send it to them and eventually start to feel poorly. Just *feel* the love and light yourself, and if it broadcasts out, which it does naturally on its own, that's best.

**FLASH!**

**Political Upheaval Part of Process**

Do not be overly concerned about the political upheaval in the United States. This is all part of the unification process for the global political system.

**Stepped-up Security Urged**

I urge all countries with chemical and biological weapons to increase security beyond the electronic means, as in the coming days the electronic means may not be 100 percent reliable. Please use greater manpower instead of or with your usual procedures. The threat of these materials passing into unauthorized hands has never been greater. This condition will exist for the foreseeable future and can only be resolved in a closed meeting of all parties speaking in complete candor, perhaps at the United Nations.

—Zoosh

# 22

# Creator Flips the Switch

Zoosh
September 30, 1998

## Women Take on Violence as Men Release It

I want to talk about this because it is relevant. As one looks at the animal world, one sometimes sees predators, but one has to look hard to see this in the plant world, though some people have found a few. One sees this in the world of the sea, and it is reflected in the world of the human being. In the past, predators have shown up as men, but these things are changing.

About seventeen years from now you'll begin to notice it as a trend, meaning it will be published, written about and discussed then. There will be evidence before then, but it may not be considered reading material. It may not be considered a trend.

What will begin to happen is that as the level of the masculine hormone decreases, men will begin to lose predatory desires. I am not talking about the sense of a man wishing to put himself forward to improve his career, but about a man as the violent being.

***So there will be aggressiveness, but not this killer instinct?***

That's right. This will begin to go away in men. It has actually begun now, which is why I am mentioning it. Conversely, what will happen for a short time (not long) is that women will become predatory for a short time.

This is not payback (though some people will say, "It serves you right"), but is rather a way to help woman as a polarized female being to move past prejudice against men for being predatory.

The men who are predatory will, granted, have had emotional, psychological problems and will have been abused (I think almost every one of them), but this is only an explanation. If a man does not have the chemical makeup to become a predator—even if all those things happened to him—he would never become one.

I am mentioning this now because this gradual shift has just begun, about three days ago. You will begin to see evidence of predatory women, though not attacking women; they will always and only attack men. I do not wish to be the bearer of sad tidings, but this will be a short-lived anomaly. Twenty-five, thirty years from now it will begin to fade, but it must exist, in small numbers at least, so that the polarized feminine being moves past all prejudice toward man for being violent to woman.

***So how will it work out? Will women be shooting husbands or . . . ?***

That occurs now.

. . . ***women abusing children?***

That occurs now. What does not occur very much now, though you have begun to see it, is serial killer or psychotic murderer. I am sorry to say that this behavior continues for a time, and then men will not be this way at all. There will be a few men like this, just like today. There will be a few women like this.

## Finally, a Resolution

When the women take that behavior over, you will then see the absolute resolution of this type of behavior—aberration, it is called, but it is called an aberration only because society rightly does not tolerate it. Even though society rightly does not tolerate it, you do not see the resolution of predatory man in society today. You see what man does (man, not woman), and it is punished. When woman becomes this way, you will see healing. That is how that will be resolved.

***That is the male/female issue that has been here since the beginning of the Explorer Race and before—the resolution of that, you are saying?***

That is a very important resolution, because many women will say "*men!*"—meaning not just men predators, but *men,* with the unspoken meaning that there's something wrong with them. This wrong thing is going to change hands. Now, all women are not going to become aggressive and all men are not going to become passive, but you are going to see this change of the guard, as it were. The change of the guard not only relieves women of this prejudice, but allows such disease to be healed in the most beneficial and benevolent way for all beings, because women resolve things differently than men—not by punishment. Women punish children and so on, but it is women's natural tendency to look for the cause, explain it and try to heal it. It is men's natural tendency to punish the action, which almost always results in further actions.

***In retaliation?***

Yes, back and forth and back and forth.

***Pretty awesome. What's the dynamics of it? Something is going to be unstimulated in the men and stimulated in the DNA in the females?***

It is cellular, yes, DNA. The switch has already been flipped—a couple days ago.

***By whom and how?***

Creator. Resolution is necessary. You cannot become Creator being while some of you are mad at other parts of you. Have a psychotic Creator? Not allowed.

***Good explanation. So the Creator can flip a switch. You don't have to get people taken up in a Zeta ship to be worked on?***

Creator can, as we say, flip a switch.

***Does that affect only humans on this planet alive now? Does it affect anybody else in the Explorer Race? Just people who choose to be here, who volunteered to work this out?***

Yes.

***Very good. Thank you.***

# 23

# Tunnels under Phoenix and White Light in New England

Zoosh
Live from the Scott Amun Radio Show
October 1, 1998

Greetings. Zoosh speaking. To your listeners in Phoenix and its environs I would like to enlist you in a project, if you choose. There has been for a long time a condition underground beneath Phoenix that causes occasional waves of discomfort for people. This discomfort is often assumed to be something personal or perhaps stimulated by people around you, but in fact it is not. You will be able to tell the difference. If it is stimulated by somebody around you, you will be attracted to looking at them or thinking about them instantaneously, whereas if the discomfort is vague, if you do not know why it is there, your mind will be blank for a moment. That's how you will know.

I want you to be on guard about this, because this uncomfortable energy that you are feeling is actually associated with a tunnel that runs underneath the Phoenix area, down past Tucson and underneath Mexico, all the way down—including underneath the ocean in parts—to the southern tip of South America. It has been used from time to time by the sinister secret government, who attempt to control every aspect of your life. You can read a background if you want to in *Shining the Light, Volume I*, but many of you already know this. So I would say this: Understanding what to do about this is much more important than understanding the background, all right?

## How to Relieve the Stress

When you have that feeling (and I have given you landmarks to know the difference between that and discomfort stimulated by others), I want you to do something if you possibly can. It is simple, therefore perhaps easier to do. I would like to you to focus on something physical. Just look at it with your eyes. If you have some difficulty seeing for any reason, if that is a challenge for you, then touch something familiar. This means, for instance, that you would stare at the sky or you might look at a familiar wall or a chair. I want you to look at something familiar because it will bring you into your physical body with perception and with sensitivity. Ideally, I would like you to look at something benevolent that has good feelings to you, but if you are in a strange place or something like that, as a last resort look at your hand with the palm facing you. Try to look at your right hand—unless you are left-handed; if so, then look at your left palm. This will tend to center you into yourself.

If you can do these things, you will get over this discomfort. The discomfort is not caused by people from the sinister secret government moving under Phoenix, for they are no longer using the tunnel, but they have electronic devices in it that are designed to control individuals who may be passing through the tunnel. Sometimes individuals do pass through there, and when they do, radiation gets stronger. That's when you will feel it.

***Who built this tunnel originally?***

This tunnel was built by the sinister secret government, using well-established (well-established now in the commercial sector) techniques of tunneling. It is deep enough so it is not readily accessible by people from the surface; yet because rock and water is very conductive, the radiations from the tunnel can be felt occasionally on the surface. Now, what you are feeling on the surface will represent at no time more than two percent of what is actually being radiated in the tunnel, but for some sensitive people that will be enough.

You might notice that during times like this there will be more agitations—not to say that there aren't other things that prompt agitations, but this is just one more thing. So if you can focus into physical reality, as I suggested, you will be able to let go of that.

Staring at your palm or at something that is known and comfortable to you physically is also a good way to let go of discomforts with people around you. For years those considered to be retarded or mentally deficient in some way have been seen doing these things, and it is considered an aberration of their behavior, something to study. But in reality what they are actually doing is centering physically. Very often these people, if they are born this way (for instance, with Down's syndrome), might be seen to do this. Down's syndrome people are always wayshowers, they are so loving. When they do this, it is to show you—the person with many distractions who deals with the outer world, as it were—the simple way to come into yourself and let go of external cares and worries, especially ones over which you have no control or influence.

***Very good. So these techniques could be used at anytime?***

Yes. If there is something you can do about the situation—for instance, a family dispute where you are in a position to do something—you will notice that this system does not work. It might take the edge off, but it won't work because it works only when the discomfort is not aimed at you or there is nothing you can do about it. This is a way for sensitive people to help themselves be more whole and complete, the only exception being when you might be influential to alter things in a more beneficial way.

***So this radiation is not deliberately being directed from this tunnel to make people above it uncomfortable?***

No.

***How long has that tunnel been there?***

About 45 years.

***What types of individuals would still be going through it? Physical beings such as ourselves?***

Occasionally, yes, physical beings—and as I say, they don't pass through very often. Nowadays the tunnels are being explored, but I would say that they are not often explored by many people because the full blast of the energy of these devices has been able to foil just about every device to deflect them. There has been some effort by secret military units to explore these tunnels and find out what they are about, but the devices that radiate these energies are not readily apparent (they are not machines sitting there, in that sense); they are built into the tunnel and cleverly disguised. The human beings would pass through there to see what these tunnels are about and where they are going and if they (from the military point of view) represent a threat. These explorations have been slow, to say the least. I might add that even sending automated devices down there has not worked, because automated devices utilize some kind of electronic circuitry, and those devices, which you feel as discomfort at the surface, have the capacity to jam electronic signals. What we are dealing with here are countermeasures.

***Since you brought up the sinister secret government, some people might think that we are talking about something they should be afraid of. I would like to give you the opportunity to discuss what you think is the proper attitude about this sinister secret government.***

The sinister secret government is what I call highly organized crime. I would grant that if you were to have the capacity, the ability or the opportunity to go over their books, you would find a lot of legitimate businesses they have a hand in. However, their sole intention is to stay in control and keep all of you dependent.

Now, they are not critically intending to keep you dependent only on *them*, but they believe that as long as you are dependent on anyone or anything, you are less likely to represent what they would feel as a threat to their way of life. This is part of the reason they are in great part invisible ("the invisible hand," if I might borrow from Adam Smith here), invisible behind a lot of these addictions.

They will sometimes provide monies, if needed by developers (if we can call them that) of addictive materials—never directly, but always through an intermediary who cannot be traced back to them. From their point of view, they do this as an investment, because the more people who are dependent on something they need, the less likely they are to be able to see the main reality of all your lives. That is, that all of you have much more in common than you have differences. And once you realize (think, feel, do) your common bonds, you will have very little difficulty in getting along with each other and will enjoy your differences. It is this they are afraid of, because then they will not be able to sell you anything and you will not be involved in the one thing they utilize as their most powerful weapon—fear. As long as you fear each other and battle each other, they believe they will be able to remain influential, in control behind the scenes, and have all the money and power they want.

Actually, the inner circle represents only 13 individuals. Then there is an outer circle, who have some or little (depending on who they are) knowledge of the inner circle's existence. Beyond that is what I would call a perimeter circle. These people have no idea they are being influenced by such a body of individuals. They are nevertheless sometimes used as dupes.

## President's Behavior Was Self-Destructive

***Would you care to give your view on the connection, if any, between the crisis surrounding President Clinton and the sinister secret government?***

I would say that this is not an example of the sinister secret government's meddling. This is simply a long pattern of behavior coming to the surface. When a person who has been involved in patterns of behavior that are ultimately self-destructive (that which harms you or somebody else), if you are less known, then it does not come out. But the more known you are, the more people want to know about you. And when you are President of the United States, many people want to know *everything* about you. Such scrutiny reveals things, and self-destructive patterns will eventually come to the surface.

If it hadn't been Ms. Lewinsky, it would have been someone else. She actually performed a great service for your country by revealing (not that this is a bad man) that this is a man whose weaknesses could be used against him and individuals from other countries could, if they chose, manipulate him in ways that would not be good for your country. This is the real reason Congress is concerned. There is no question that laws were broken, but this is the real reason.

***Would you not agree that many other peripheral things, other issues, have been processed, worked through or brought up for many, many people in the country because of President Clinton and this scandal?***

Yes, there is no question that the U.S., being a young country in terms of your political method and so on, is still struggling with the people who founded your way of life here. I am not talking about the Quakers; I am talking about the Calvinists who did not believe that smiling was all right and continued from there. So you are struggling with that. However, I would certainly say that while sex is all right (after all, if Creator had intended you to not have sex, you would have had a short-lived civilization!), nevertheless, I would say that, as it has been done by this man, it has often been self-destructive. His tragedy, however, will allow your country to grow a little bit.

## Cynicism Makes Us Easier to Control

Now let me say another thing. It is very easy nowadays to get cynical and say, "Oh, they're all like that; they *all* do that." I want you to understand something when you are saying that. This is no different from any other prejudice. You will think, Oh, I am just being honest, or I am just being sophisticated. But in reality, you are just being prejudiced. It's no different than saying, "Oh, blacks are all this way," or "Jews are all that way" or "Filipinos are all that way." It's no different at all. It's just an attempt to head off future disappointment.

Now, I want you all to do something (extra-credit homework): I want you to write—in red if you can, or whatever pen you have available—*cynicism* or *cynical*. Then I want you to draw a big red circle around it and draw a red bar through it, the way they have on traffic signs. Cynicism will ultimately keep you from happiness. Any opportunity to achieve happiness might be headed off by your being cynical so that you won't be disappointed. Be sure that you remain vigilant about that, my friends. And while you're at it, look up the meaning of *cynical* in the dictionary and look at yourself honestly. Are you exhibiting those qualities?

***Very good. I was planning to ask you about that very topic, Zoosh, because I have enjoyed your writings in the past in which you encourage us all to flush cynicism out of our system as much as possible. It seems to be an almost pervasive sickness.***

Yes, and it is a way to play into the sinister secret government's hands, isn't it? If you miss the subtle signals of beauty and friendship and kindness and love, the sinister secret government will be happy, because you will be so much easier to control.

## Resistance to Life Lessons

***Another important point that relates closely to this, which you have mentioned, is our resistance to lessons and the movement upward from the third dimension to creating a fourth-dimensional world. You have stated in the past that one of the main things that stops us from that is our resistance to the lessons we have come here to learn. Any general advice you could give to everyone about getting over that resistance?***

Yes. It is very difficult for you, and I appreciate that because you do not remember your other lives, you do not remember your natural continuity. It is not an accident that Creator does not allow you to live past 100, 110, maybe 125 years, for those who are getting up there. This is because this is *school*. This is not nursery school for people who don't know any better. This is the Ph.D. school, because you are exposed constantly not only to lessons, but to temptations, to distractions and, most importantly, you are exposed to responsibilities, to actions that have consequences. You must consider how to be, how to not be and what is right for you, what is right for others. This is what happens in college in the Ph.D. program. That is what this life is all about.

Understand that you have all lived before this. You will all live after this. You are not allowed to remember these lives, because if you remembered them, you would then resolve all the problems here exactly the way you have resolved them in previous lives. You would not grow one bit. The reason you are not allowed to remember these past lives is so that you can re-create your reality and invent new solutions to problems you have faced before, though to a lesser degree.

Here they are more dramatic, but they are more dramatic to call your attention to the fact that they exist. What might be a minor annoyance on some other planet can become a major disaster on this planet, because this is a planet of polarity and a planet on which to learn. This is the material-mastery planet. Material mastery does not mean control over all things; it means learning how to be in harmony with all life.

So recognize that the lessons you are facing in this life are fleeting in the overall continuity of all your lives. You are all immortal. And what is immortal? Is it the soul, as the Bible calls it? Yes. But what is the soul, besides being a portion of Creator? It is your immortal personality, how you know yourself, how you recognize yourself. This lives on. You will live on, you will get past all of this. If you have lessons, embrace them and realize that they are only temporary.

***Thank you, Zoosh. Could I ask you to clarify something? When you mention that we are not allowed to remember these past lives so that we won't try to solve problems in exactly the same way, some people, including myself, might say, "I do remember things about past lives." How do you explain that?***

What occurs when one explores past lives? It is that one is truly exploring a matrix. This is like a therapy system. It allows individuals to explore probable past lives or potential past lives, because you are in a time now when both the past and the future are being recreated. So the therapeutic recollection of past lives allows you to support, sustain and resolve lessons you are working on in this life. In that sense these recollections are valid and useful. But if you were to ask me, "Are these absolute recollections of past lives?" I would have said yes 20 or 30 years ago. But today, because the time sequence you are on is in flux, I would have to say, yes and no.

***So because our time system is changing, it's more difficult to look at reality, even past reality, as being one particular way?***

It is not desirable to maintain a rigid fix on the past or use the past to suggest the future, because your future is in fact anchored by benevolent energies that love you and that represent you. It is this time line you are getting on now, with lots of probabilities and things that could be or might be. But the old time line, which is anchored in strife and difficulty and war and conflict, is a line you are all letting go of so that you do not perpetuate these actions between each other.

***Zoosh, in times past you have given a number scale to indicate your view of where we, as a whole on the planet, are in the movement from the third to the fourth dimension. Would you care to do that and give us a thermometer update at this time?***

Yes, you are now at 3.47.

***Have we been staying steady then for a while there?***

## Time to Choose

Yes. You are now at a point where you as individuals must begin to make your choices, which is why the sinister secret government is attempting to keep you in the third dimension, or at least as close as they can. But, of course, ultimately they cannot prevent your transformation, planet and all, into the fourth dimension. However, as is common at times with the people in power, they want to hang onto their power and influence as long as they can. What you are in now, from 3.47 to 3.52, is the time when you must choose. Most of the energy that was used to get you to 3.47 has not come from you. It has come from other allies, supporters, planets, Mother Earth herself, angels, Creator and so on. Now you must choose. Do you feel able?

Let me tell you what will need to be changed: the way you treat your children, the way you treat your old folks, the way you treat your sick, the way you treat your emotionally and physically wounded, the way you treat your prisoners, the way you treat each other, the way you treat yourselves. In short, every day find in yourself something you can love and respect and appreciate, some quality in yourself that you feel good about. If it's more than one, fine, but at least one every day. Then at least two or three times a week, find a quality like that in somebody else that you can love and appreciate. This will be a good beginning.

## Healings through a Comatose Woman

***Thank you. Zoosh, I was wondering if you would like to field the question about something I just saw in the news recently. Anything you might like to say about it would be interesting. There is a woman in Massachusetts who is in a coma, and some people believe that they are actually receiving healings from her. Would you talk generally about comas or about this particular woman?***

Yes. Coma is a state of consciousness that allows a vast amount of spiritual freedom to the individual's soul while the body heals and sometimes even after the body is healed, if the person is involved in spiritual work.

This is another coma patient who is involved in spiritual healing. She is not in fact using her energy to heal anyone, because her individual energy, while it may feel like her and have her personality characteristics, is not enough to stimulate the healing process in others. It is because in her comatose state she has connected with benevolent gold-light beings of a beautiful world beyond the veils. I might add that these worlds are common beyond the veils that protect you and them from your actions here. She is functioning right now for a time as a thread between those places.

You might ask, "Wouldn't that represent interference from other places?" I would say yes, but not in this case. In this case the beautiful place is an angelic place, and the energy she is bringing through or helping to bring through is angelic energy. And since the angels have lessons involved with you as a people here on Earth, they are allowed to influence and generally provide benevolent energy at every opportunity they can. Also, because their energy is so benevolent, it's not harming her and in fact is helping her. So in short, yes.

### Message to New Englanders

Can I make a brief statement to the people in New England? My friends, those of you who live in New England just north of the northeastern boundary of the United States, deep within the Earth there is a beautiful white light that is growing. I would like you to send white light there if you can. Ask it to go there, don't send it from yourselves. In three months from today you will be able to reach out to that area and pull the white light from there. It will supply a great amount of white light for the northeastern United States and Canada.

***Wonderful! Does this relate to any crystal deposits or mineral deposits, Zoosh?***

Fortunately not, so it will not be interfered with by any mining.

***Could you briefly say something about the value of prayer and petition to Creator, to Mary and to any of the angels?***

Yes, please speak to these beings as if they are your friends, which they are. They love you and want to be treated as equals just as you do not wish to be treated as if you are different by your friends.

So strike up a loving friendship with the angelics and others of such benevolence so that you can feel they are truly your close friends who love you, which in fact they do. In this way there will never be any fear of them. Fearing them cancels out anything you ask them to do or anything they can do for you.

***Wonderful! Thank you very much, Zoosh. I am very honored to have had you on the program today, and what blessings I have, I wish to give to you as well. I hope to be speaking to you again at some time in the future.***

Thank you very much, and good life.

# 24

# Soul Mechanism: Weightlessness Equals Death

Zoosh
October 29, 1998

Let me briefly say that this issue of concern by NASA—astronauts showing signs of aging in space—is less about the conditions of the spacecraft than about a simple case of weightlessness.

When the soul departs the body at the end of anyone's natural cycle, it most often does so gradually, if it is a slow and natural death. Yet there are times when death occurs more quickly. In both these cases, however, one thing occurs all the time. The soul itself is, by your standards, weightless. As a result, when it is in contact with other weightless things, it is not attached to those things. On the other hand, when you are in your physical body during your lifetime, the soul is tethered to you not only because of the spark of life within you, but on a more fundamental basis, because you have mass or weight. When you come to the end of your natural cycle, the soul recognizes that that weight is becoming part of Mother Earth's body again.

Mother Earth reaches out, as it were, and engages that physical body you have resided in, and the soul recognizes that it is now in contact only with what is weightless, not your physical body, and will tend to gravitate toward its natural objectives. The soul also does this when you are dreaming and sleeping. It will go to various places where it has things to do, since the soul does not require sleep. But it remains tethered to your body weight.

## Artificial Gravity Necessary in Space to Tether Soul to Body

Now, in space we have a phenomenon that is a temporary challenge for the soul. I predict that the next major effort in the exploration of space will be creating artificial gravity, not because Uncle Zoosh is saying this, but because of the realities of the situation: The soul finds itself in a state of being within people who are still experiencing their natural cycles, but it is surrounded by a weightless physical body, which it ordinarily recognizes as an opportunity to move on and go elsewhere. But, of course, the spark of life is still in residence in these astronauts, so the soul gets confused. The soul "thinks" or experiences that the physical person is in a gradual death cycle. When you have the opportunity to have a slow, natural death, which sometimes occurs over some time, the body is gradually reclaimed by Mother Earth and the soul experiences a diminishing weight of the physical body, so that when the soul finally exits, the physical body is weightless.

What is occurring now in space is that the soul feels that the physical body is in some kind of death cycle. As a result, it tends to spend less time in the physical body; or when they sleep, the sleep is either fitful (associated sometimes with moving toward the end of your natural cycle) or unusually deep. Not to put too fine a point on it, without gravity, the soul senses an artificial death cycle, which is why there are accelerated symptoms of aging in space.

In time, this is going to be a serious problem. On long trips, say, events to Mars, it would be conceivable that a young, healthy, vigorous astronaut would experience a catastrophic impact on his physical health regardless of exercise and diet. So I am afraid you are going to have to rethink your space program to Mars and other places. You will have to have a vehicle that can sustain some form of artificial gravity, and by so doing, allow the physical health of the astronauts to remain more intact.

I know you are going to work on this in the space station you are planning to build. I hope you can manage to get it funded, because I feel you will find a good interim system that will hold you until you have discovered ways to improve the artificial gravity system. It is perhaps the most important challenge that will be faced by astronauts.

***In the meantime, can't we delegate some angels to talk to the guides of these souls and explain the situation to them?***

The souls do understand. You have to remember that the soul has its own understanding of life and it has built-in mechanisms. It would be like this: If you were standing at the top of a tall cliff and suddenly fell off, even if you understood on the way down that it would have been better to stand farther back so that you didn't fall off, that thought would not prevent your hitting the rocks below. So understanding is not sufficient.

These are actual built-in mechanisms that are in effect only on this planet. Remember that this planet does not have the typical mechanisms one finds on other planets and places where benevolence reigns supreme. One finds almost nuts-and-bolts mechanisms here on Earth. You need to have material mechanisms in place, third-dimensional materiality at that, which does not allow a great deal of flexibility in the mechanism of the soul being in the body.

If the mechanism were changed (and we have to allow also for the shift in the dimensions), this is the hazard that would present itself: Souls might get buried with the dead body.

***Ah! This is like an eject button on a jet plane?***

That's very well put. So while it would not be a disaster for the soul, it would slow down the soul's natural progress, and it would be very lonely and stressful for the soul. So the chance of this mechanism being changed is almost nonexistent.

# 25

# No Mining! No Drilling!

The Collective Consciousness of All Earth Guides
November 28, 1998

Mining is the greatest danger to your societies. You are not the only people who bury what you don't know what to do with. Mining brings up these parts of the past misery of others.

Perhaps a passing ship leaves something buried deep within the Earth, perhaps not so deep as in the past—that's what caused the plague that killed millions, although the cause runs deeper. Deep mining expeditions and drilling ventures are now hitting some of these deposits. They are not all dangerous to people, though some have devastated various plants and animals.

### The Recent Release of Three Organisms

Three organisms have been released recently, however, that could potentially destroy human life as you've known it. One affects the birth rate, making it unlikely that certain people will be able to reproduce. These people are of the heart and mind. It is most often these people who guide or lead your peoples away from hazards and precipices of risk.

Another affects the skin of *all* peoples, causing you to lose your resistance to the Sun's effects. It could ultimately stop surface living.

The last is potentially the most devastating. It can literally cause the glue of life, the DNA, to become recessive, to shrink from its capacities and become submissive to all forms of mutation. This would initially seem like disease, but that is only a symptom. Ultimately, all life would be affected.

Mining must be stopped. The industry must be altered. This can be done by embracing shamans or mystical people who can feel what's safe and where it isn't, or by declaring off limits to mining certain areas such as deserts or rain forests traditionally occupied by few people.

Last and most important, mining the Moon or desolate or abandoned planets and asteroids must be avoided at all costs. As it is, it will take many, many more years to remove toxic substances from the Moon and Mars. This has been an ongoing activity ever since Earth citizens began showing an interest in exploring the stars and skies above.

We are watching and praying for the most benevolent actions to be acted upon by you all.

# Mining, Drilling and Benevolent Magic

Zoosh

November 28, 1998

## ETs Bury an Enzyme near Europe about A.D. 1300

All right, Zoosh here. Let's talk about this topic. A broad hint is given that a certain culture, not knowing what to do with a certain enzyme that they had more of than they knew what to do with, came to Earth some time ago and buried it in a place they thought would be safe for the citizens of Earth. People were on the planet then. This was about 20 to 25 years before the Black Death, as it was called in Europe.

The place they put it, however, turned out to be a spot where occasionally there were earthquakes—and in fact, there *was* an earthquake. Now, the material was buried about 35 feet below ground, which ought to have been sufficient. It was in canisters that by today's standards would be considered safe to bury. But earthquakes, of course, change everything.

The main thing that changed was a crack in the Earth. Although it was minuscule, it cracked one of the containers and allowed a very small amount of this material to escape. But the amount was equivalent to a chemist's description of the impact of nerve gas, meaning that a very small amount could be devastating.

This was something that wasn't done as an act of war against the people of the Earth, but as an act of desperation. The civilization was required to release this material. At that time they were not able to put it on the Moon or Mars because there was still some surface civilization functioning on Mars, so if they had approached Mars with it, the civilization probably would have attacked the ship.

They thought they were being very careful, but it didn't work out that way. Now, the civilization that did this is nowhere near this planet, but they heard about it sometime after the plague, went back and retrieved the material to avoid any future such happenings. Being honest, they reported their actions to their government. Even though their government applauded them for removing the material from their own planet, the entire planet felt responsible and informed the elders they consulted with about this act, and a judgment of penalty was withheld.

That withholding took place because the people were given an option, an opportunity. Those they felt were most responsible (not all the people of the planet) were given an option. They could serve the Explorer Race in some capacity or serve Earth as a planet or serve her peoples, animals and plants in some way. If they could not do it in their current life, they would do it in their next life. This is what most of them did.

After all, you can't erase the suffering and bring back the lives of the people who died. Of course you could say that the largest spiritual effect of such a plague would not have to do with its physical cause. Nevertheless, one cannot overlook the physical facts.

***Where is this planet? In this galaxy?***

No.

***What were they doing here? Aren't there other empty places between there and here?***

There are lots of empty places, but this particular enzyme had an effect on their people and other people nearby, and it was believed it would not have such an effect on the peoples of Earth. Of course, they didn't know what it *would* do to the peoples of Earth, but it is an enzyme that, once it comes in contact with people, will linger even if every last portion is removed by millions or billions of miles. It is insidious in the sense that it tends to migrate into the DNA of these beings. Basically, it would migrate into the DNA of any beings who were sensitive and without any form of immune system. Since the people of Earth were known to have an immune system, the beings who brought it here thought it would be safe even in the event of a problem.

***Where did it come from? Where did they get it?***

It was produced as a byproduct on their planet when they were involved in the creation of an energy source for another planet. This was a planet where what you would call very high-tech manufacturing took place. This is not very different from your own problematic circumstances, only on that planet there were rarely any problems. But there *was* a problem with this one. Remember, I said it wasn't a virus or a germ, but an enzyme. Enzymatic action tends to perform a catalyst type of action. As an enzyme, of course, it was a living, functioning being that's always perceived. It could be taken only if it wished to go, and that was honored.

***Is it still here?***

No, they came back and got it all.

***But you said it got in the humans' DNA?***

No, I said it got in *their* DNA, but it didn't do that in humans. It gave humans the plague.

***The black plague.***

Yes, which is still in existence on Earth in various places, but not as overpowering, of course, because antibiotics didn't exist then.

***So it's still here?***

The black plague is still here.

***So the enzymes stimulated something in humans, and even though the enzymes are gone, there is still an effect?***

Yes, it had a residual effect. I'm not ruling out a causative factor of its being carried by fleas and so on on the Earth. I'm just saying that that's where it came from. Fleas existed on the Earth before that and they didn't have the plague then, but all of a sudden they had the plague. That's what happened with the enzyme. The enzyme didn't come to human beings directly. It came from the little insects. You might say it affected the little insects, but of course it devastated the human population.

***What actions did the people on this planet take then?***

Oh, that's in the history books. I'm not going to go over that. People initially just started burning down everything.

## Making Amends by Incarnating Here to Become Guides

***The planet from which the enzyme came—what actions did those people take to make amends?***

Some of them decided to become guides, and of course they had to train long and hard—meaning they had to have incarnations on Earth. Some who decided to become guides for plants had to have incarnations as plants and so on; some who decided to be guides for fleas or the little animals had to do that, too. They altered their reincarnational cycles to include responses where they could provide service to Earth peoples.

***Beautiful! So some of them incarnated?***

They had to. You cannot really be a very good guide if you haven't been the type of being you're trying to guide. You can't really speak from experience. You can only say, "This is my opinion."

***So did any of them affect history? Have we ever heard of any of them, or did they keep a low profile?***

They always kept a low profile, of course. If they affected history, it would have been indirectly, as any guide does. You could say that guides have affected all your history, but that would rule out inspiration and application.

***I know. That's why this earlier message about mining came from the oversoul of guides, because the guides themselves were the ones who knew about it, right?***

## Your Unknown Hazards

Yes, and they felt a certain urgency to say something. I believe Speaks of Many Truths and others have commented on this in the past, but the situation is becoming more urgent. It is a hazard; it has always been known to be a hazard when people live on a world in which they are not, on a physical, conscious feeling level, fully aware of their surroundings as you are on other planets.

The hazards are that you can essentially destroy yourself before you realize you have done so—meaning destroying plants and animal life, destroying the function of the planet so that her cycles become strange and destructive to surface life, for example. This is a possible hazard when you are cut off from knowing what Earth feels. Those who have trained themselves to be sensitive to this or who are born that way, which occasionally happens, will know it; but average citizens, unless they strive to know so, will not. Therefore, you could inadvertently destroy something on Earth that is irreplaceable, or perhaps in the course of mining uncover something that was meant to be buried indefinitely. Ultimately, of course, these challenges serve another role, a role that, you might say, could be in your favor if you decide to proceed with benevolent magic.

## Making "Impossible" Changes through Benevolent Magic

Benevolent magic, of course, changes things and produces results that react to the impossible. For the impossible, I always bring up the example of nuclear waste, which your civilization has no real means to transform right now. You can't take a wafer of nuclear material you are now using that is highly toxic and perform some benevolent magic on it to make it completely benign, but benevolent magic *has* that capacity. These courses and trainings are very important, because as you continue to have more and more complex problems, you will eventually be faced with one conundrum after another. You can either throw your hands up in the air and say, "We're all doomed," or you can begin practicing benevolent magic designed to transform the impossible.

***What courses and trainings are you discussing?***

We've begun doing some classes with people. We've talked about it in books, which you are putting out (of course, the next book [Shamanic Secrets for Material Mastery] coming out will focus on that), and it is my intention to stimulate this and talk it up more in the future, giving various homework lessons to support benevolent magic and its potential good effects.

## Native People Affected by Another ET Organism Released from Underground

***There's a series here. One of these organisms affects the birth rate. Can you say what that is, where it is, what we can do?***

These people are people of the heart and mind, people with strong hearts or brave hearts, this is true. I grant that these qualities can be encouraged in people who might not otherwise have them, but there are also people who are actually born with these potentials so strong in them that even the slightest amount of encouragement will amplify to the point where they become unimpeachable (politically speaking), meaning it is ever-present in their personality.

People of the heart and mind are very focused in heart energy. They can produce things mentally, be they theories, applications or actual ideas produced in technology or what-have-you or social or intellectual dissertations that are geared and structured toward heart causes, meaning that which is of love for all beings.

These particular beings are particularly sensitive to a certain form of mutated virus that has been accidentally released by an expedition that was drilling deep into the ground—I think strictly for the purposes of science—in order to see what's down there and how long it has been there. While I understand these ventures—one always wants to know more about oneself or where one is living—nevertheless, there is a built-in hazard, especially when this particular virus does not have an immediate impact.

People are not stupid. If it had had an immediate impact, they would know and try to cap it off, but in this case, just bringing the material up and examining the core samples has released this mutated virus. It has a certain function, which is unfortunate, in that it takes about four or five years to have physical effects. During that time, of course, cycling through the bodies of different people, getting into the water, the food chain and so on, it will tend to decrease the population of those beings.

***You mean reproductively, or kill off the ones who are here?***

Reproductively, not kill off the ones who are here.

***What is it? How did it get there? Who put it there?***

It was buried on Earth. You have to remember that you have been burying stuff for a long time. It was buried on Earth a long time ago—before the populations that you now know on the Earth were here, but after the Earth had established itself in this solar system. It was buried by another passing culture who looked at the Earth and said, "Well, there are not that many people there. Perhaps if we bury this very deep (several hundred feet down) it will be completely safe, especially if we put it in this particular canister." It was put in a canister of crystals so that from all apparent examination from the surface by a passing civilization (ultrasonically and so on), it would appear for all purposes to be crystal, meaning a crystal or rock.

It was buried simply because it was a waste product, not being damaging to any civilization. They needed, and it needed, it to be put someplace where it would not damage anyone.

***And they didn't know its effects?***

They didn't really analyze the future of human life on this planet because they weren't expecting human life here. You have to understand it was years ago. They had been told that life on this planet would probably be plant and animal life, not human life. It would be a sanctuary for plants and animals.

***Thousands? Millions?***

Many thousands of years ago.

***What can humans do?***

## Mining Companies Need to Use Sensitives/Dowsers

You need to be more vigilant about mining and drilling. The guides suggested this, and I will support that. Even now, today, drilling and mining operations often use archaeologists to say, "Drill here, drive here, go here, go there" in order to avoid places where artifacts are in existence, not necessarily only because the company has public service or public spiritedness in its makeup, but because there are laws to prevent such things.

I would recommend two courses. One, that people think about passing laws. It could be simple, really, when you think about it. You could say something like: "No company shall knowingly, in the course of mining or drilling, bring anything to the surface or let it get in the water, that is damaging to the population of Earth." Something like that. I think it's all right to say "knowingly," because I realize that mining and drilling companies might not know about something unusual. It's not a matter of liability, but a matter of being careful for its own sake.

Then I recommend that companies begin to use sensitives in a different way. For quite a while people have been asking various sensitives, "Where is the gold? Where is the silver?" Sometimes these sensitives are known as dowsers. Of course, many of you have asked dowsers, "Where's the water?" Dowsing works, of course. Yet these same people and others might be able to tell you where it's safe to dig or drill. Now, I recognize it would be better if you didn't dig and drill at all, but I understand the practical realities of current technology. If you had someone to say, "Go here, don't go there," you could not only discover things that might be useful to you as a company, but you could also avoid making catastrophic mistakes that would perhaps be very damaging to your own company, to say nothing of catastrophically damaging to all populations on Earth.

## Another ET-Buried Hazard from Ancient Times

***They said, "Another affects the skin of all people, causing you to lose your resistance to the Sun's effects. It would ultimately stop surface living."***

Yes, it actually affects the pigment in the skin. You have now these people who have very pale skin and light-colored eyes. These people must be tremendously careful when going out in the sun, their lives being somewhat ruled by that. If everyone were like that, you would probably see an end to surface living.

***This could cause everyone to become albinos?***

It could.

***Where is it, then, and how did it get here?***

Again, all of this is just civilizations passing and dropping stuff off. This stuff was buried deep within the ocean, but you have to remember that it was dropped off a hundred thousand years ago and put in what was then believed to be permanent containers. But most of these civilizations didn't understand earthquakes or volcanism.

***Did they know there was a movement of tectonic plates?***

That's right, they didn't really understand that. As a result, that's how a lot of these things happened, through the impact of Earth motion. It ruptured and gradually trickled up to the surface of the ocean floor, got into the fishes and ultimately into the people. I don't think it represents an immediate threat, but it certainly represents a threat in the next 17 years. However, it is my intention to have many practitioners of benevolent magic functioning by then.

A lot of you scientists are attempting to resolve disease through genetics. I think, however, that as science discovers its true God and its true heart, it will embrace benevolent magic. Right now it would feel awkward with it.

***So has this started affecting people? Are there cases on the Earth right now?***

No, but there might be a potential in the next few years.

***Not from drilling, but just accidental release?***

Yes.

## The Most Hazardous Release of All—This Year in the U.S.

***The last one is potentially the most devastating. It can literally cause the glue of life, the DNA, to become recessive in its capacities, and become submissive to all forms of mutation.***

This is very dangerous. It was released accidentally in a coal mining operation. The miners were not particularly impacted because this is the type of thing that tends to have its impact on the succeeding generations. In each generation it becomes stronger. I realize that generations are measured in say, ten-year cycles, although they occur on a daily basis. So it's not a daily impact, but the risk tends to expand every ten years or so.

***When did they mine it?***

It was recently released, I think in the past few months. It was that last release that prompted this sense of urgency by the beings who gave this message.

***Can you say which country it's in?***

It was released in the United States.

***Coal mines in the United States. So what do we do?***

## The Only Cure: Benevolent Magic and Mapping the Planet Anew

There is no cure that you now have. I do not think genetics can treat it. It will be necessary to use magic, benevolent magic. When I say magic, unless I'm talking about something sinister, always say *benevolent magic*. It is essential to do this, otherwise people, the reader, can get confused about the type of magic. We're not talking about illusion here. We're talking about physical changes. I know that *you* know this, but I'm saying this for others.

***So you're saying deserts and rain forests should become off-limits?***

Yes, what has become desert, in terms of ancient deserts, and what has become ancient rain forests, even though these rain forests are being seriously impacted, are areas where much of this material has been buried; also in the very deepest trenches of the sea. So that's a certain hazard.

I will encourage scientists who are able, perhaps geologists and others who are able to track where rain forests may have been, to map this thoroughly, because you all know that rain forests are now being wiped out for technical and agricultural purposes. But some rain forests were wiped out before you got here—that is, through some form of natural disaster over the years. Therefore I recommend you to track where rain forests may have been.

***And you say, no mining or drilling there especially.***

Especially, yes. It might be possible to do some small amount of work there, but it will be essential to use a sensitive—not just any sensitive, but people who have track records not tested by science. A practice of the heart cannot be tested by the heartless for accuracy. Be aware of that. That is why science practically never comes up with proof that it finds satisfactory in accepting certain spiritual or psychic practices.

So I'd say, use shamans or mystical people if they wish to participate. They might be able to help. In the coming years it will be particularly important to find sources of fresh water. It will also be necessary to utilize benevolent magic to create water, since more and more water is being turned into technological byproducts, breaking it down for the hydrogen and oxygen and so on.

***Are they doing that?***

I am not the only one who has made this warning, but this is going ahead. It is a big hazard. Benevolent magicians will need to be legion.

***Are you working with others on this project?***

I have begun some workshops, and I'm intending to give homework through this magazine and other outlets to encourage such abilities. I encourage others who can teach these things to continue.

***Are you working with other beings on other levels to train people who come through other channels?***

No, I'm not.

***Wouldn't it be good idea, since this is so necessary?***

There are others who have the capacity to teach such things. I do not claim to be the singular source.

## Toxic Dumps on the Moon and Mars

***They talked about toxic substances on the Moon and Mars. Let's start with the Moon. What is buried there?***

A lot of the mining that has been either seen or speculated on on the Moon and Mars is actually extraction. For years and years your society just looked at the Moon, and there was no real action toward getting there. But in recent years, there is action toward going there and maybe setting up some study colonies—and, of course, mining the Moon, which is the ultimate intention. At just about every moment you'll uncover other people's toxic waste, so a lot of the so-called mining on the Moon is removing material. Some of it is mining per se, but a lot of it is service-oriented [storing toxic material for safety reasons].

***What should they do with it?***

Get it away from you. Take it to some other desolate place and put out a notice that this is a place where such material is stored. And don't expect to store it indefinitely like this, only until you find out what to do with it.

Remember, the Explorer Race's job is to expand not only your own abilities, but the abilities of *all* beings. Ultimately, when this great expansion takes place, the mental knowledge and the inspiration will be available to transform these materials. But right now it's not there.

***But they don't know that.***

Oh, I think some of them know it, yes. The Explorer Race and what you are doing here is not a big secret. It has been somewhat of a secret to the people on Earth, but that has been necessary so people wouldn't simply wait for it to happen.

***But just a couple of years ago, when the expansion was first discussed, it seemed that most people didn't know that these things were part of the expansion.***

Well, a couple of years ago. On what time line? It depends.

***The time line we use here. And Mars, too. So you're saying if we were to go to the Moon right now, it would be toxic for us.***

It might be, though not every place. When areas are cleared and cleaned, they will also be sterilized. The sterilizing will not alter the Moon itself, but would tend to keep the material of the Moon present, simply sterilizing it, eliminating from it the material that was stored there, like other sterilizing procedures. It is not likely that any near-term projects from Earth would be at risk, but certainly in 50 years, when Earth has permanent colonies and is in deep exploration on the Moon, if nothing were changed, you would be at terrible risk.

***So will we need benevolent magic on the Moon?***

Yes, you will need benevolent magic everywhere. Benevolent magic is not so unusual in the universe, but most planets do not utilize it. They have no reason to because everything is already benevolent. You could say that floating an object for the purpose of teaching your children, as the Pleiadians might do, is benevolent magic. It's used in a very benign fashion; it's not necessarily used to create something that is urgently needed, such as your eventual need to create water. It might be to create something of beauty.

***Or to detoxify something. And Mars has been used as a dump, since it hasn't had a surface civilization.***

That's right. You need to be aware of that when you go there. Fortunately, I'm not worried. You're not going to go there and walk on the surface with no protective suit on. You will be careful.

***This is kind of gloomy.***

It would be gloomy *only* if there weren't a cure.

## Recycling

***So what about all the people who need to mine?***

For one thing, you really need to recycle full blast. You need to be absolutely certain where all your dumps are right now, because all those dumps can be mined. Almost everything in those garbage dumps can be recycled. That would be a good outlet for mining companies, by the way. You can dig all that stuff up and use it over again. There's no reason not to be into absolute recycling, and there's no reason for mining companies not to be involved. It would be a tremendous stimulus to the economy. In the beginning it would appear to be too expensive, but if there's no fresh material coming from mines, it wouldn't be so very expensive.

# 26

# Need for Control Makes You Vulnerable to SSG*

Zoosh
October 3, 1997

Just so you don't think that I ignore what you say, I have something to say about the sinister secret government (SSG). Now, what binds all you citizens here to the sinister secret government is that element in yourselves that is equal to their cravings and desires. As individuals, the sinister secret government wants nothing more than to control, you might say. You might say they'd like to control everything, but in reality they just want to control enough so they won't have any surprises and are able to maintain a constantly increasing income—but more importantly, to increase their control or power base.

You've asked before why the citizens are susceptible to these beings. What I want the readers to do is to look inside themselves. Because you are a human being on Earth and because your life has been out of control from time to time, you will find in yourself a desire to do the very same thing—to be in control, to have power over your own destiny and to keep from having unwelcome surprises from outside yourself.

So although your desires are not exactly equal to the sinister secret government's, it is a fact that because so many people *do* have these motivations within themselves that the SSG is able to capitalize

* Excerpted from *Shamanic Secrets of Material Mastery,* 1999, and published in the February 1999 issue of the *Sedona Journal.*

on your mostly inner cravings. If you take a cold, hard look at your life and the way you run it, you will notice that you do have a tendency to attempt to control. By control I do not necessarily mean manipulate. What I mean is to provide certain levels of activity in your brain, and hence into your world, that are designed to keep your world in a predictable state.

Interestingly enough, most of you, even though you might wish to be more wealthy or healthy or what-have-you, do not apply those wishes in your control mechanism. Mostly what goes into the control mechanism is the desire for predictability, taking no particular account of whether that predictability is positive or negative. Now, this does not mean that you are foolish or not very bright. It means that because most of you have had experiences at one time or another that are so out of control and so completely unpredictable, you are living in a constant state of anxiety, thinking about those circumstances or dealing with circumstances if you're in them now.

You might say that the aspect of control is really under the heading of self-protection. Yet for those of you on the spiritual path, or even on a path that allows sudden benevolent change for you, many of you know that letting go is one of the best ways of having almost instantaneous improvement in your life.

Here we have a dichotomy: (1) letting go and improvements that may follow, and frequently do; and (2) the need for control, which is a reaction to previous or current circumstances, and the knowledge that you do not actually filter your wishes, hopes and dreams to improve circumstances into that control, whose objective is predictability.

The SSG uses your primary self-protection motivation (control) to plug in to you. You could say that they stimulate fears in the background and try to manipulate your reactions so that you frequently have that knee-jerk reaction to want or need to be in control. I'm not going to tell you to give up control, because it is very hard to give something up. If you've been reading anything I've said for a while, you'll know that I do not recommend giving something up, but adding something new and beneficial. The more you do the new and beneficial thing, the less you'll use the older, somewhat self-destructive thing. Then you'll easily be on your new path.

What I recommend is that you think about what you want and need and try to keep it simple and basic, such as a need to be wealthier or healthier or living in circumstances that are more benevolent for you—like that. Keep it simple and say it out loud somewhere where you feel safe and comfortable and where no one can hear you.

If you live in a crowded situation, you can whisper it, then work on letting go right after that. Say it and mean it, but then release it.

## An Exercise in Letting Go

Some of you will be able to just let it go and go on with your lives and not think about it anymore. That's how it works best. But for those who have trouble letting it go and want to think about it, here's what I want you to do. It's very simple. Just grip something. It can't be another person, but it could be the arms of the chair you're sitting in or even the support, the bed or bunk you might be sitting on. Just grip it, and after you say what you want in your life, then do two things: Gradually release what you are gripping, which signals your body that you are letting go, and try to put yourself into the physical feeling of giving up. Giving up and letting go is exactly the same feeling, only you have a judgment about giving up.

If you loosen your grip on whatever you are gripping and giving up (which for most of you is infinitely easier than letting go), you will be able to release it. Then just go on with your life and don't think about it. You can do this once a day for a week or two if you want to. You don't have to say exactly the same words for what you want and need, but remember, try to keep it simple. Also remember—and this is essential—never ask for what you *don't* want; always ask for what you *do* want.

If there is something you want to get rid of in your life or something that's hounding you, then ask (for instance) that you live a more benevolent lifestyle. That covers a lot of ground, and it will sustain you. I'm not predicting miraculous results, but for a lot of you it will help. Say it once a day for a week or two, then you can say it again once a week or so for a while, or as often as you need to in order to feel better. Saying it more often and then letting go does not necessarily bring it to you any sooner, though it may make you feel better when you are doing something for yourself. I recommend that as homework for everyone.

I also want to remind you that the sinister secret government has very little power of its own, but because it's able to tap into the fears and anxieties of the general population, they draw their power from that. It's an odd thing, but if you took the sinister secret government and just dropped them off on a planet where everything was benevolent (granted, it wouldn't be good for that planet, but I'm talking theoretically), they would immediately lose all their power because they wouldn't have any anxiety and misery to pull on.

You can see what my underlying agenda is: The more comfortable and benevolent your life is, the less energy the SSG will have to draw on, and, of course, the less powerful and less influential they will be.

# 27

# A Lesson in Benevolent Magic

Zoosh
January 23, 1999

•

All right, Zoosh speaking now. Let me talk about the next installment of a series on benevolent magic. Let's start off with that.

You know, it is time to take a conscious, aware step toward changing your reality. It has been useful in the past to experience what exists, then unconsciously change it or work with it. Now one cannot wait anymore for changes to occur.

I'm going to suggest what to do to change your reality. If you are around children, this will be easier. If you are not around children, then you will have to wait for your opportunities. Your opportunities are as follows.

When people around you are laughing, cheerful, happy or joyful, just take note of it and observe them from a distance. If you are involved, note your cheerfulness, your laughter, and be that quite sincerely. If you are, however, observing, look at the happy people, especially if they are laughing just for fun or because they heard an amusing story or because, being children, they are having a good time. Focus on it, then turn away and look at something else. Try to look at a neutral scene such as trees, the sidewalk, cars—whatever is available—and stay in that feeling of joy.

What is going on in your society all the time are moments of joy and happiness. These moments of joy and happiness are bursts of happiness, yes? But they are not sufficient anymore to sustain benevolence for you all, so I'd like you to begin to spread it around. After you have seen this (just glance quickly), notice that it cheers you up. It is especially important to smile at it if it cheers you up. Then look at something that is neutral. If you can, glance back to that cheerful scene and again look at something neutral. Hopefully, it will be something in your environment that you see every day. Now, this will not work if you are looking at a moving picture, a movie or a television program. The emotion has to be demonstrated by *living people*.

If you can, next look at something that is either unpleasant or that usually annoys you, and you will notice that it doesn't annoy you as much. This is not a profound revelation. You all know that if you are laughing and look at something that annoys you, it doesn't usually annoy you as much. This is a way of becoming *consciously involved* in that process so that you are like a farmer—you are reaping the excess happiness. You are not draining it from people, you are just an observer. It's just like picking an apple off a tree that has many apples, and one will not be missed.

When you then look at something, it might be annoying or usually annoying. Just look at it for a moment, don't dwell on it. Then notice that it doesn't annoy you as much. When you can do this around your home, ultimately things that annoy you will not annoy you so much even if people aren't around who are laughing.

This is really a way of seeing your world and making your world different. It is simple. You will not remember to do it all the time, but when you do, it might be something to experiment with. Consider it an experiment, because we will build on this later. It is interesting to note that the electronic media (such as television) are not something you can draw energy from. It has to be people. It can be people laughing at the television, but it must be *people*. It can be people laughing at something on the radio, but it cannot be pulled *from* the TV or the radio. If you do that, you will simply pull the electromagnetic radiation and not feel very good.

It is not that there is an immediate crisis, but there is a tendency now to become overinvolved in the dramatic. The dramatic is there to catch your attention, to relieve you of the need to create dramas of your own. But it is necessary to begin making an effort to change your reality, not through your will, but through a conscious effort to utilize excess joy. There is not a crisis. I just want you to begin to do this.

## Hang onto That Smile

**1.** When people around you are laughing, cheerful, happy or joyful, take note of it and observe them from a distance. If you are involved, note your cheerfulness, your laughter, and be that quite sincerely.

If you are observing, notice that it cheers you up. It is especially important to smile if it cheers you up.

---

**2.** After you have focused on the cheerful scene, turn away and look at something else. Look at a neutral scene such as trees, the sidewalk, cars—whatever is available—*and stay in that feeling of joy.*

If you can, glance back to that cheerful scene and look again at something neutral. The emotion has to be demonstrated by *living people.*

---

**3.** Now look at something that is either unpleasant or that usually annoys you. When you can do this around your home, ultimately things that annoy you will not annoy you so much. This is a way of becoming consciously involved in the process of reaping excess happiness. You are not draining it from people, you are just an observer.

---

This is really a simple way of seeing your world and making your world different.

—Zoosh

# 28

# SSG Manipulations and a Temporary Astral Processing

Zoosh
January 23, 1999

## SSG Experiment with Benevolent Subliminals

The sinister secret government (SSG) has put subliminal messages on TV in the past that were destructive or harmful. Now they are attempting another project. This is not public relations for them, but in a world in which many of you are surrounded with discomforts and challenges, they want to see how things would be if they prompt you with subliminal messages that are benevolent. They want to see if the action and the reaction (the action being the message and the reaction being your response) is as swift as that toward the negative.

So for the past week or two and for the next five to six weeks and possibly longer, the subliminal messages (not what advertisers put on the screen) that some of you might notice occasionally whether the set is on or off, will be benevolent. They will say, "health, healthfulness, good health" or something like that. They might say "happiness" or "cheerfulness," things along that line. They won't be orders. They won't say, "Get healthy" or "Be happy." They will just be suggestions.

This is an attempt to see how you respond in given situations. I'm mentioning this, not to say that the television is required watching right now, but that as of right now it is less damaging than usual because of this subliminal program.

***But this is January 23 and won't be published and available until the first of March. You're saying that it is going to be over by then. Is that true?***

It might or not. It might be extended. If it's extended, it will run for maybe eight or ten or possibly twelve weeks, but that decision has not been made. Even so, it might be interesting for people to remember how they felt during that period. It's up to you. I state what is of the moment, and you publish what you feel is relevant according to your deadline.

### A Bubble in the Astral Veil

***Your comment about looking back is valuable. Is there anything you want to say about where humans are right now and what they are going through? They seem to be going through a lot of drama of their own.***

Human beings now are processing things within themselves that are running threads to past lives. Normally I do not talk too much about past lives because it is very easy to become overconcerned with a past life, but some of you have been having the following experience. Let me describe the basic symptoms.

For no apparent reason a person might wake up in the middle of the night with fear or nervousness or with symptoms that might be considered anxiety by a trained professional. But some symptoms won't seem to have any relevance to that. Some people might have cold sweats. Other people might feel that they've got to run around the block and that if they do that, they'll be fine.

This is not madness, and it is not usually associated with anxiety or panic. I'm mentioning this because I want to put the psychologists, therapists, even analysts, on notice. This will have medical symptomologies, and it is perfectly acceptable to provide therapies to your patients (especially to individuals who have not shown or complained before of such nervousness or panic) and give treatment, but it is not a sudden wave of anxiety, as if anxiety were a virus that people were catching—although you might, in more radical moments, think that it could be such a "crazy" thing because of the spurts of patients. Sudden spurts of patients will report these symptoms for no apparent reason, and people will, rightly so, look around to see what it is.

I will talk about it. Right now many of you are processing past lives that have taken place on Earth or—for some who are strong and whose health is normally good—you have taken on other people's past lives. You have done this because the current soul incarnation of a person is not strong enough to take on those past discomforts, or else those past-life individuals do not have any current incarnations on Earth. Thus you are processing for others. This will be a short-lived phenomenon. I want you to understand that, because it will not last, and it is perfectly acceptable to use whatever medical or therapeutic treatment you require to get through this time.

We are going through what I would call a veil. It is an outer-boundary veil of what is sometimes called the astral. (I do not talk much about the astral because this has been overworked at the moment. This has also been an overworked concept in the past by well-meaning spirits, guides and other individuals.) There is an area that exists between the third and the fourth dimension where the unresolved sometimes, not always, is in residence. If the unresolved becomes overwhelming, if there is too much for that area, there will be a flexing that expands the boundary of the unresolved, potentially partway into third-dimensional reality. That has actually occurred, and it will be relieved over the next few months by many of you who have volunteered, just as one relieves pressure from a pressure cooker with a pressure-release valve.

The unresolved is always under stress to be resolved. It is the stress or oomph (if I may use a word that is not a real word, but you get my meaning) that calls attention to it, and will make it easier for those who help the unresolved be resolved. As the Explorer Race, you have now completed all your karmic lessons and are prepared to begin applying your knowledge and creatorship lessons. This is why I've been talking about benevolent magic, which is a creatorship lesson. I want you to consider this. I'm not asking you to volunteer for it, but if you have been picked and have begun to show these symptoms, be alert to the fact that you have volunteered on the soul level and that it will pass.

This processing is a profound thing. To be involved in it is to be acknowledged as a person who has achieved enough on your own throughout all your incarnations, plus this life, to be able to process the pain of those who no longer live in your now time. The reason you initially feel it as anxiety, fright, panic and so on is that it is the expanded version of stress—in this case, in this level of the astral.

The astral is not a place one goes to because one is being punished. It is simply a place that functions as a safety area for the unresolved when it is not yet prepared to be resolved, or when it is at odds with itself and cannot be resolved in the moment. Understand that this will pass; it is not a permanent fixture.

I might add that, given your current position at 3.485 (a little bit of movement there), the astral exists generally where one does not expect it [draws], right before 4.0, but it is . . . I'm showing it as a dotted line. If there is too much in that area, this is what occurs, although this is just for the sake of illustration. It creates something like a stress bubble, and this "outer band" between this [3.485] and this [4.0]. The astral is normally just a thin membrane.

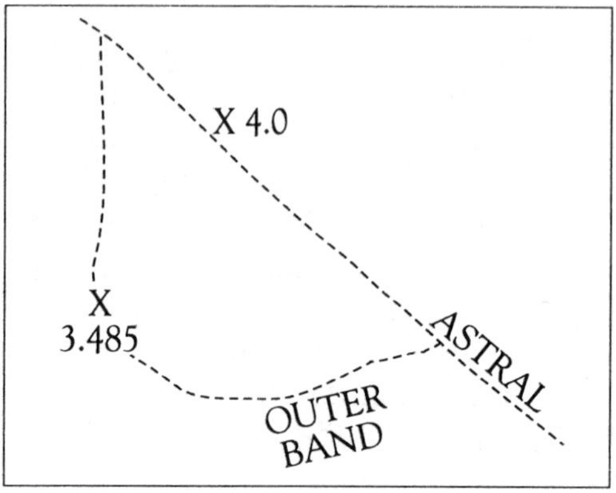


***But it is below 4.0. That's important.***

It's very close to 4.0.

***Some people say it is the fourth dimension, but that is not correct.***

It's important to say this, because some people have stated that the astral is the fourth dimension. I want to have it published like this so you can all see that the reason people have said that is perfectly understandable. We can see that the position of the astral is practically on top of 4.0 on this particular two-dimensional map. It is an understandable perception by some, but the fourth dimension is *not* the astral.

We must understand that the unresolved (which is what I prefer to call the astral) must be close enough to a source of potential resolution that its stress does not ordinarily become overwhelming and create these bubbles, yet far enough away from the place where it was originally put into an unresolved state, which would have been the third dimension. Therefore it's as far away from the third dimension as it can get, yet as close as it can be to the fourth dimension without interfering with it. In this way it is sufficiently close to where you are so that should it bubble out like this and create an outer band, you can be tested as individuals on the degree of creatorship ability you have now.

So for those of you who now have or might have this experience, it will be short-lived. Don't assume that you have suddenly succumbed to panic and anxiety, which are very real conditions. For those of you who might have panic and anxiety as part of your makeup, this will probably not become worse for you. It is something others will experience, so continue the therapies you are utilizing that are helping you. I am talking about individuals who do not normally demonstrate such symptoms.

***How can someone reading this know the difference between working on their own past lives or if they are volunteering on some level to clear the unresolved for others?***

There is really no way of knowing. I would say that it really doesn't matter, since you are all one anyway. The differentiation between your own past lives and volunteering for the past lives of another is really unimportant, because the symptomology and the results and the duration are the same. There is really no way by which you could know it.

## Hate Anchors You to SSG's Enslaving Radio Wave

I want to also mention that the sinister secret government is able to influence you, not only because of your being exposed to the many manipulations they use toward you, some subtle and some more direct, but by an anchor they might have in you or by putting something in you.

***Like an implant?***

No. They have discovered how to create a temporary anchor that relates to your feeling body, which relates in turn to your physical body. Of course, their actual goal is to tamper with your spiritual body, although that is not likely to occur. They will anchor hate in you anytime you demonstrate it, whether openly or by just feeling it and saying nothing.

Hate is a profound feeling. Sometimes it is partly anchored in the mental, other times it is connected to a strictly visceral reaction. Sometimes it is very fleeting, such as when a child says it hates a parent and gets over it quickly, or in a relationship where you might hate each other momentarily, but you get over it.

Other hates may be over a lifetime, such as prejudice based on a reasonable argumentative or advocated prejudice—when everything the person has ever experienced about this particular issue has always been unpleasant. This is not to say it is an acceptable prejudice but to compare it to a prejudice based on ignorance, one that has no physical evidence to support it, yet causes the individual expressing it to feel better in some way.

Hate in all its forms is an actual resonance. The sinister secret government has discovered a way to radiate a wave similar to a radio wave, which will anchor into anything that feels hate. Generally speaking, this would have to be a human being because animals do not feel hate. Animals might get angry and attack, but they don't feel hate. Land does not feel hate; it might be agitated or upset, but it doesn't feel hate. Only human beings feel hate. This is something the SSG can create a temporary anchor into to manipulate you profoundly.

Know that if you hate something for whatever reason—even if you can stand up and explain, "Zoosh, it's this, it's this, it's this," and I can easily say that it is completely understandable—you are still basically shooting yourself in the foot every time you do this. That radio wave is being broadcast twenty-four hours a day, and every time you hate *anything*, whether it's justified or not, you immediately become susceptible to a slavish devotion to sinister secret government causes, which will *always* be detrimental to you and others. I think you ought to know this.

## Broadcast from Undetectable Underground Caverns

***What about the radio wave?***

It is emanated from underground caverns inside the Earth and disseminated through various places on the Earth's surface. It is difficult to stop because sourcing the signal for purposes of destroying it is almost impossible on the basis of the current technology of various governments. Certain governments, I might add, have actually made an attempt to stop it. They have on occasion noted the wave, and there have been one or two research projects that have correlated this wave to increased hate, anger, riots and so on. There have been some attempts to stop it, but right now surface governments have their hands tied, not only because of monetary constraints, but also because the technology to locate the source of the signal does not yet exist for them.

You can locate where the signal *was*. You can locate everything but the point of origin. Even if you use the most sophisticated weapons technology, the chances of your actually being able to stop the radio wave is almost zero. Battling it has to be something that is not controlled through technological means. It has to be either benevolent magic, at least the core of it, to get people consciously aware that if they want to guarantee that they will become slaves to somebody else's cause—a cause that is *guaranteed*, and not just occasionally, to be detrimental to you and others—then they can just hate.

For example, let's say that you get angry about something and you hate something, anything at all, for about thirty seconds. That radio wave, always being present, will mean that for the next two hours you will be unconsciously but slavishly devoted to the sinister secret government. This might or might not prompt you to do something they would like you to do, because there are other factors in your life that, for example, might keep you from doing things that are benevolent.

When you are living on the edge or in an extremely difficult environment such as any prison anywhere, you don't need much to tip you over the edge. That's why I'm mentioning it.

***That's very powerful. Shades of that hate would be resentment and all sorts of other levels of it.***

Yes, and the sinister secret government knows this. Other people manipulate with hate and prejudice, but the SSG knows this absolutely. As long as they can keep you fighting amongst each other, they know that you will not unify. Unification, even *moments* of unification (not all the time in every moment) have a profound defeating effect upon them. If everybody were happy for a moment—such as at New Years, because great numbers of people sometimes get happy then even for a short time—this would create an impact on the sinister secret government even though it is like a momentary episode of shortness of breath. They immediately lose a great deal of their influence and power. They know about this, because there is a significant amount of unity at New Years Eve even though it is not a universal holiday. Any form of benevolent unity between human beings, even if for short moments, is something the SSG fears mightily.

***So that's why worldwide meditations have become very potent, right?***

Yes, that frightens them. Religions add to moments of great joy and happiness as long as they are not driven by hate and fear (there are some like that). But religious joy and happiness also work. One must guard very carefully in respect to religion, with the hate, fear, restriction and rigidity, because those aspects play into the hands of the SSG and tend to stifle the creative element of the human spirit.

Religion was always intended, as you know, to lift you out of depraved and horrible conditions. To some extent it has accomplished that, but because of mankind's attempt to interpret the Creator (not to reflect, support and encourage belief and appreciation in the loving Creator) based on the human being's interpretations, this is where religion sometimes goes wrong.

# 29

# Crop Circles

Zoosh
February 26, 1999

***What is the purpose of crop circles?***

The purpose is purely to activate, and it works on many levels. Obviously, those able to enter into or at least close to one (very close would be within 2 to 3 feet of the actual circle) would experience a profound effect on their spiritual bodies.

***Do you mean the edge of it or the center?***

The perimeter, it is not necessary to actually go inside if the circle is fresh, within 12 to 14 hours of its creation. Now, that is the primary impact. However, the secondary impact is the actual sight. There have been many comparisons to ancient diagrams, especially on Native American lands, suggesting a correlation between messages given to ancient peoples of many lands and more contemporary messages. Certainly there have been many methods of analysis applied to these particular messages. But as you know, without a common language it is often necessary to use signs and pictures, which are seen frequently in ancient cultures.

Many years ago the ancient cultures of the world—at about 3000 B.C., then 1500, then about 700, then about A.D. 200 or 300 (depending on where you were) up to about 700, different groups of people around the world were approached and given various signs and symbols. Some of the peoples had the foresight to make a permanent record of the symbols. Some did not, and made either a temporary record or passed them down from person to person in accurate ways. However, should anything happen to the people, which did happen, many times these messages were lost.

## The Wiltshire Oval and Key Codes

One might ask why the most well-known and frequently cited crop circles happen in what is now call the U.K. This is because certain principles function there and certain identities will be there in the future. One knows about Stonehenge, but all over the U.K. there are stone circles and monoliths and so on, all aiming their primary energy to an area that runs in somewhat of an oval (hard to describe verbally) that includes Stonehenge. So you often find in this area—Glastonbury, Avebury, Stonehenge—many of the more profound crop circles. The circles were initially designed to catch people's attention, and for those who were able to approach them, to greatly accelerate their spiritual capacities in this life.

But ultimately (I'm condensing this greatly), they are designed to function as key codes. You all know that the brain does not operate at its full capacity. This is intentional, so that certain information and wisdom, which you were born with but is inaccessible at this time, can be maintained. When you see certain things, certain codes will unlock, not the knowledge of what the circles mean (that is really almost unnecessary), such as spiritual capacities, which will accelerate your current history so that you get through the more difficult and heartbreaking aspects of it as quickly as possible while you are developing these capacities on Earth as you are now.

***I'm glad I'm going there in July!***

## Walking Inside Depletes Their Energy

Yes, if you have the opportunity, please remember that everyone will want to rush inside the crop circle. This is entirely unnecessary, especially if aspects of it are circular, which they usually are. You can tell friends, if you have them on the trip, that the most profound means of experiencing the circle is to walk around the outside of the circular portions—say, within 1 to 2 feet of the crop circle, but not touching the circle itself. You will hear from many people who go inside that it is very powerful, but it is in fact no more powerful inside than it is close to the outside. I might add that it is not intended for people to go inside. If people simply walk around the outside of it, the circle's energy will last much longer, but if people go inside, the energy will be depleted very quickly. This is not widely known and has not been published, as far as I know.

There is a tertiary purpose: Many parts of the world, especially those roughly opposite to the U.K., are steering energy to that part of

the world, but when the crop circle takes place, if it is able to maintain at least some of its energy up to the 36th hour, meaning a day and a half, then it can feed back some of that energy to those areas on the other side of the world that have been giving all this energy to the U.K. For thousands of years. This has been promised and would be good to do. That is why in the past there have been crop circles in such obscure places that they have not been noticed at all. Some people feel that there was a loss, but it was not a loss, even when the crop was burned or mowed by the farmer because it was time to harvest it. Even those that might not have been seen much by human beings were seen by animals and birds. (You are not the only beings here.) The circles would have fed back a great deal of their energy to the other side of the world, and if they had not been seen by humans, they would have been reproduced at another time.

Ultimately, the purpose of the crop circles will be fulfilled. Those who are not interested and who cast aspersions on them, it is simply for them to get the experience some other way. It is not unlike music; some people like rap or rock and roll, yet the intention of music has always been to expose you to certain tonal or rhythmic sounds that affect your spiritual growth. These sounds might come in the form of an opera or a simple ditty sung in a bar, yet the tones do come. They are most effective when you make them yourself, but they do have some minor effect when listened to, especially in person. This is a very good analogy.

***Could you give me more detailed information?***

## Subliminal Messages, Sub-Key Patterns

Current history, as you know, is full of strife and conflict and all kinds of confusion, yet at the same time there are plenty of good things. The intention is that it works almost as a result of what I would call a sub-key message. The idea of subliminal messages is based on sub-key, but sub-key is a little more to the point. When an individual is born on Earth, the patterns of the brain, while they are mechanically set, are not set in terns of society's conditioning. This takes place over the first 3 to 7 years of life, depending on lifestyle. During these times your brain, your nervous system, your feeling body, your physical body and your general sense of self are keyed into your surroundings, your life, your reactions to life and in general, those who are in your life. This is the key system. This system in the past has stayed in effect throughout a person's entire life.

But this has changed. The change began in the late '40s and has been increasing—or let's say accelerating, in terms of potentials for change, at a gradually accelerating rate. Now, in the late "70s it started to become noticeable; people's thought patterns, their ways of reacting and interacting, began to change noticeably. Now, one could also say that this might have to do with what society was going through at the time. That certainly must be considered. However, what I'm talking about is something that can be measured.

I'm mentioning this especially for those individuals who might have been running long-term research projects. For those who might have been doing that, if you check magnetometer or magnetic readings—taken from the brain patterns of individuals you may have been testing, you will notice a definite trend toward more expansive or more receptive patterns in the brain, which also measures the nervous system somewhat. Yet there would not be any apparent difference in intelligence quotient, because the patterns—the keys, as it were—were being changed to allow a broader potential use of the brain and the nervous system involved with the potential that your scientists and most people now know seems to be unmeasurable or unused.

These sub-key patterns started being expanded in the late '70s. It has continued through the '80s and reached its zenith in the year 1997. That zenith will be maintained over time to include the years '98, '99, 2000, 2001. These pattern changes, you understand, are not cut in stone. They may continue to hold that zenith for another four years, depending on historical needs of the moment. These needs have to do with what's going on, basically. If by that time there has been sufficient spiritual and feeling growth in individuals' day-to-day practical lives, the zenith will begin to retreat. If, on the other hand, there has not been sufficient growth in the spiritual and feeling self as experienced through practical, day-to-day physical life, then another level will begin, building to a new zenith right around the year 2005. It is not likely that will be necessary, but it is a contingency.

## Acceleration in Interacting with Spirit

You might ask , what does this have to do with crop circles? Crop circles in the very beginning had to do with immediacy. That is to say, for those who would fly (in the case of birds) or walk (in the case of animals or people, but meant mostly for animals), it was meant to have a local impact, and acceleration and openess and a change in the sub-key patterns that would accelerate and allow for more encompassing motions. What does that mean? Greater encompassing motion means that instead of just interacting with your immediate physical reality on the physical, mental, spiritual and feeling plane, as you expand your sub-key patterns, you would have the capacity to interact with what your spiritual self is guiding you to do, what your imagination builds upon and what the sacred intentions for Earth are patterned to be, and it would become more possible to bring those things about. Because this is a polarized world at this time, there is another factor built in: the potential to manifest becomes more likely.

## The SSG's Reaction

Things have become so intense, so apparent, so almost overwhelming because that which is imagined, if it is built on something unpleasant, might have, though with less possibility, considering the comparison to the overall power of spirit, a 15% greater chance of coming about. The sinister secret government has utilized this possibility in attempting to corrupt individuals, desiring what is corruptive at its very core: encouraging you to be more reactive in an unpleasant way to each other. In short, it encourages patterns of self-destruction. As you know, I define self-destruction as hurting yourself or someone else, including all life.

We have, however, an increase of about 40% in the spiritual manifestation potential, far greater than the 15% increase in potential damage. This is why there has been a gradually increasing interest even amongst individuals in cultural, sociological, political and nationalistic circles where such interests have not been part of the tradition of those cultures. We have, then, a greater capacity for manifestation along benevolent and beneficial lines, with that echo effect in the polarized world of the potential unpleasant manifestation also being slightly magnified. This has created an accelerated history for you.

As more and more individuals see crop circles or pictures of them or, best of all, walk around outside the circular portions (not the angular portions), they will have a much greater capacity to have their personal spiritual vibration increased. The sub-key patterns of spiritual manifestation can be increased from the 40% potential all the way up to 55% or even 65%, though the average individual would most likely not go beyond a 58% increase. Those who are involved in practical applications of spiritual activities (not just thinking, bu doing) might have their capacity increase to 63% or 65%. What about going into the crop circle? Wouldn't that increase it more for an individual? No, it does not, because when you go in, it begins to immediately deplete the energy.

The crop circle, then, is intended to have more than one impact. The decrease in energy comes about as a result of penetrating the membrane. The arc portion, the circular portions of the crop circle, function as a membrane between the actual pattern and the surrounding grasses or crops. This membrane might break, once it is punctured by a large human being (any human that can walk; a crawling baby would not have that impact). If a steer or a domesticated cow entered the circle, it might or might not break the membrane, though this might happen with cows that are overly chemicalized. But if they are able to walk about in a field with a considerable amount of freedom and are not too close to slaughter time, they are less likely to break the membrane, though it's still possible.

This is because cows have such a close tie to the human being. If a human being were more respectful of cow, appreciated them more for their great sacrifice to support you as human beings, it is unlikely they would have this impact. They are like a test being, because when human beings get to be more appreciative of cows and treat them better, and when slaughtering them for meat do it in a very respectful and kind way, one at a time, not mechanistically or by people who hate their job or are corrupted because of it, this will be a sign of spiritual evolution.

As a human being, when you go inside a crop circle, you will immediately create a rupture in that membrane, causing the energy available to emanate to other beings to deplete quite rapidly, until about 48 hours later the energy will not likely be noticeable. Even within 12 hours it will be greatly decreased. If you can, try to preserve them. Just walk around outside, but only where there are curves. Ovals are acceptable, but most of the curves will be arcs or actual circles, sometimes connected to the rest of the pattern. So there is that immediate impact.

You might ask, what about animals? When birds fly in and land, they will become about three times as spiritual or as magnetic as they normally are. Thus when they fly about in the area of human beings, they will dissipate that energy gradually over the period of an hour to an hour and a half. The same for insects and small wild creatures who might walk in, though they may walk around it.

### An Exercise For Looking At Crop Circles

Now, what about the pattern, the shape? This has a secondary impact, and for those who cannot go to tho crop circle, which is the majority of people, if they can look at a photograph and turn it very slowly, they'll notice something interesting. Maybe you are in your living room looking at individual photos of crop circles, which are ideally taken directly overhead from an altitude of at least 500 feet. (You can use a telephoto lens; the plane would be a minimum of 500 feet above because it might otherwise interfere with the radiating energy.)

Try to get comfortable, relaxed. You can meditate if you want to before you look at the photos, but be relaxed. (Try to turn the phone ringer off or unplug it so it won't interfere with this little exercise, and do it at a time when you are less likely to be disturbed.) The photos are face down on your left. Once you are relaxed, pick up a photo, look at it for a time.

If you don't feel exactly right, don't just discard it, turn it slowly in your hands, very slowly. Turn it either clockwise (right) or counterclockwise (left). I'd recommend turning it slowly toward the left and notice how you feel. The most prominent feelings will be in the area of your heart or solar plexus because they dominate your immediate reaction to your physical world. Notice, if you can, if the crop circle comes to feel more comfortable. If it does not feel comfortable no matter how you turn it, place it face down to your right.

Do this with each succeeding crop circle, separating out those that cause you to feel the best. Once you've separated out the ones that do not feel good to you no matter how you turn them, set those aside. Let's say you separate out three of the ten you have. Of the remaining seven, go through them again one at a time to see which ones cause you to feel the most benevolent. This is a physical reaction and it is very important. Some of you might have a spiritual reaction, a gentle energy you feel. That's good to pay attention to also. That energy might be felt on your face, head, neck or other areas. Take note of it, and if it feels pleasant, then put it in the pile of the ones that feel the most pleasant. Eventually you will find the two or three that feel best. (If there are fewer or more, that's fine.)

While you are going through the process of elimination, hold the pictures by the edges; be especially careful not to touch the crop circle in the photograph. If they are cut out of a magazine, use the same process. It is better to have actual photographs because a magazine will have printing on the other side, which could affect the process. Then take note of the parts of the crop circle that are spherical. Some crop circles may be mostly spherical, perhaps with tabs or lines connecting to other spherical shapes. You might like to touch the photograph.

After you have touched the spherical or circular parts of the crop circle, touch it with your left hand—the fingertips or the palm—and notice how you feel. At that point you can either relax and experience the good feeling, take notes about what you felt or tape-record your comments. You might choose to touch it with the fingers or the palm of your right hand, but I think most of you will get the most out of this experience by using your left hand and palm. If there are portions of the crop circle that are angular, jutting off from the round portion, *do not touch those* at all.

## Angular Parts of the Pattern

You might ask, why does this exist if it is apparently not something to be touched? It is understood by those who leave crop circles that you are living in a polarized world. So this tangential portion or abridgement, as it might be called, is intended to deal with the discomfort polarization on Earth. It is almost like a grounded antenna so that the round portions could be experienced at their most beneficial.

Now, if you are physically present where there is a crop circle, it is safe to come within five feet of those portions, but if you should happen to touch it accidentally or unconsciously or step through it, it might drain your energy. It's not likely to cause harm, but it might cause you to feel less energetic, and if you are unhappy or have an ache or pain, it might become more prominent. These areas are not intended to be touched, but to have a grounding effect so that the rest of the circle can have its benevolent effect.

There are some larger crop circles where the angular portions are seemingly predominant (we're calling them crop "circles" for the sake of simplicity), which are intended to transform discomforts in general in such a way as not to directly impact human beings. Avoid touching the angular portions if at all possible. What about the lines that go from one spherical portion to another? Try to avoid what I'm calling the tabs. These are angular, not intended to be touched. Once or twice, maybe more often, you might find angulars inside a crop circle, one or two types, perhaps more. Again, try to avoid touching them. If you have touched them in the past, don't be too concerned. Any discomfort amplified by these angular portions is likely to dissipate within 60 to 90 minutes, gradually decreasing over an hour, so that after 18 hours it has no impact whatsoever.

It is important to warn you because this angular portion can be dissipated by people touching it or walking through it. It is intended to have an impact—partly on Mother Earth, to help her cope with all the excessive energies on her body these days; partly on your societies; and partly to simply ground the crop circle on a polarized world.

## New Overflight Problems

***There are new British restrictions on planes that photograph the crop circles.***

Part of the objection to planes flying over crop circles is the noise and annoyance factor, and also having too much unregulated air traffic. So make sure the plane is at least 500 feet above, though it would be better at 1500 feet. Of course, there is also the idea that this is an unknown phenomenon, which any governmental body will treat, regardless of public announcements, as something potentially dangerous. As such it will be a topic for debate in various governmental and military circles about safety to the local population, so understand that it is not just some attempt to prevent contact.

## "Grapeshot"

***Many crop circles have smaller circles around the perimeter. Is it necessary to stay two feet away from those circles?***

If there are smaller circles around the perimeter of a large circle, look first to see if they are outside the boundary of the main circle but within one or two feet. If they are, then walk around the little circles as if you were walking around the main circles.

***Would there be enough energy then?***

You would have to come within 18 inches of the little circles. If such a phenomenon occurs, sometimes it means that it is intended that people give the main circle a larger berth because it will be radiating on its own, intending to keep you at a little distance. If, on the other hand, the small circles are six to eight feet or more away from the large circle, it would be possible to walk around the perimeter, the arcs of the large circle. (Of course, as you do so you will be changing the pattern.) Ideally we need to have the photographs taken before people do that, but ideal conditions are not always possible. What makes the difference is, if the little circles are very close to the main circles, keep your distance.

***Are the older circles ever completely depleted?***

## Gathering Crop Seeds and Compensating the Farmer

Yes, if the older circle is depleted, the energy of the circle itself, the shape, the form, is no longer radiating. However, the crop seeds—wheat or oats, perhaps—might be extracted by the farmer or others. Try to extract them in the field using no mechanized equipment; use old peasant farming techniques. These seeds can be planted elsewhere and will have potentially powerful spiritual effects, not only in terms of what is ultimately consumed, but the effects of the plants growing.

I recommend that if the farmer is looking for a way to make up the loss in revenue for that part of the field from not only the crop in the circle, but the traffic of people coming and going, it would be perfectly acceptable to gather the seeds and sell a 10- to 15-seed packet for a reasonable fee.

I'd like to make a comment to those who take tour groups into those areas. I think this is a good idea. It is also very important to make alliances with the farmers or have local representatives who have such alliances and have consideration. Farmers, after all, are trying to grow crops to feed people, and one needs to consider such an honorable profession. Therefore, if there are any crop circles on his farm, the farmer deserves to be compensated in as many ways as possible—not in crassly commercial ways, but certainly there needs to be some kind of a fund set up so that access could be readily obtained by those who would teach about crop circles. Perhaps individuals might wish to contribute so that a bounty is paid (for legitimate crop circles only) to the farmers or those who lease the land to grow the crops. This would allow some compensation for all their work and the lost crop.

I'd also like to congratulate those who are leading such forays to these areas. This is a profoundly spiritual thing to do. Even if you're doing it for the curiosity value, try to recognize that your alignment with your true purpose in life, in the most benevolent and beneficial sense, is useful. Try to encourage the people you are leading on the tour to be conscious of their true purpose or some benevolent or beneficial circumstance that would be good for all people as well as themselves and their families. It is not so much a wish, but holding and focusing on benevolent and beneficial thoughts and feelings. This is more important close to the crop circle. Teaching can take place within 50 feet of the crop circle, but once you are closer than that, it is best to be quiet so the mind does not have to think, simply absorbing the experience. Once you have stepped away 50 feet or more or gotten back into your vehicle, the teaching can continue.

I also strongly recommend that those who gather seeds from these crop circles be encouraged to set up a fund to support their activity, be they farmers or individuals doing this. I am not inventing something here; these practices are happening now. But people need to be either compensated or offered compensation. If people wish to turn it down, that's up to them, but the offer needs to be genuinely made in all sincerity.

## Addendum

March 26, 1999

In the next 12 to 14 months there is at this time a 45% chance (and perhaps that chance will increase) of further crop circles, not just in the usual places, but now they will begin to show up in the more remote areas of Australia, Europe and northern Africa. These circles will be profound. They will also be highly unusual, in that some of them will be very large and others so small that they will easily go unnoticed. These particular circles are intended to perform a function largely for the Earth. Because of the removal and the transformation and the recombination of Mother Earth's iron ore deposits, her surface magnetic energy has been greatly interfered with.

Now, the human being cannot function in a climate that does not have a significant level of magnetic energy. The heart is, in its own right, a magnetic instrument, as are many other functions of the body's physiology and even chemistry. Some of the blood cells cannot exist in a field without magnetic energy. You might say that would seem highly unlikely. Yet if the magnetic energy is even troublesomely confused or lowered or over influenced by other field effects, similar problems can occur: Blood flow in the human, the heart's near-elliptical circuits not working properly and also certain combinations of body cells, to say nothing of the immune system, can be seriously impacted.

Yet the physiological circumstance for the human being is but a microcosm of the larger picture for Mother Earth. Her magnetic fields need not only recharging, but they require linking up to other star systems and planets in ways heretofore unmentioned. The planetary bodies in this solar system are not exclusively performing their own functions. Some of these bodies are performing functions that may be called upon by other planets in times of need, especially Earth, because of her unique situation in the solar system. Therefore, excess magnetic energy that is often seen, such as the great spot [on Jupiter] that is so often pictured in astronomy textbooks, is an effect of excessive magnetic energy. These planets, then, are producing and have the capability to produce significantly more magnetic energy than they need. So these new crop circles will function as a short-term link to other star system, but mostly to solar-system planets to replace and temporarily recharge certain areas in Mother Earth's body that used to have significant iron ore deposits.

This is an important factor, because there will be side effects, especially in northern Africa and Australia. The people who live in these areas are likely to feel significantly greater levels of magnetic energy. It will not be so great that signals you use now for communication will be interfered with. Certain things might take place; it is possible that body chemistry, endocrine functioning and blood chemistry might become improved in these areas.

Curiously enough, it will not be easy to locate these areas except by highly sophisticated equipment, some of which might be found in certain classified satellites and other equipment clusters that might be found even in aircraft which might fly over. But for the average human being to find these places would be difficult except for individuals who can function within the universal "range-finding system" of the instinctual body, where one feels one's way. Individuals who can do this might be able to lead others to places that are very powerful.

If you find these places, please do not walk in them; walk near them. If you can detect the ground pattern , which you may or may not be able to do, try to walk around it without getting too close, and generally follow the protocols laid out for the interaction with crop circles in the above article. These individuals who can come within, say, six feet, if they cannot walk around the perimeter of the crop circle, can even sit. But if you need to sit, try to sit in something that is not metallic. That would tend to ground the energy. Try to sit in something such as a wooden folding chair or on the ground, if you can. This might be perfectly adequate for some. If others cannot, then do the best you can to stay away from metal. It is not harmful; it will simply negate the effect.

These crop circles will work only temporarily for Mother Earth because other systems are gradually being put into place by stars that are connecting with Mother Earth to support her magnetic field. This has been discussed in previous issues of the *Sedona Journal.*

***You said there is a 45% chance it would happen. What is the dynamics that it might not happen?***

The chance of its happening has increased 45%. Given circumstances that unfold in the future, the chance might become greater or lesser, but I cannot say because the circumstances have to do with events associated with the human being. It is not associated with anything connected directly and exclusively with planet Earth herself.

# 30

# Reach Out to a New Friend and Global Unity Will Follow

Zoosh
April 7, 1999

For those of you on the Internet who talk to people around the world, please make an effort, to the best of your ability, to reach out to people from the other side of the world, other cultures. Make an effort to do so because cooperation on a government-to-government basis for coming events, as well as those already happening, is most definitely needed. If you as citizens have communicated with people in other countries, to the extent that people in these governments feel their citizens can accept and will be comfortable with economic and political alliances between another government and your own (one you have been told for years are the bad guys or one that you are constantly told how bad they are), your governments will feel encouraged.

This is not only for people on the Internet. Once upon a time people had pen pals, and maybe they still do. It doesn't require a computer. But write, communicate in some benevolent way with people in other countries, so that when your government says, "Well, we're making an alliance with . . ." and names the country, even if you have been told for years and years that these people are bad, you can say, "Oh, wonderful!" That feeling of benevolence will be felt at some point up the line of government people. Then they won't have to feel that they have to sneak behind your back to make these alliances, which is exactly how they feel now.

They have been told for many years by their economic advisors and even their most esoteric advisors that unity amongst the countries of the world is *essential* and that even though it might begin as an economic unity, it will have to take a very strong and unified turn toward being a political unity even though you disagree with the way each other does things.

So get to know other people—even if you can't pronounce their names!

# 31

# Oxygen-Eating Meteoroids

Zoosh
April 7, 8 and 20, 1999

It is most important that the U.S. and other countries begin to develop means to deflect the meteoroid* barrage that will begin to show itself in five to seven years from this point of time.

### Tiny but Dangerous

The initial meteoroids will not be very dangerous; they'll be very small, but they will essentially be a leading edge for the catastrophically dangerous ones that will follow. These meteoroids that follow are not dangerous because of their size, but because of their content. The organisms they contain could spell an end to life as it is known here on Earth.

These organisms do not represent a direct threat; they are not going to attack you or cause you to become ill directly. But they are oxygen-consuming, and they re-create themselves with alarming speed. If these meteoroids are allowed to strike Earth, the most likely places they will strike will be the polar regions. They will be quite small, perhaps none of them larger than the size of an orange. On the one hand, landing there will be advantageous because of the

* *Meteoroid:* A solid body moving in space, smaller than an asteroid and at least as large as a speck of dust. *Meteor:* A bright trail in the sky caused when a meteoroid burns up in the atmosphere. *Meteorite:* Matter that falls to Earth's surface from outer space. *Asteroid:* Any of numerous small celestial bodies that revolve around the sun, with orbits chiefly between Mars and Jupiter and diameters between a few and several hundred kilometers.

sparse population. On the other hand, it represents a greater threat in some ways because there might be a feeling that there is time to deal with it.

But know this: Once they strike, there will not be time to develop anything to contain them. One would assume that simply finding them and placing them inside a totally sealed container would work, but the problem is that within five seconds of their striking the Earth, they will begin to cycle the crystalline/organic material to their surfaces. They are not exactly eggs, but they are involved in re-creation effects. If someone does not arrive to place it in a sealed container within 45 minutes, some of that material will escape into the atmosphere.

Here's the critical factor: *If even one micron escapes*, it can consume, in terms of its constantly reproducing cycle (and its cycle of reproduction consumes the greatest amount of oxygen) *all the oxygen on Earth within 45 to 50 days*. These are Earth days, 24 hours. This means that the effort made to capture them cannot be seen as a first line of defense. The first line of defense must be deflection. Be aware that even if these meteoroids are within five to six thousand miles of Earth's atmosphere, any attempt to blow them up could still cause some of these organisms to find their way into your atmosphere. What is needed is something that can deflect them without harming them.

### Their Original Purpose

These meteoroids were originally intended to seed a planet that was in this position (where Earth is now) many, many years ago. Originally they would have consumed, on that planet, all the oxygen, which would have been good, because the plants, the animals and the people that would develop on that planet would be poisoned by oxygen. The irony here is that this is something that has been moving in this direction for thousands and thousands of years and was intended to save people, plants, beings. But because Earth occupies this space at this time, it represents a hazard.

Rather than hit the panic button, such technologies to deflect even in the most minor degree are in the process of being developed, though they are in their infancy. As any astronaut or astronautical engineer knows, any object approaching the Earth, if deflected even slightly, might very well miss Earth completely, possibly by a wide margin.

What is needed, then, is a crash program. It will require cooperation between governments in the initial stages of achieving alliances.

The cooperation and alliances that are absolutely required to achieve the best effect for all the peoples and all the plants and animals of the Earth will need to be between the United States, Great Britain, Australia, France and China. China is the most vital ally, and it is fortunate that there are long-range plans already being applied to accept China as a working partner diplomatically, politically and otherwise by the nations mentioned. But this process may have to be speeded up. Even though the U.S. and other countries have some difficulties with China's policies and governmental programs, nevertheless China has the will, the resources and some of the technological breakthroughs that, when combined with technologies being developed in the other countries, can put into space—create the actual deployment of—the necessary technology within four to five years. This, of course, is if all stops are pulled out.

It's important now for us to realize that the cooperation that has been gradually forming, even in the face of dramas you are constantly exposed to, is *intended*. Just as the Y2K problem is intended to create unity amongst all nations in order to support each other, this is another circumstance along those lines.

What we have here, then, is not only an opportunity to create unity, but something that is driving you toward it. The Y2K crisis would best be considered a training opportunity to learn how to work together, even with people and countries and governments with whom you have nothing in common but with whom you also have ongoing complaints and problems. When these meteoroids show up, you will have to not only be prepared, you'll have to be used to working together in the face of your differences.

Now, this five- to seven-year arrival time sounds critical. Know that the first wave might very well burn up completely in the atmosphere, but as stated before, this is very risky. While the probability of the material in its initial form—this crystalline-genetic material that eventually becomes simply genetic material—getting through in five years is very small, those chances will increase at an accelerating rate from the fifth year to the seventh year. That's when you'll need to have something in place.

Now, it is possible to destroy or at least deflect these incoming objects. Of course, you won't be able to tell what's what immediately through the use of current technology, but the speed of these objects is the problem. Not only will you not be able to tell what's what, but you may not be able to define it until it has *already passed by* your detecting systems. The objects that are dangerous will all be small; as stated, none will be larger than a good-size orange or a small grapefruit. And most of them will be *very* small. This will not make finding them any easier. However, it is important to give you some kind of coordinates. First, know that they will all be aimed for the poles.

**The Space Coordinates for Detection**

Now for the plan, which is helpful: If you draw a line outward in your solar system to the star system you currently call Alpha Omega 3, you will have the line by which to tell where these objects are coming from. They are not actually coming from Alpha Omega 3, but are moving from a line roughly 50 to 80 thousand miles from there. This gives you an approximate targeting area to look for. Obviously, the long-term protection system will be some kind of field effect around the planet that will deflect (this is the simplest way to do it) anything coming to Earth that is physical and is moving at a high rate of speed.

This is the safest thing to do because extraterrestrials and other benevolent beings who might come for the purposes of diplomacy will, by the time they get to within 15 to 20 thousand miles of Earth, have slowed down greatly. So the deflection system will not affect them. Generally speaking, anything that is benevolent to Earth will be moving fairly slowly by the time it gets to that deflection system. So the system ought to be geared toward objects moving at a high rate of speed. Certain openings might be a potential for returning space capsules and so on, but exceptional areas could be created through boundary-effect fields. This is understood. This is where to put your long-range energies.

**A System of Antennas Needed**

With the crash program in place, deployment of such a system, although it seems like science fiction right now to the general public, would still be possible within 25 to 30 years. It would require, of course, absolute unity, because antennas/generating stations for the field effect would need to be mounted on fairly tall and sturdy platforms that I am calling antennas. These would have to be perhaps from a minimum in high places of 50 feet to as much as 500 feet in certain low-elevation places, with varying heights in other places. Most importantly, the initial field effect put into place will require these platforms and generating stations to be no farther than 50 miles apart.

Now, this is suggestive. Since Earth is a water planet, what about places where there is water? It will be possible to plant these generating stations in an entirely sealed manner at the bottom of the ocean and perhaps large lakebeds. You can look for places that are higher rather than lower—you obviously don't put them in ocean trenches—and use a system of buoys floating on the surface. The buoy would be the antenna or radiator of the generating station. Such buoys would need to have around them a minimum of 1000 to 1500 feet so that vehicles do not penetrate that space. There are two reasons: (1) it will damage the field effect in that area, and (2) it might be hazardous to the health of human beings, animals and plants that are being shipped or are moving through that area.

This is the long-range plan, and it is what is recommended.

✧ ✧ ✧

April 8, 1999

***I'd like to get a little piece here to add to last night. Why are these meteoroids coming to the poles?***

That's really a simple reason. The poles are like poles of a magnet, and they will tend to attract first anything new that is coming to the Earth.

***We saw the picture showing where they go in and then go out.***

The poles are really as close as you can get to the center of the heart of Mother Earth. It's almost a surface of that, because the poles project directly from within the planet to pretty close to the surface, in terms of their power. Granted, at the surface you don't have that much power, but you do have magnetic effects, phenomena in the sky. You might feel a little funny if you were there, but if you could dig down a little farther (which I don't recommend), you would feel it increasingly powerfully as you went down. This has been done by shamans just to see how it feels, but one does not go too deep.

The poles have an attracting mechanism, which is really to your advantage, because if the poles didn't exist for some reason or another, the little meteoroids would go straight into the ocean or onto the continental landmasses. If they go to the poles, where population is scarcest, there can be, if not a warning system, at least some kind of mechanism that will tell you to take cover or something. You'll have time to react.

✧ ✧ ✧

April 20, 1999

## Deploying a Deflector Shield

***The asteroids are coming in five to seven years, but you said deployment of the deflector couldn't be ready in 25 years.***

Yes, there's some capacity for handling these objects, but it would require a great deal not only of physical effort on the scientific front, but also a lot of people working in concert to deflect these objects. For the first few years of their impending contact with Earth, it will be possible to deflect them using shamanic techniques. Most of the world's mystical people will be working on this by then, amongst other things. There will be a lot of energy put in to deflect them, not to destroy them. This is something that your people have not yet fully grasped: that it is infinitely easier to deflect something or be deflected from something (which is slightly different)—meaning that the object coming toward you moves or you move so the object misses you—than it is to destroy it. For one thing, destruction is never complete anyway; it just alters the substance. And as indicated at the beginning, destroying it might still allow some of the material to get into the upper atmosphere.

Part of the problem is that the elements inside these little meteoroids are not common to the Earth. Therefore the simple solution, the understanding of how this chemical works with that chemical and so on, is not readily available. So be thinking *deflection*.

***We're going to see the leading edge in five to seven years?***

Yes.

***And shamanic techniques can deflect it until 25 years from now, you think, when the deployment is in effect?***

Most likely there will need to be some deployment at the poles before then. Total deployment will take 25 years at least. But even some deployment at the poles or at mobile vehicles near the poles might be able to take care of the bulk of it before then. Look for shamanic techniques to take care of it perhaps for the first three years, possibly seven years. But then it would be necessary for deployment to begin. I indicated total deployment in 25 years; total deployment is a lot.

But this will be only temporary. You see, after the threat is over, then it will be possible to use the shielding device for other things. For one thing, it can create at least a partial shield for the Earth in other respects. Defense industry people will be intrigued. Alternately, it would probably be used to create a navigational system for the Earth. Right now the idea of moving the Earth is strictly science fiction. And while I don't recommend that the Earth be moved, you will at some point want to do something about the wobble. Far-thinking minds might try to utilize it to do something about the wobble in Earth's axis. I can say no more at this time about other uses.

***The field effect—it is a radiating field of what?***

It essentially involves a magnetic effect. The reason the term "bi-polar" was used is that the effect pushes things away, but only slightly. You know, the same theory that causes homeopathy to work to some extent with most people (a minor amount of medication having a good effect) will work in the same way with a minor amount of polarized magnetism—the kind of magnetism that pushes away. This kind of technology now is top secret. The reason I say total deployment in 25 years is that by 25 years it will no longer be top secret, and within ten years others will know about it, including various allies and groups. The poles are largely being used for military purposes anyway. Such top-secret technology might be acceptably utilized at the poles without compromising confidential scientific matters.

***So we'd have the technology—rudimentary or complete?***

Not rudimentary, not complete.

***When you speak of other groups and allies, do you mean those on Earth or off Earth?***

On Earth.

***Would that be the countries you mentioned earlier?***

Yes.

***You have stated in other channelings that there are ET scientists on Earth who are already teaching various scientists how to deflect asteroids and meteoroids. Can you say more about that?***

The teaching is going on, but it is very low-key, and some of it has to do with larger objects. The technology used to deflect smaller objects will not be the same as that used to deflect large objects. Larger objects that pass less than 80,000 miles from Earth could create certain disruptions on Earth. But the technology being taught by those beings is more for objects that would pass closer to Earth or strike a glancing blow or even (a much, much more remote possibility) hit Earth solidly.

This technology uses a different effect entirely, which is involved in an energy (this is really shamanic) that *pulls* the object from a remote location. Right now you're used to the idea that things are difficult, meaning that in order to throw the ball from person A to person B, it requires a certain effort. But what if person A wants to play catch with himself? He could conceivably throw the ball to a point in space and then, before the ball arrives there, create enough of an effort to *pull* the ball back to him, not push it back.

## Techniques Using Creativity

What I'm saying is this: The techniques being taught will be less reliant on technology as you know it than the utilization of the totality of a person's capacity to create, at least on the level at which you might be expected to create here on Earth. It is not unlike bilocation, but instead of simply being in two places at once, you are exerting an effort in that other location to *change* the motion of an object but not destroy it. This cannot be used to destroy; it can only be used to change the motion in such a way that the object can still arrive at the place it is going to.

Let's say the object, whatever it might be, actually has a destination. Your science likes to believe in the random effect, but this is still a theory, even though people have been attempting to prove the theory for a long time. Now physicists are moving away from the random effect, theorizing that there isn't any randomness to the motion of even the smallest particle. So if you want something to move because you have a need for it to move and you are working to help that object, even the largest meteoroid or asteroid, to avoid hitting the Earth or even come close to it or anything else, you can work with the moving object. You would not extrapolate scientifically, but you would create a path through the solar system (if it has to pass through this solar system) that would allow the object to get where it's going. You would set up a temporary effect around planets and asteroids such as moons and other aspects of the solar system that would be missed if something happened to them. This would cause the meteoroid to move in sort of a weaving pattern through the solar system. It works easily when you work with the meteoroid, when you work with something that is feminine technology. But if you work in opposition to it, that's what creates crises.

Generally speaking, *on the physical plane opposition can create crises, whereas working with something so that everybody wins creates solutions.* Never forget that!

***Are there many scientists from many different planets here on Earth teaching this technique to our scientists?***

No, very few.

***From how many different planets?***

One.

***Are they working with all the governments on the Earth or just one?***

They're working with the governments that give them the most attention and the most freedom.

***You can't say which ones.***

No.

***Can you say why you can't?***

No. Why do you think?

***I haven't the slightest idea.***

Yes, you do. Think. People have preconceived ideas. Any unnecessary preconceived ideas placed upon anything would deflect the project from its goal or at least slow it down. Let's say a youngster feels reasonably confident, is reasonably intellectual, is planning to go to college and is getting good grades through high school. If people around him or her think that she doesn't have what it takes to get through college even if she does, it will make it that much more difficult for her to do so—even if it's entirely unspoken and no one says anything to anybody.

***That explains a lot of things, then, that people have to work against in families and social situations.***

That's right.

***You said some years ago that the secret government time travelers went to Mars, and deep inside the planet was machinery set up long ago to deflect asteroids and meteoroids. These time-traveling scientists thought it was a weapon and dismantled it. Can that be put back together and used?***

## Your Unexpressed Kinetic Energy

No, and in a way that's good, because it's time that you all here begin to participate. A lot of you have been feeling a lot of nervous energy lately. For some, you've felt it as agitation; for others, it's been interrupting your sleep cycle; and for still others, it's simply creating difficulties and confusions and so on. A lot of this nervous energy has to do with kinetic energy, unexpressed energy that is or could be used for motion. It can either be expressed as that motion or it can be held, thus creating nervous tension within the body. When you don't know what to do with it, when you're not normally very athletic or when the degree of physical motion that you perform on a daily basis is fixed, nervous tension builds up because you have more capacity than application.

The reason I'm saying that it's good, in a way, that this mechanism cannot be repaired and that you cannot be saved by some unseen device and go on your merry way, is that you all now have to make an effort. Some of you are doing this unexpectedly, such as taking naps for no reason, suddenly, unexpectedly. You have to sleep. Or some of you are feeling the need to do something physical.

I'm going to give you some homework. I want you to try this, and it is not that difficult. I want you to use yourself physically to do it.

It might mean moving your arms about. If you can imagine touching something at a distance, do so. Those meteoroids I mentioned are on the way here now. Even though they are light-years from here and moving at a very high velocity, you can begin to deflect them *right now.* Here's your homework.

### Exercise: Using the "Long Touch" to Deflect the Meteoroids

First state your intention to deflect these meteoroids away from Earth so they don't strike Earth, and to allow them to go where they need to go without causing any harm. Put it that way, because when you do, it will tend to create a navigation that will move them around things. They have the capacity, but you have to reach out. You can use your long touch; Speaks of Many Truths has talked about this. If you know this, if you've had homework in this and you know how to do it, do that. But if you don't and haven't been shown, then reach out and do this gently.

***Right hand with thumb up, hand vertical, moving it laterally.***

Yes, laterally, from side to side. In the place you are on Earth right now, depending on the perspective looking at Earth, you could call it the center of Earth (not the center of the planet). You are in the center, in that sense. But let's say you were over here. If you change the point of view so that you're looking from a different direction, you are then in a different center, as in any two-dimensional drawing. That's why we're going to move the hand laterally, like that, back and forth.

Now, I don't want you to just stick your hand out and wave it back and forth. If you know the techniques, you can do it like that. But not knowing the techniques, I want you to reach out and *try to feel* something coming toward the Earth. Imagine it, then move your hand from side to side. Imagine something that's moving toward the Earth that causes you to feel nervous or upset in your physical body.

***In your solar plexus.***

In your solar plexus, yes, or possibly in your heart. Then you're going to deflect that a little bit. You ought to notice after you do this deflection, moving the hand from side to side like this, that that part of your body—the heart or the solar plexus—relaxes a bit and feels better.

***And it also helps use up the kinetic or nervous energy that's accumulated.***

That's right. And if you've done it for just a couple of seconds and those parts of your body don't feel any better, then keep it up for a little while longer until those parts of your body do feel better.

This can also be used to deflect danger from you. It cannot be used to *stop* danger, but only to deflect it so that it goes around you. I won't say any more about it right now, but Speaks of Many Truths can be asked about that for the next shaman book. Make sure you ask it in as much detail as possible, and he will show how it is done.

### More on the Original Purpose of the Meteoroids

***Where are these particles coming from? Why are they at such a high speed, and where are they going?***

They're going to a planet well beyond this solar system. They were originally, however, coming to this solar system to this planet, as indicated earlier. They were going to eliminate oxygen, and while that would be threatening to you, it would have actually protected the people on the planet that was here before. Now that things have changed, the particles have a different planet to go to, and when they arrive at that planet, they will do the same thing: They will eliminate oxygen.

There is a planet along that line as indicated, from that point to Earth and beyond, where the people on the planet have been very gradually reduced in their life span. It has caused some alarm. Part of this, although they have not discovered it yet, is due to oxygen bubbling to the surface. This, as you know, creates oxidation, which reduces the life span.

This planet, which is in Zeta Reticuli, will be served by these objects. So for those of you who want extra credit, you might, after deflecting the objects, turn around the opposite way. Try to turn toward Zeta Reticuli, which is viewable in the Southern Hemisphere as part of the Southern Cross constellation.

If you know where to point to it, do so. If you don't know where, then just imagine it; perhaps get a picture of the Southern Cross constellation and do this. Make a throwing motion with the right hand after you've done the deflection in order to encourage the objects to go to the Zeta Reticuli planet where they will serve.

***Can you say where they came from? Or does it matter?***

It doesn't really matter too much. All needs are fulfilled.

***The planet that was here before the Earth came from Sirius. What did those inhabitants breathe?***

You know, what they breathed is less important than the fact that it didn't have any oxygen and they had a long life span.

***I've asked you before about this planet and you don't want to talk about it, right?***

For good cause.

***It's on the time line that goes to the past.***

It might be possible to rescue it, and the less you know about it, the better—maybe eventually, once you get anchored to that future benevolent time line.

***There's a reason you don't want to talk about it—you were associated with that planet?***

There's always a reason why I don't tell you things. It's not capriciousness, though it might seem that way.

***That's the one you were connected to, right?***

Yes.

***Earth has been here 65 million years, so these . . .***

. . . meteoroids; they're too small to be asteroids.

***. . . meteoroids have been on this course for more than 65 million years. Is that true?***

No, I can't really say they've been on this course for that long, but they've been on course for quite a while.

***But they wouldn't have been set in motion once this Earth from Sirius was in this position, would they?***

You're not taking into account other dimensions. You're only taking into account third dimension.

***This is so incredibly important. How is this going to be announced? Is it going to be kept hidden? Is it going to be in the newspapers? Are there going to be articles about this? Nobody's going to know what they are, right?***

Spiritual, mystical and medicine people the world over will begin to talk about it more openly. This has been predicted in some cultures for some time. There will be some discussion initially in the intellectual press on the basis of what-if and what we would do. But you know, I'd say that it is less important for the global population to know this, because a few thousand people can do a lot toward deflecting these objects, and they might just be able to succeed entirely without the need for a technical system of deflection. I feel that the technical deflection system might possibly be a way to unite the countries because ultimately it would be used to create a safe environment on Earth for everybody.

## The Zetas, Who Are the Receivers

***The Zetas we've talked to all these years—is this oxygen leakage part of the reason why their bodies didn't work as well and that they had shorter lives and were concerned about dying out?***

I knew you'd get it if I said Zeta. That's part of it, that's right. Even though there are spiritual reasons for things, there have to be *physical* causes and effects so that the physical can represent the spiritual.

***So with all their sophisticated scanning and technological equipment, they weren't able to figure out that oxygen was coming to the surface?***

It's such a minute quantity—no, let's quantify it. There are other things going on here. There's a degree that oxygen is affecting it. The quantity of oxygen, if compressed but still in a gaseous state (not liquid), would fit nicely into a five-gallon tank.

***And it's affecting the entire population?***

Yes, because they are *very* sensitive—and the planet is quite a bit larger than this one, actually.

***Oxygen is toxic for them.***

It's not toxic in the sense that it would kill them if immediately faced with it, but if they went into a room that was solid oxygen, it would cause rapid aging, not the kind you could see with the naked eye, but their life would be greatly impacted. So just a tiny amount would have a long-range effect. You have to remember, on Earth you've got factors that consume oxygen—human beings, animals . . . there are various organisms that consume oxygen. But there is nothing on this planet in Zeta Reticuli that consumes and transforms oxygen, so it's there as a pollutant.

***And more keeps coming all the time.***

Very slowly. My challenge to you all, who have been paying attention to the sinister secret government (and we might have more on that tonight) is, here's an opportunity to do something to save the Earth, to save the populations and yourselves. People might think, "Well, we can go underground, we can be safe." Not true. If anything catastrophic were to happen to the surface atmosphere, it would affect you underground unless you had the most technological capacity—if you had an inexhaustible supply of water that you could convert into atmosphere. But ultimately, of course, you'd have to have a fixed amount of water simply to drink.

## The Sinister Secret Government

***This brings up another question: If the shamans and mystical people have known this for a long time, then I assume that the secret government has also known it for a long time.***

Never assume that the sinister secret government has the capacities of even any individual shaman, much less many of them. Shamans have their capacities because they believe in the sacredness of all life. When you have this belief, it is not necessarily engendered by your philosophy or culture; it could be taught to you by your teachers, be they physical or spirit. When you do have it, though, you will then be able to be trusted to receive methods considered impossible by science, but that's because science is still focused in masculine science (that some things can't be done). In fact, once you are trusted, you are given these techniques by your teachers or your spirit teachers or both. You are trusted because you believe that all life is sacred, and it is not strictly a thought, but something you put into action on a daily basis.

The sinister secret government does not have this belief, and they are not trusted with these techniques. They will find out now, of course, because I'm talking about it. But they don't know it. Don't assume that they have greater capacities than they do. They are very single-minded, and much as they would love to have the abilities of even a novice shaman, they don't because they don't have that honoring of all life. They *have* to have that.

***It will be interesting to see how they react, then. They will start doing everything they can . . .***

They've already been doing that.

***. . . with technology to come up with a solution, right?***

You mean a solution that would harm the population?

***A solution that would save themselves.***

They think they have that already.

# 32

# Don't Let the SSG Draw You into a Malevolent Time Line

Zoosh
April 20, 1999

What if there were a future malevolent time line that has been anchored? This is what the sinister secret government has been doing; this is what they've been up to. They've been attempting, using their time device, however rickety it is in terms of its capacity to function, to anchor a future malevolent time line and pull you along into it.

### Anchored in 1967 and Now Aided by Fear, Fictional or Real

Now, while they cannot actually bring the whole population of Earth, the Explorer Race, onto this negatively anchored time line, they have in fact anchored it. Every time there is some negative or catastrophic event or war or some disastrous thing, like what is happening in Kosovo, for example, they will at that time—especially as people find out more about it and worry about it and wonder, Has the human race made any progress at all?—be putting forth maximum effort to push (they can't pull, you know) you onto this negative time line. They have been working on this since 1947, and they anchored it in 1967. But anchoring it did not mean that anybody was on it except them. It does, however, explain very nicely why you can't find them: They are here on this planet, but they are anchored in a different time line.

It's like this [draws]. Here is the past-anchored time line and here is the future-anchored time line. They're trying to [anchor their malevolent future time line to our present time line].

There has been a lot of effort to resist this by many beings who work to help you on this planet and a lot of you also, working in

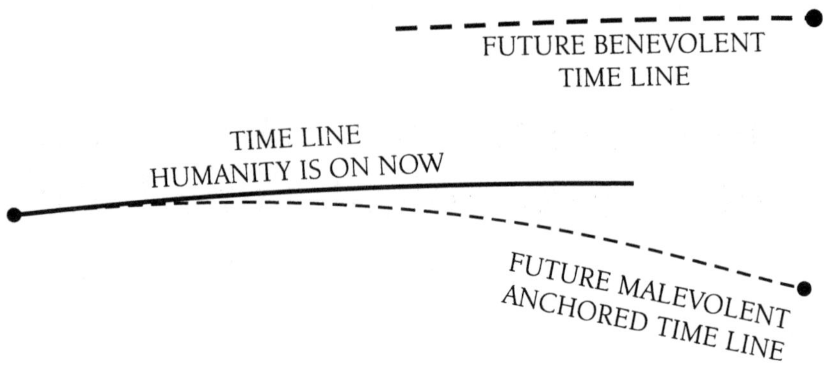


your sleep state. Yet think of all the things that have permeated your thoughts and feelings and all the discomforts that are hurled at you on a regular basis, whether it comes from factual reality, meaning something you know is true or something you hear from a reliable or trusted source; or whether it be fictional, meaning something that somebody made up (but you don't know that) or something intended to be fictional, such as a story or movie. All these things are being hurled at you, but the physical system of creation in your physical body, which is anchored in your solar plexus, does not know the difference between factual and fictional unpleasantness. You get just as terrified in a horror movie as you would if that horror movie were real and you were in it. The effect in your body is exactly the same.

### The Cumulative Physical Effects of Fear

Be aware that these effects are cumulative. On the one hand, if you are a soldier in a war, it teaches about your instinct and, if your commanders are conscious enough, what to do about it. (They may or may not be conscious enough.) So all of you who are "enjoying" horror movies or frightening movies or fictional things that are frightening in general, are creating within your physical body a general antipathy toward your fellow human beings, because even though you know consciously, mentally, that your friends and family and the people you trust can be trusted, all this malevolent input fills up this creator organism in your physical body and causes you to have suspicions about those you would normally trust.

Remember, you take it in through your solar plexus first on the physical level. You're screening everything you take in and to some extent what you create, which also comes out through the solar plexus on the physical plane. You're screening it in both directions—reception and creation. You're screening it through this discomfort, this malevolence. When you do that, you might have unrealistic suspicions of people around you even though you mentally, consciously, know there is nothing to be concerned about.

## Transform It with the Heart-Heat and Other Exercises

I mention this to you because it is something you have to pay attention to. For those of you who like this kind of entertainment, it will ultimately be something you'll have to transform. You'll have to deal with it because it will try to work itself to the surface so that you *must* transform it. It can be transformed by that heart-heat exercise, and it can also be transformed over time by other exercises and by simply interacting with your friends and family and continuing to reassure yourself that these people aren't really monsters trying to kill you. I'm mentioning these things because all these malevolent impacts on you can, especially when something horrific is going on such as what's happening in Kosovo, have a tendency to draw you toward that future malevolently anchored time line. This, I might add, is an actual threat.

For instance, last night we couldn't channel. There was a herculean effort going on because there had been progress, from the sinister secret government's point of view, in dragging you onto that malevolent time line. This herculean effort [by those who help you] was to try and correct that slip. These things are going on. There is help for you all, and some of it is from other places—teachers, benevolent beings and so on. But you all have to do something. I want to say that I know some of you like horror movies and think they don't affect you, but they do. I'm going to suggest that you think about giving them up.

## Gold Light, Its Function and Purpose Here

***Anything more about what was done last night? Were they pouring golden light into the time line? What were they doing?***

All over the Earth they were flooding it with golden light. Golden light, while it is the Earth-mastery color, has been greatly depleted on Earth. It is actually intended to function only slightly for human beings; the bulk of it is meant to work with parts of Mother Earth and other natural life here—life that isn't learning anything, such as plants, trees, animals, microorganisms and so on—that which is here to guide you but is not here to learn. Most of that gold light is intended for those beings plus Earth, but the vast population of human beings, especially those involved in things that are artificially malevolent, such as malevolent entertainments or imaginations, are draining the gold-light reserve.

The intention was to flood Earth with gold light. White light is unconditionally loving, meaning that it will love anything, no matter what. Gold light has unconditional love within it, but it will change anything it touches into being benevolent. Maybe not immediately, but eventually. So it is *light with a purpose.*

***What was the result of last night, then?***

## If You're Easily Depressed, You're Being Affected

The rate of your culture's movement toward that malevolent time line was slowed, that's all. Now *you* must take responsibility to stop it. I'm telling you these things like this because urgencies come up, and you're all being tested now. As anybody who's ever taken any kind of test knows, when you are tested you must produce. But this is not a test where you are made to feel badly because you didn't get all the questions right. You may not even know immediately if you didn't do it right, but you will know eventually.

How will you know, on a practical level, whether you are moving toward that malevolent time line? Even if you've slept well, even if you are in ideal conditions, meaning the right balance of oxygen to your atmosphere, cheerful outlook, you won't have as much physical energy and stamina. I understand that other things may be affecting your stamina, so I'm going to give you more [of an indication] than that: Even if your mood is elevated, if you are cheerful, it will take only a very small malevolent thought or unpleasant feeling or piece of information or news to drop you down into the doldrums, even though it might be temporary.

So those of you who have noticed lately that it's hard to maintain cheerfulness, it is a direct result of the sinister secret government's attempt to drag you onto this malevolent time line.

## Earth Depletes Her Needed Gold Light by Helping You

***What is the anchoring of this time line doing to Mother Earth?***

It's depleting her gold light. When this happens, she must take gold light from her own needs and put it into you human beings so you do not cascade into this malevolently anchored time line like water over a waterfall. Remember, your physical bodies are part of her physical body, and when she does that, she's doing that to protect her physical bodies as her own physical self that she has loaned to you. The net result is that then she does not have enough gold light to maintain herself, and the animals and plants are also not fed enough gold light.

That's why many of them have been dying out lately. It's not only ultrasonic and microwave interference that's been causing problems with animals finding their way to various places or getting lost or beaching themselves (in the case of sea lions or other creatures) or getting sick and dying for no apparent physical reason. It also has to do with the fact that they're not getting their usual food of gold light to supplement their other food and the air they breathe and so on. This is also why some sensitive and not well-protected (compared to a beetle that has a shell of armor) plants or very sensitive or frail animals are dying out as a species.

***What can we do?***

## Heart-Heat Exercise with a Group

Do your heart-heat exercise, and do more than that. Try to do it with others; it will then be easier to obtain the heat and radiate it. The minimum number for this would be two, but I recommend three or more. Always face each other, though you can close your eyes. Closing your eyes is perhaps a good idea.

Let's say there are several of you. If you are in a circle you would face toward the center. Even though the ultimate intention is to radiate the extra energy, you would face toward the center. In that way you would first feed each other, which is good, and then the excess would be radiated out of the center of the circle up, down and all around. Remember, don't *send* the heat out. Just feel it and notice it. It will radiate naturally.

***Is this gold light?***

It isn't gold light, but it is a component that maintains gold light, like a food. It will make it easier and more gentle for other beings in your neighborhood—everything in that area, plant, animal, planet, human, atmosphere, condition. That will feed it. It is like taking a supplement.

## The SSG's Hiding Place

***The remaining members of the secret government are now where?***

They're anchored in that future alternative malevolent time line. It's not in 1967; that is when they succeeded in anchoring it to the future, but nobody's there in '67. That's why they can't be found. They're here on Earth, but they're on a different time line, which has allowed them to remain completely safe. They have access to your

## THE HEART-HEAT EXERCISE

- Practice feeling love as heat in the chest. (Use your hands over your chest to help focus energy.)
- When you can hold this warmth, add the feeling (not visualization) of gold light.
- Keep practicing back and forth until you can feel both at the same time, then hold it for at least 10 or 15 minutes.

After you learn to do this, while you are feeling this heat or love or both, say out loud:

- **"I give all beings permission to be of love, to be fed, clothed, healed and comforted."**

You can add other appropriate things, but keep it simple. The heart heat will naturally radiate even when the gold light is absent.

Because one of the most important levels of creator training is to be able to feel what others feel, you might have nightmares and wake up with horrible feelings or have other experiences that result in such feelings. As soon as you can, ask:

- **"Let benevolent love bless and transform all I am feeling."**

Then feel gold light. This is alchemical training to transform the pain of others through being aware of their feelings.

When you come together as a group to feel heart heat and gold light:

- Talk about what's bothering you so you have some feelings to transform.
- Focus on the physical warmth in your chest or solar plexus, which is the physical evidence of love.
- Strike a chime or make some signal, then imagine gold light there while you feel the heat with total focus so that the alchemical transformation can take place.

In a group these feelings are amplified. This exercise can transform any discomfort that arises and you will feel ecstatic; it is the closest feeling to the Creator energy that you are. The larger the group, the wider the area it will transform to cheerful, loving feelings. Eventually it can become first nature to you and you will feel it all the time. It will lead to unifying all beings everywhere.

past-anchored time line as well, but they have to be very careful. In order for the core group and many of the people around them to move together from that malevolently anchored time line to the past-anchored time line you are on now requires a great many steps, and it's hazardous. They very rarely attend or visit the current time line you're on because it's hazardous.

***Can you say when in our time?***

They started doing this in 1947; they succeeded in anchoring it in 1967. What does that suggest?

***That they went back in time.***

That's right. When you can travel in time, there's no point in my saying . . . I could say right now that something has not happened. But I could also now say that not only has it happened, but it happened a long time ago, given the capacity of beings to travel in time.

***But keeping on our time line now, it's been two or three years since we talked about the SSG being underground; they were under Las Vegas and other places. So it has been since that time that they have gone back in time?***

Yes and no. They've been working on this project since 1947 in your time line. They succeeded in achieving this goal in 1967 in your time line. But they've been functioning in both areas. I just couldn't talk about it until now.

## More Tests on the Way

***Was there some catalyst or event that allows you to talk about it now?***

Yes. It's time for you to be tested in a way whereby you could do something about it. You'll be getting more of these tests, so don't think that you've passed this test and then you're okay. The tests will, by the way, get exceedingly more difficult. They have to get more difficult because you have to apply what you've learned. When I say difficult, I mean difficult in your mind, not in actual application.

***Were those who guide the Explorer Race, yourself and others, aware of all this years ago?***

Certainly. I and others like me are aware of a great many things that we don't tell you right away, just as a parent might be aware of something about a child that they don't tell it right away. Or a manager might be aware of something about an employee but doesn't tell that employee right away because the time isn't right. How do you know the time is right? When the people you are talking to have the capacity to do something about it—not to hear it, but to *do* something about it.

***So this is part of the great test. We can't be pushed from 3.47 to 3.51 or some-***

***thing. This is where we have to do it ourselves.***

Yes. You have to pull yourself forward.

### Emergency: How to Slow or Stop the Rate You're Moving into the Malevolent Time Line

***Now, if we get anchored to that future benevolent time line, everyone who puts energy into that is going to defuse and lessen the ability of the secret government to manipulate our time line. Is that true?***

Not exactly the way you said it. It's not "defuse"; if you defuse something, you stop it. But everybody who puts energy into the benevolent future time line will *slow down the rate* at which the sinister secret government can move humanity onto that malevolent time line. If enough people do it often enough, it will stop the rate, and the more people who do it will finally turn it back. Right now, though, you are here [draws an arrow]. If you look closely, you can see that you are moving slightly onto the malevolent time line. That's why this is a red-light emergency.

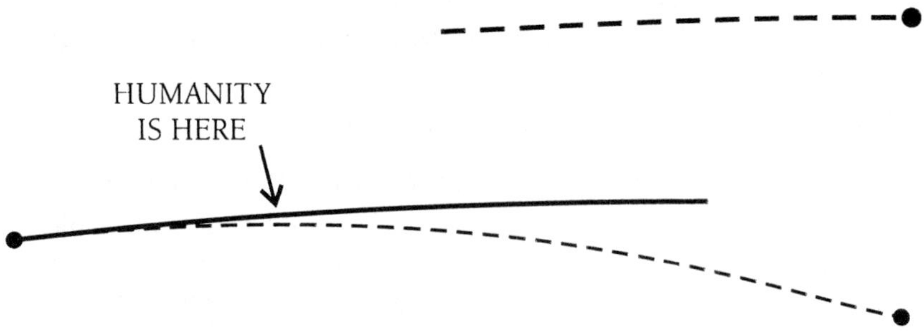


***For the first time.***

Yes, that's right. Remember the way to notice it: You can be cheerful, then somebody says something, you hear something sad or upsetting—I'm not talking about something that is *very* sad, just something slightly sad, such as that your friend broke his arm but is feeling better. You dip way down [emotionally], and it takes you awhile to get back up.

***Can this be quantified? Are there people actually attacked? Have they pulled some people onto this thing?***

No, it's all or nothing. Everybody moves at once.

***You said before that some people can't move to the ultimate future.***

That's right. It works the same way for this.

## Your Extra Energy Is to Meet This Challenge

***But every bit of energy we put into attempting to do it helps pull up all humans onto the future benevolent time line.***

That's right. It's challenging. I *want* to challenge you. You need to be challenged because you have all this energy, more than you need right now. I know a lot of you feel exhausted; you don't feel like you have a lot of energy, but that's because the energy you have is intended to be used physically—but also, for lack of a better term, for these magical purposes.

***There was a point in time when we were talking about the alternate negative future reality, then that was taken care of by the warrior of light. That's different from this one?***

Yes, different.

***The warrior of light said that in the inner circle of the sinister secret government was an Orion who kept changing his shape. The Mother of All Beings said that there were only humans in the inner core. Does that mean that the warrior of light was able to remove the Orion?***

Yes.

***Does that have any long-range positive effect on the leadership of the SSG group?***

No. Why would it?

***I thought he was the leader.***

So what?

***So they just continued his policy even though he's not there?***

If everybody is dedicated to doing something malevolent, that's what it takes—dedication.

***Where is the warrior of light now?***

On the job elsewhere.

***On this planet?***

No.

***He was going to help discreate some of the negative past.***

He did.

***I actually thought the warrior of light would make a difference.***

It did make a difference.

***But not enough to help us that much.***

It made a difference; it helped you in a big way—*big*. But that doesn't alter the facts that are presented before you tonight. Let's say a doctor does exploratory surgery on what he believes to be a patient's cancer, and while he's in there he removes as much of the cancer as possible, but he knows that there's more.

***Okay, there's more.***

## Your Energy Gift

There's more. The more challenges, the better, because people have all this energy. It would be better for them to use it in some benevolent way so that it doesn't simply make them nervous and upset and agitated, which can lead to more malevolence.

***But why do we have all this energy?***

Because you're expected to *do* something with it!

***So it's been given us.***

That's right. You're not being burdened with it. It's a gift, but as with all gifts that are not obvious, instructions are required. If someone hands you a beautiful, smooth stone and every time you turn it, it changes colors a little bit, you might like it very much, but if you have to carry it around all the time, it's going to get heavy. Unless, of course, you find out that it can be used to lighten your burden in other ways!

***When did we get this gift of energy? Recently?***

It started coming in about 16 months ago. It's building up, so much so now that just about everybody's aware of it. A lot of people are aware, but on an uncomfortable level. But it has a comfortable, let's say, purpose.

***Will it continue to grow?***

It depends. If there is success moving you off that motion toward the malevolent time line, it won't increase. But if you keep moving onto that malevolent time line, it will get stronger and stronger and stronger.

***Until we have to use it.***

Until you have to use it benevolently. What happens if you don't use it benevolently? You use it . . .

. . . ***malevolently.***

Yes. You're on a polarized world. Gifts have a potential malevolent aspect. You must choose, and you must know how to use it in a benevolent way.

# 33

# Kids Will Lead the Movement to Embrace Outcasts

Zoosh
May 1, 1999

***Is what is happening in Kosovo, and what happened at the high school here in Denver, simply a wake-up call about the futility of violence and hatred?***

Not about futility. It's more of a wake-up call, not for the youngsters, but for the generation that produced the current generation. That generation was really the first one raised in this country with the influence of existentialism, where the pursuit of the individual is much more important than the experience of the group. Although this country seems to have been founded on individual rights, that was never the case. It was founded on covenants of what's best for everyone. So this generation was the first one that was actually raised, exposed to, grew up with, and is still living that philosophy.

***Are you speaking about the flower children?***

I don't want to say that, because most people did not participate in that; that was a very small percentage. What I'm talking about is, generally speaking, the generation where you'd find the parents today to be 30 to 50 or 55 years old. That's a loose statistic, with some flexibility. It's a wake-up call for them, not for the kids.

The kids have been awake to these facts for a long time. They've been upset about it and that nothing is happening about it and no one is doing anything. It's not just that individuals aren't doing something, because individuals would, but that mass group attention has not been paid to this, and it's not just the availability of guns.

You see, even now that's the focus: "Oh, let's do something to keep guns out of their hands," but that's not it at all. The kids are very clear that it's about some kids being made outcasts. That's the bottom line, regardless of the available technology of monstrous video games that are designed to create and support violence as an intoxicant. That is the profound intention. Not everyone can be intoxicated, from the intoxicator's view, by violence and its graphic imagination as it's stimulated in your mind. It's another form of intoxicant, and it is definitely not, for most manufacturers, a conspiracy. As far as the sinister secret government goes, they are supporting it directly and indirectly. I don't want to call it simply a conspiracy. All the manufacturers are participants; it's not a conspiracy, but that's how it's working out.

Kids are very clear that this is the problem, but it's still being treated the way most diseases are treated by the adult community: "Let's treat the symptoms because that's all we can do, and maybe someday we can cure the disease." The problem is still being treated as a "maybe someday . . . but let's get the guns out of their hands. That's somehow going to make it all better," as if knives weren't readily available. I'd say that the generation that is now trying to do something about the guns still hasn't awakened. The average high school kid knows what the problem is.

***I think the children are starting to do something. They've gathered together in Denver to do something about the lack of funds for the schools because the money is going to roads and other things. They're speaking up.***

Yes, that's good. It is important. You know, for the longest time your culture—not the culture of all Earth peoples, but the culture you were raised in yourself—has had a very fixed point of reference about children: that the adults have the authority, and children are a possession to be cared for and nurtured, perhaps, but not to be considered in any way a participant. Ultimately, adults are not prepared at this time to listen to those most affected, who are the children. It will change *when the children change it themselves,* and the wake-up call on that level has been heard in Colorado. We'll see if it will spread. Remember what it says in that Bible, that "a little child shall lead them" [Isaiah 11:6]. Ultimately, the people who are going to change the circumstances of the world will be children who say, "We're going to do it because we can't wait for *you* to do it. You don't listen to us, you don't hear us, you don't understand and, most important, you don't remember." Let's hope this is the time when children all over the world will lead.

The youngsters are going to have to understand that they will not be supported by the adults. Ultimately, they will have to do it themselves. The interesting thing is, the tool for such international movements is now readily at hand, and that's the Internet. If it becomes a cause celèbre on the Internet for youngsters, then you might see something happen. But it will require discipline, on an individual basis, and healing; it will require what I would call the nation of children, which is international, and they won't just be children. Some will be very young and others will be 17, 18 years old.

***Do you see this happening soon?***

I cannot say. It is up to them.

***Are there very many teenagers who are involved with the Internet?***

Enough. You understand, the Internet is not the method. It is simply the tool of supportive communication and requires a minimum of adult interference. You see, adults will want it to be done in a reasonable and structured fashion, but that's not how things work for youngsters. For youngsters, it has to be done as a feeling thing. It *has* to be. The dedication is with the feeling. It's not that they can't think, not that they cannot do things the way adults want them to, but it has to be done, if it's their own, with feeling and passion, and adults are generally afraid to do this around children. This does not make the adults less, it's just that they have good reasons to feel this way. So the cause will have to be led by those who are most likely to be affected by it.

# 34

# Practicing Shamanic Gestures near Crop Circles

Zoosh
May 22, 1999*

***When you said that the purpose of the crop circles (the current issue of the* Sedona Journal*) was to activate and increase one's spiritual capacities, is the way the activation occurs related to what Kryon channeled [in the June issue] about "the cosmic lattice and the constant communication between the 12 strands of DNA and the 12-segmented crystalline memory," which he says is at less than 15 percent efficiency now?***

I suppose that's one mechanical way of describing it, but I'd rather think of it this way: Imagine a light bulb and imagine there is a shroud completely covering it. You know the light bulb is on because you've turned the switch, yet there is no light coming from it at all. Then you take a pin and poke a hole in the shroud (it is like cardboard)—and bingo! There is some light coming out. Then you take that pin and make many holes. It is more like that. It is something that is already on, completely. It requires a physical action on your part to welcome it. If you think of it that way, it becomes less complicated. It's very easy to imagine it that way.

***You say it requires some physical action. What action is required?***

The purpose of the book *Shamanic Secrets for Material Mastery* (and, to some extent, the previous Explorer Race books, but this book specifically, and in larger quantity in some of the books to follow) is to encourage you to do physical things that will allow you to metaphorically make more holes in that shroud—actions by yourself

* From a personal research reading.

and others that allow feeling that improves the overall living conditions of all beings.

***I was doing an exercise today from the book that involved the left hand and the elbow in a certain position, making a circle. Is that the sort of thing you are speaking of?***

Yes. Also, you'll find another section in the book where Speaks of Many Truths talks about the basics of his life in very simple ways—not because he's talking down to anybody, but because he's trying to connect his way of communication to the most easily understood method in print. We'll talk more about that in future books and also give more elaborate things to do that involve physical actions that integrate or stimulate spiritual results. Remember that. It's a very important point.

***In other words, the action may not be a specific one, but one that intuitively comes to me to do?***

Exactly. That is why there are so many exercises given for different points on the Earth. In future volumes, if there is enough interest in the first volume of the Material Mastery series to make it worthwhile for the publisher, we will cover other places on the Earth and perhaps points beyond. But most likely they need to be spots on the Earth that people can, in some way, reach physically if they choose.

## Separating the Subgestures When Practicing

***What if I make the wrong gesture?***

First, practice the gestures. (This is difficult because you are not here to see physically, but the way to practice the gestures is as follows:) There is often a series of gestures: "Do this, then do this." If you're going to practice and you're concerned about making an error—say there are three gestures, for example, or a gesture followed by three motions—you would practice the initial gesture and the first two motions, but not the third. Then you'd stop and wait at least five minutes. After that, you'd practice the second and third parts. You see, if you do it that way, because there is no immediate continuity, it's clear that you are not attempting to create.

Now, if you are concerned and you want to make sure, then the thing to do after you practice the initial gesture and the next two gestures, per our example, is to wait five minutes and draw an X in the air in front of you where you've been making the gestures. Then wait another five minutes before you practice the second and third steps. You don't have to do that, but if you feel a powerful energy or feel like something is happening, that's one way to do it.

On the other hand, if you feel a powerful energy and it feels good when you're making the gesture and you think, "Pretty good," then complete the process.

***Without the pauses?***

Without the pauses, without the X, nothing. Then stop and sit down. Put your hands in your lap with your palms on your legs or else cross your palms—one hand on top of the other or facing your body, whatever feels best. Then wait. If you're feeling the energy or the heat or the effect, just wait as long as it feels good. It might tingle or feel pleasant some other way. Just wait until you don't feel it anymore. Don't try to eliminate it, and don't think, if you can help it. If the phone rings, don't answer it. Eventually the feeling will go away and then you can go on.

***So if I practice these at home and continually get the same feeling from a particular set of actions, that would be the best to do at the crop circles?***

I'd say this: Don't make a mental decision here. Once you get to England but are in the privacy of your room or when you are somewhat refreshed, then try it. You might discover that what has felt good in your home state will feel different in England. Because geography, not the mental kind but true physical fact, will also have its effect; and your position in relation to other things in the Earth and the stars, physically speaking, will also have an effect, to say nothing of the energies and the spirits in that area where you are staying. That's the time to make your predecision.

## At the Crop Circle

When you get out to the crop circle, first do at the crop circle what we have discussed before. And don't be a policeman. (If you see little children running through the crop circle, just say to yourself, "All right, that's not my job.") Recognize that other people might be told to do different things. Lots of people are being told to get in the center of the crop circle and do this or that. Don't worry about it.

After you have done what you are going to do by the crop circle, should you be able to approach one, there are the fine points, you know. (We didn't put the fine points in the book because they have to do with either the individual or the circumstance or the place.) Very slowly make a miniature version, pointing your fingers toward instead of away from yourself. Do the first step or two, not the whole thing. Or you can point your fingers toward the ground (not by the crop circle but within 10 feet is okay) to do the first step or two and see how you feel. If you feel good, wait for a moment; in 10 or 15 seconds you ought to have a response, probably immediately. If you feel really good, do that gesture. Try not to do more than one gesture in, say, a twenty-minute period.

When you're by a crop circle it's best to be quiet, but people feel they have to talk, and to some extent the reaction, the surprise, the beauty and so on prompt them to talk—that's normal. But if you have to step away to a quieter part, then do it. Go through the gestures you know. Maybe you've photocopied a few pages and brought them along so you can try it. Whichever one feels right or best to you, not as a mental thing but as a physical feeling, that's the one you do. When you do one, you wait, just like the other steps. You won't be able to sit down, but wait until the energy passes.

Now, when you're going to do the gesture, you can walk up to within 3 to 4 feet of the crop circle. If the energy is too strong, step back to within 6 feet and try to get somebody on the tour with you (by that time you will have made some friends) to keep people from walking between you and the crop circle. (If somebody is walking inside, you can't help that—just let that go.) When you complete the gesture, wait until the energy passes. If the energy is very powerful after you complete the gesture, you need to step backward, so make sure you wear some good shoes that give you good balance so you can step back easily.

That's another reason it might be good to have trip buddies who can watch out for you so you don't bump into somebody, not because it would harm you very much, but because the energy will be blasting through or around you and might cause other people to feel temporarily dizzy. They might even fall. So this is for the protection of others. Ideally, if someone is within two or three feet of you, if you should be so overwhelmed by the energy that you need to sit or flop down for a moment, they'll catch you. Probably that won't happen, but you have to take that into account.

Normally when one makes this gesture, one might feel energy, and that energy would be manageable. You might sit down, but the best way is to back up. If you feel it's not safe to back up, then turn to your left and step away from the crop circle, perhaps 4 or 5 feet, so that you are 10 or 15 feet away (it shouldn't be necessary to be more than 15 feet away). Then continuing to turn in that same direction, face the crop circle again. You will have made a counterclockwise circle.

Normally I wouldn't encourage a person to do these gestures at a crop circle, but I know this is something you want to do, and you won't be doing it every day, so it would be worth trying it once or twice.

When the energy passes so that you feel only the energy of the crop circle or your normal energy, wait 20 minutes before you consider doing another gesture or series of gestures. I'm not saying you *should* do another one; I'm not even saying you should do *one*; you could, but it's up to you.

### Inspired Gestures from the Material Mastery Book

Now, there is one exception here. Normally I say, do the one that feels best. However, this is the one exception: You haven't had formal shamanic training, so I'm not giving you infinitesimal details. I know you are dedicated, so I'm giving you this much. If you feel that there is some gesture in the book that would be appropriate to do for the sake of all beings or the sake of mankind (depending on the events of the day), which might come to you, then I encourage you to do it at a distance of 10 feet from the crop circle or even away from the crop circle entirely, but on the land. And try to get at least two others to do it with you.

The reason I'm leaving this kind of vague is that something could come up while you're on the road; you won't be completely out of touch, you understand? You might hear something, or people are doing this or that: "This is needed" or "that is needed" or simply an inspiration. If you do it, you're going to follow the usual instructions plus what's given in the book. If there are at least two others with you (you might have five or more), make sure the individuals wait until the energy they are feeling passes. You need to have a minimum of 5 feet and ideally, 8 to 10 feet between you when you are doing this.

Now, some of you will feel the energy more profoundly than others. If so, whoever no longer feels the energy personally, aside from whatever energy they normally feel, can step away from the group. Try to take at least the first two steps backward. It's okay to look over your shoulder. If it doesn't feel safe to step blindly backward, then turn counterclockwise, step back, then step away. If you have turned counterclockwise to retreat and want to look at the group, then turn farther counterclockwise in order to look at them. You might wonder why. I'm mentioning it because something political or something you feel is necessary might come up, and if people in the group are intrigued by this whole business, other things might come up.

***Well, I know I'll be learning a lot from this book.***

The interesting thing about this book is that it's not a book that's only meant for reading. A lot of the books that preceded this were meant to stimulate and intrigue and even prompt. This book is really meant for all of that and more: it is meant for action. People have been asking for a long time, "What about an action book, how to do it?" So this book is the next step. I've given homework before; so has Speaks of Many Truth and Isis. But this book is homework from one end to the other. It doesn't demand it, it's optional. It's "this is what this place is about" and so on and "if you want to do this, then here it is." It's kind of nice this way—no demands.

***Well, I imagine each of us would be drawn to different things—some things more than others.***

That's right. That's why some attempt was made, however minor, to mention places in the world other than the U.S. People who live elsewhere or who have particular cares about other places might choose to nominate places. A lot of places were very lightly skimmed over, if touched at all. There are many, many sacred spots all over the world, but this book is like an introduction. In time, if there is enough interest, people might write and ask, "What about this spot?" or "What about that spot?" A whole list of spots will be accumulated, ideally with photos and map references. That way they can be shared with those who read them, and that will go into the next volume.

Turkey is a place that is packed with places like that and, as far as I know, is not mentioned in the book.

## Artifacts Found in Crop Circles

***Some people are using a magnetometer inside crop circles and finding metal objects that have been there a long, long time. They are encrusted and have the same pattern as the crop circles.***

I realize that on the surface, digging appears to be doing damage. One must make sure that this is carefully documented. In terms of the Roman coins, they need to be given to the property owner or the state or a museum. Perhaps there can be some kind of reward or recognition. My feeling is that it's probably not a good idea to do this, but people will find out about these artifacts. There will be those who will try to fake this. I'm not saying anybody has, just that there are those who will try. If this is being done legitimately and being documented, it's probably a good thing for people to know about it.

After all, crop circles are not new. This is quite obvious by the pictographs and pictograms that can be seen in various places in the world. One often finds exactly the same crop-circle shapes that were left on the rock hundreds if not thousands of years ago by other human beings. It is as if someone was saying, "Look, we saw this. What is it?" Or "Look, we saw this and we know what it is. We want you to know it was here, and if it shows up again, pay attention." This is happening, and lots and lots of research is being done on it. It would be good for people to know about it because it's pretty obvious, isn't it, that the same crop circle was either there in that exact spot before in times gone by or (even more interesting) that someone knew that crop circle would be there someday and buried that object there to attract the mechanism that creates the crop circles so the mechanism can find it.

### Best Investigated by Experts or Meticulous Record-Keepers

Now, obviously I'm going to say, don't go digging in the country in places where there haven't been crop circles. Wait until the crop circle shows up. I'd really like to see a university-inspired project that gets published about this because this is something that ought to be documented by antiquities experts. That way the knowledge and general information could eventually get out to the public, to say nothing of the professional interests. The obvious answer would be not to do this at all, but that's not the idea. It's *intended*, but it's very important who does it, what happens, whether it's documented and, most important, how it's followed up. These are not intended to be souvenirs, even for well-intended people. It's intended to be researched by intellectuals or scholars, and it's vital that it is documented, photographed and mapped, and that the exact point of retrieval is pinpointed. Try to use the best mapping system available, even the electronic systems, because eventually it will be like a connect-the-dots picture that will reveal something else. It's really like the prize in the box of caramel corn.

***You say that some of it could be real and some of it a hoax?***

I'm saying only this: that as the information gets out, there will be those who try to hoax it, but the hoaxes will be very obvious to a trained eye—that's the key, to a trained eye. That's why it's important to document it. I'm not saying that spiritual groups shouldn't go to the crop circles anymore or that the whole thing ought to be studied by university people. Rather, I'm calling the university people to arms and encouraging scholarly people to go to the crop circles to examine them when searching is being done. If they're not present, then whoever is doing it needs to make meticulous records so that the objects can be studied at a later date. It's very important when the objects are taken out of the ground that they not be touched very much. Eventually it will be important to touch them because they are sacred objects; I will say much more about this in the future. Right now I'm just giving an advisory.

***The "people from the universities"—what should their discipline be, archaeology?***

That will be up to them to choose. It will start unofficially and then become official. I'm not saying that people who are meticulously documenting this process should contact the university. Ultimately a university will be the most likely place to get this information out. However, if universities are not interested (which is always a hazard these days), it must be documented and the objects must be kept very carefully and exposed to the air as little as possible. The whole thing can deteriorate very easily. That's why it's good to apply a professional method of research. If it's going on, try to do it in a good way. These objects that were buried were *intended* to be found. If any of these objects happen to come into your hands or the hands of someone you know, encourage them to touch them as little as possible. The artifacts have powers that, when combined in certain ways with certain gestures (you know it's important if I'm *singing* about it) can have very specific effects. I'm purposely being vague. It's not likely they could be used for anything harmful, but it's profoundly likely that they can be used for something of great usefulness. That's the word I'm going to use right now.

***Intriguing!***

That's the intention.

***Am I to ponder that?***

As always, we're doing a session that ought to be published. Part of the reason is because your group is not the only group doing these things. I'm not trying to restrict their freedom, but I'm trying to keep this from turning into a "let's find the gold" situation. It's not about silver or gold or wealth. It's about knowledge, application and ultimately, benevolent magic.

# 35

# Sand as Crystal Libraries

Zoosh
May 22, 1999*

***I have a question about the Great Sand Dunes in southern Colorado. I read some time ago that these sand dunes are what is left of a great library, that each grain of sand contains the knowledge of the whole library and that people came and destroyed this. Is that true?***

That's a nice story, but if you look at sand . . . pick up a handful of sand next time you go someplace, especially lighter-colored sand. Take out a magnifying glass and look at it. The grains of sand *are* crystals.

***Yes, that's what Archangel Michael said.***

This story applies very nicely—it's a nice story. *Every* grain of sand everywhere has this capacity.

***Wow! To have all that knowledge?***

To have all *applicable* knowledge. If it had *all* knowledge, it might take you forever to pull it all out unless you knew how to get to what you need. It has all applicable knowledge, meaning all that you would need for any given circumstance for where you are and when you are. As an aside, there is a famous incident where a UFO was seen by a sheriff in the U.S. He was driving along and saw this object land. He saw a person get out of the object, scoop up a handful of dirt—and sand, of course—run back to the ship and take off. It sounds kind of strange, but in fact, this thing that is stated about

---

* From a private research reading.

sand is known just about everyplace other than Earth. There are some on Earth who know about it; that's why it's mentioned from time to time.

Sometimes when knowledge is needed that isn't available to individuals, or when the raw material of sand or dirt itself is needed, such a happenstance will take place and the individual getting out of the ship will do just exactly that. Then they take the sand into the ship and put it in something that looks like a small table. The table is actually like a receiver (I'm putting it simply), and this device will sort out the wisdom in that sand to find the particle that contains ("contains" is not quite the right term, but it's the best at the moment) that needed knowledge, which will then be applied and used. The rest of the sand will then be sorted to see if there is any other usable knowledge. Then the proper thing to do is to put the sand back.

Now, if the sheriff had not happened to be driving by and saw the event and drove closer because he was curious, the person would have taken the sand and put it back on the ground and left. But because he was interrupted and didn't know what the witness was about and didn't want to cause any more of a stir than necessary, he had to take off. He has been unable to return that soil, but it has been sitting in a container on a distant planet and will be returned when relations are well under way on a public basis between the people of Earth and that other planet. It will be returned in a very ceremonial fashion. The sheriff's relatives or friends or family will be invited to attend the ceremony, at which time the sheriff will be honored for being the witness to this in some way.

You know, people laughed at that sheriff, but they didn't laugh completely, because he was, after all, an official and was willing to say what he saw. He didn't make a fuss about it, but that's what he said. He needs to be honored, just like all witnesses need to be honored and appreciated for coming forth and saying what they saw.

***This is wonderful! If that sand was going to be put back, how did they record the information?***

It's not that much different from the way information is retrieved from a computer disk and put into the hard drive of a computer, which can be accessed by the user. It's not the same mechanics, but the analogy is the same. Something touches something else and the knowledge is transferred on the basis of what's needed. The table part of the device knows what's missing, what's needed, and the sand is "mined" for that information. It's not broken down or damaged in any way. It's now sitting in a container on the planet, and there is a label on it. It's inside a box and has a mission statement: "Return to Earth when possible."

So that will be quite an event. There will be banners and people attending, diplomats and political and global government officials and lots of fun and lots of children.

***Am I going to be here then?***

Well, probably in spirit, at least.

***I take it this is going to be a long ways off?***

It will be a ways off, I should think at least fifty years, but possibly as soon as thirty-five or forty.

***So it would be this man's relatives who would be there.***

Most likely it would be his relatives who would say "Hey, how about that! He's finally getting credit" and all those good things.

***It sounds as though there will be a lot of progress in fifty years.***

Most likely.

# 36

# An Invisible Hand Brings Together China and the U.S.

Zoosh
May 22, 1999*

You know, an interesting is going on right now, politically speaking. Look at the situation with the U.S. and China. You might say there has been an invisible hand shoving the U.S. toward getting involved with China, but if you back up a bit, you have to see that the invisible hand has been working for years and years with other countries. Other countries have been somewhat involved for years as trading partners. It's an easy way to get involved with a government or with people whose system you may not particularly approve of. You can get involved by buying their products and they can get involved by buying your products or by simply trading cultural things, too.

For a long time it has been known by many people (certainly by inner circles of many people) that the U.S. and other countries need to get along with China. Here you have a circumstance where all these things are being revealed about China spying on the U.S.—not that other countries and the U.S. don't do that.

Why are they a most-favored-nation trading partner? Many people know that in order to be included in the Union of Planetary Cultures and other such groups and to receive the great benefits of such cross-cultural exchanges—including the clearing up of all diseases

* From a private research reading.

and a great improvement in the general health of everybody on Earth and so on—that such steps have to be taken. The most basic requirement is that Earth must be united.

So the "invisible hand" is here, to quote the famous author economist [Adam] Smith. This is really insider knowledge, and things are being revealed, not because President Clinton is a traitor or because President Bush or President Reagan were, but because people must know, accept, be all right with it, then go on. Certainly the same thing is going to have to be done with North Korea, Libya and other countries that the U.S. has problems with, but it's happening. Granted, the people have been somewhat conditioned to allow it to happen, but it's happening intentionally, so that you can speed toward being a united planet.

The economic and trade organizations are really beginning to establish a planetary government now on a corporate level. It may not be the ultimate global government, but it is a beginning. When you have a united planet, you will not only gain the rewards of contact with other planetary civilizations, but you will be able to share what you have to offer as well. On that note I will say good day.

# 37

# U.S. and China, an Opportunity to "Mine" Feelings

Zoosh
May 25, 1999

***Would you comment on U.S. affairs with China?***

Zoosh speaking. I want to talk to you about something that's very important for you to know because it's a factor of Creator School training, which I've been talking to you about for some time. Right now you are experiencing something I'm going to call mining. You all know that mining is digging around for something that (hopefully) you can use.

You have all needed to use your feelings more lately, but in order to use them, you need to clarify them to know the difference between thoughts and feelings and be able to apply your feelings in ways that work for you rather than against you or that harm others. Right now you are in the time of "mining" the feelings. This circumstance between the U.S. and China now is an example of this opportunity for both U.S. and China citizens as well as other people around the world who are worried about the possibility, however remote, of a nuclear exchange—which would, of course, affect everyone.

Now, the reason these feelings need to be mined is that the animosity between the U.S. and China is largely based in the past even though China has not changed its form of government in any major way. It has liberalized its form of government, from its point of view, though maybe not from the U.S. point of view. If you look at it squarely, there is a significant movement in the U.S. to run the government more conservatively; at the same time there's a movement (albeit on the q.t., as they used to say) in China to liberalize the way the government runs things. Even those who wish to keep things conservative in China favor a gradual loosening of government enforcements. This is not to say that the system in China will change, because China and its current government take the long view—not just forward, but backward. They don't have to look back too far to find the old feudal system under which most people in China suffered and only a very, very few did well. Even though communism as it's applied in China is often ruthless and is, to outsiders, apparently rigid, it represents an improvement over feudal times from both the government's point of view and, overall, the view of China's citizens.

Now, the U.S., either the government or the average citizen, does not use the long view going backward. As a matter of fact, the U.S. is famous for not particularly paying attention to history, so it is more likely to be distracted by what might be and what is. What might be and what is are not only distractions, but in the U.S. they are often based on the entertainment industry, which has been applied perhaps too liberally to all segments of the community.

Now, I'm not saying you should live like the people in China; what I am saying is that you need to pay more attention to other points of view as they are applied to other people. Understanding that as a groundwork, what does this have to do with mining the feelings? Your attitudes toward China (except for those of you who are elderly citizens who remember China as an ally at points during World War II) have largely been created by the Cold War, which is very fresh in the minds of many. Let us understand that spying on friends and foes takes place by most countries most of the time, so the U.S. is hardly an innocent child here who has been betrayed by a powerful taskmaster. Please let us get away from that posturing.

## External Prompts Needed to Face Your Fears

On the other hand, I can certainly see that the cares about "what if" are perfectly legitimate concerns. However, you now need to have a circumstance where you can feel the full range of your feelings—all the old fears as well as all the new desires for world peace, open trade opportunities and many chances for the good life for many more people. You need to have all those feelings confront the feelings of real danger and risk. In short, *you need to feel external prompts.* These prompts are meant to give you the choice to react either with totally excited and extreme feelings or with a calm, benevolent, long-range outlook toward the ultimate resolution of bitter feelings that have accumulated by both sides against each other. You need to have a full range of potential testing based on old fears that were especially profound during the fifties and sixties.

Now, in order to do that you need to have the progress you've made on a global scale philosophically and politically, but also spiritually. You've made a lot of progress spiritually in recent years. In order to test that, you need to start having these buttons pushed. *This is a test!* It is not intended to end in World War III, nor does anyone really expect that, but it is a worthy test of your capacity to create a well-routed, benevolent ending of the current shock situation between U.S. and China. This is something that needs to be resolved someplace beyond the United Nations. The United Nations is a worthy body, an organization that will resolve it. But what is going to come out of this and other crises such as your current crisis in Yugoslavia, ongoing situations in Africa and so on, is a clear-cut recognition that there needs to be something besides the United Nations, something that strives for peace and has the capacity to authorize a concerted effort to generate peace. In short, what you are seeing is literally nothing less than the beginning of a recognition of *the need for a global government.*

### Recognizing the Need for a Global Government

This has been coming for a long time. It is not a desire for a global dictator, nor is it a desire to live in the Garden of Eden immediately, but rather a desire that global conflicts, be they small or large, have a method to talk about them and create solutions that may or may not come to pass (such as what has been going on in the United Nations with the best of intentions), but also to create solutions that will solve the problem, at least in part for all sides, and maintain the peace. Not just create it, but maintain it. Such a thing would require a global government.

Now, I know that it is not clear how that is going to come about, but you as human beings have the capacity, the ability and, perhaps on the spiritual and now feeling level, the desire to make it happen. For a long time many people (very quietly behind the scenes in all countries, especially countries involved in diplomacy) have known that the only way to truly establish world peace and harmony, to a degree at least, and the good life and free trade is to involve all countries of the world in a global economy first, then in a global peace-making mechanism. It is that intersection you are at now. Look at your world! You do in fact now have a global economy. Granted, it could be improved upon; it could be made more efficient, but time will take care of that, plus experience and ongoing diplomatic efforts between different governments and also between corporations and governments.

With that in place now, it has given every government, every country and almost all people a personal stake in maintaining this move toward a global economy, with the ultimate intention of improving the quality of life of every human being on Earth. This was once a pipe dream, science fiction, but it is now believed to be true by people all over. This is a very important step; it is progress. As I said some time ago, the first form of world government would be economic; it would be a form that involves everybody, where everybody actually feels connected and so on. You can read about it in the Explorer Race books. I talked about that at the beginning of speaking to you about the ultimate resolution of your challenges here, which is the Explorer Race concept, its ideals, practices and, ultimately, fulfillment.

Now, what is going on for you is that this crossroads is really a *time to choose:* Are you going to hang onto old resentments, or are you going to build a new time line into the future that will allow you to experience, not just a move toward a better life for all people, but ultimately a form of forgiveness based on the understanding of feelings and motivations? This does not simply mean a historical study, because that often just digs up old wounds, even though it is useful to some degree.

To understand why China spied, why the U.S. spied, why Russia spied, why France spied and so on, is useful to know. It is important to be discussed in a way that the general public hears it as well as those of "elite" status in other circles of the informed on Earth.

### Homework: Claiming "the Good Life"

There needs to be an acceptance that "the good life" is deserved by you, all right? I think that there is an acceptance that some people deserve to have the good life, but there needs to be an acceptance on a personal level that *you* deserve to have a good life and that you can most easily attain it if everyone in the world has that same opportunity and feels and knows that it is possible.

Now, the good life will be different for different people. Some people will see it this way, some that way, but it is important for you to see that it is possible. In this way you are personalizing this experience globally. It is very easy to see it in an impersonal way: *they* are to do this, *they* are to do that. But what ought *you* to be doing? I'm giving you the homework assignment now: I'd like you, as an individual, every individual, to say, "*I claim the good life for me.*" I know many of you will be working on world peace in your own way; however, it is essential to personalize it and recognize that the benevolent global economic government is in place even though it does not always appear benevolent nor is its motivation necessarily benevolent. In the big picture it is benevolent because it is a link that you can all agree on and it has value to you. Whenever you can all agree on anything, it's a good start.

You must take it out of the impersonal or global and bring it down to the personal. I think you can all agree that you would like to have the good life. If you can't all agree, if you do not feel that the good life is right for you at this time (and there will be a few of you who feel that way), then you can say that *people* deserve to have a good life. You will be able to say that easily. Some of you will be startled when you say, "I deserve to have a good life" (or you might say "*the* good life," either one or both), because you find that you feel uncomfortable.

This is important to know because you are *mining your feelings* when you do that. You will discover that you may feel uncomfortable about the experience of "the good life." What does that mean? "Do I get to ride around in a limousine and live in a penthouse?" Maybe so, and does that make you uncomfortable? Then you are quickly alerted to the fact that you are blocking yourself from this good life on a personal level and that you are living vicariously these good life experiences of others. While it's good for you to cheer them on to their successes, it is not good for you to block that from yourself. You do not have to compete with them; rather, you need to recognize the possibility, even if you think of it as science fiction, that you can *all* have the good life, you can *all* live in nice apartments and nice houses. You can *all* have a limousine ride; you can *all* have everything you need—fresh food, clean water, nice houses, good friends, happy families and so on.

It may sound like a pipe dream, like science fiction, but it's true. Right now I want you to build a time line toward the future. The step is to say, "I *can* have," to say, "I deserve the good life. I deserve a good life for me." Saying both things is the best, but you can say either one if you prefer. If you feel good when you say it, that means you don't have any blocks in the way at that moment for it. You don't have to say it many times; just say it once—maybe once a month or something like that.

It is not a prayer; it is not something you say over and over. It is something you say to mine your feelings. If you say it and then feel uncomfortable, that means you need to learn how to get out of your way or move through your blocks to feel better about your potential for having the good life. If you feel good when you say it, then you've mined your feelings successfully. You've discovered that you're open to it and you can make strides toward achieving it.

That's your homework. Those of you who know how to do the love exercise—the heat in your chest [see page??]—if you feel the blocks when you say, "I deserve the good life," then by all means go into that heat and loving exercise. It will help support you, and after you've done it for a time and feel the heat, then gently say afterward, maintaining the heat while you are saying it, "I deserve the good life" and add, *"I am safe; it is safe for me to have the good life."*

You see, that's the key. When you feel physical discomfort at some inner level about saying you have the good life, it is not to be disciplined out, but to be confronted, to be worked with, for your physical body is your material-mastery teacher. It is to be worked through using various methods that others have discussed and that I will talk about more in the future. If you do not feel safe about having the good life, that is why you feel uncomfortable when you say that. Of course, many of you will feel fine.

That's your personal homework, what you can do right now about the political crisis with China. And let's not overlook the U.S. bombing the Chinese embassy in Belgrad. How do you think the U.S. government or the citizens of the U.S. would feel if the U.S. embassy was bombed somewhere accidentally? "Oh, sorry, we didn't

### Claiming the Good Life

Accept on a personal level that *you* deserve to have a good life and that you can most easily attain it if everyone in the world has that same opportunity and feels and knows that it is possible.

Say, **"I claim the good life for me."**

Build a time line toward the future: **"I deserve the good life."**

When you feel good as you say it, that means you don't have any blocks to it in the way at that moment.

If you are uncomfortable saying it, do the love or heart-heat exercise [page 230].

Then say, **"I deserve the good life. I am safe; it is safe for me to have the good life."**

mean to bomb you; we meant to bomb somebody else . . . uh, a short distance away." Do you think you might be just a little bit upset? I think their being upset is completely justified. They do recognize mentally that it was an accident, although there are people—and you must know this—in China's government and military circles who question that and think the U.S. might have bombed the Chinese embassy *because of the spying* China has been doing. Some people felt that it was an intentional threat. Now, I'm not saying whether it was or was not, but those feelings exist, and there is a great deal of behind-the-scenes political negotiation with China to say that this is not the case.

But put yourself in that position. How would *you* feel? You just got caught with your hand in the cookie jar and you were told not to have any cookies. Then suddenly someone gives you a mighty vicious slap on the wrist. Wouldn't you think that the two things are connected? Of course you would. Understand that position and you will understand that their reaction is only human, and it is certainly political in these political times. Political does not mean bad; it simply means understanding the way people think and act based on their thoughts.

But now we need to unify people based on their feelings. That's why this time of mining the feelings is associated not only with Creator School lessons for the Explorer Race (which is all of you), but also with moving into a common language that you all share equally. You all have different thoughts politically—*my* government, not *yours*; *my* beliefs, not *yours* and so on—but the function of your feelings is the same for everyone. And when I say everyone, I don't mean only Earth human beings (plants, animals, stone—Mother Earth herself, since stone *is* Mother Earth), but also ETs on other planets, everyone. Feelings work exactly the same way for everybody, but thoughts do not always work for everyone the way they do on Earth.

Your common language is feelings. That's another good reason to start mining them; you can weed out the feelings that don't feel good. You can discover why they don't, not dump or suppress them, and find a way to heal them, not by rejecting them for that discomfort but by finding out what would make them feel better.

When a child is hurt, that child needs the parent, the adult, the guardian, to do something for it to make it *feel* better, not just dress the wound. The child needs a hug because it has had a shock. When you're very young and you get hurt—maybe you fall down and hurt yourself—you discover that life is not only to be discovered and enjoyed, but there is also pain. In those early days especially, the first few years of life, many people, if they are not immediately given love, a hug, a kiss, soothing words, will identify life as pain and die young or sometimes get distorted on their path.

When children are shocked like that, they need reassurance, and when you do not reassure them, they might turn out differently, step off their path and recognize life as pain or that life is something to be feared. That can change things. But even though they have had some pain, if you reassure them, if you give them a hug, a little kiss *and* dress their wound, then you will be doing not only the physical thing, but the *feeling* thing that will help them maintain their good feelings about life.

It is time now for you to mine your feelings and address the results, then utilize the knowledge and abilities you have to bring about a feeling of safety for yourself and others. Now, *that's* what China's all about.

# 38

# August 11: What Happens, What It Means

Speaks of Many Truths
July 26, 1999

***Tell me about the effect of the August 11 lineup of planets. What is the aftermath? How will this affect humans?***

To me, aftermath always means application of what you have learned in new and oft more useful ways. It means this time you have been living through. [It] has been meant to strip from you your old adaptation. You must, as a soul, adapt to Earth ways when you come here. [You] cannot do things the way you have done on other planets with the same wisdom and enthusiasm. Must do things here the way they are done. Sometimes not much fun, but you get better and better at it, then after a while you don't remember that you ever did it another way or that there *is* another way.

## Discomforts Bring up New Skills and Strip Away the Unnatural

You have come to moments in the past that have been intended to bring up your soul and spirit skills—usually in [a] dramatic situation, as you know, in emergency, this disaster, that disaster. Then suddenly everyone works together for the betterment of all beings. But that type of thing can only happen so much, until disasters cause more harm than good—and you have seen much of this. So now is better for you to have opportunity to become aware of things you have been doing that can be done in a different, better way that is in greater alignment with what is natural for you.

This time you have been living through has been designed to

strip away the unnatural, just as an actor would leave the character he or she plays in the theater, then go home and be himself as best he can. Is the same way for all people. Many of you will have had some discomfort through this time recently, but sometimes that is to get you to ask for help if you don't know how or are ashamed. Some of you have been taught to be ashamed to ask for help, as if there was something wrong with you for asking this. This is unfortunate in your cultures now, but it is a fact. Sometimes you are put into a position where you must ask for help, then you discover that it's not so bad. People are often happy to give it, and they give you new, better ways to be and to act. Then you don't have to do things the way you used to, which was ofttimes painful or uncomfortable. You got used to the pain because you thought that was the only way to do it.

For those of you in situations like that, you have had to unload some behaviors that you could do in different, better way or other people could do for you. You have had to say, "Well, that's just how it is." Others of you have had different opportunity. Maybe you have lots and lots of skills you want to offer or didn't even know you had, and you were put into a position where those around you, or people you maybe didn't even know, suddenly needed you to do something and, much to your surprise, you discovered that you could not only do it, but that you were good at it! That's the time you have been living through most recently.

Don't feel bad about some discomforts that come up. These are all intended to lead you to the same place—to do what you naturally do best and let go of what you don't do so well. You have all had to learn how to do many things that you don't do so well. Sometimes it was necessary. Other times it gave you some compassion for those who will be continuing to do these things when you don't have to do them anymore.

You all begin to learn now that a finger can be a finger and a toe can be a toe, and sometimes toes can do things like fingers and fingers can do things like toes, but is always easier for fingers to be fingers and toes to be toes. (That's something we say to our youngsters, but is very profound.) Some people can do something very well and other things not so well, but they try.

You are all being reminded that you do not have to do the same things. Some of you can do some things and others other things. You are being reminded that some of you do some things easy because you were born to it, and others, if you don't do a thing so easy, there's probably something else you were born to. If you haven't been asked to do it yet, you *will* be, so you'll discover it if it's remembered. Generally speaking, if it's hard to do, if it seems completely unfamiliar, if you feel completely lost doing this thing, most likely you were not born to it. Things that come easy, natural to you, this you were born to.

## A Time of Rediscovering the Whole and What Skills You Were Born With

***I always thought that the things you were born to were the things you had done before, and that in this life you were to learn new things. Is that not the way it works?***

My understanding is that in this life, yes, you are born to *discover* new things, but now you are in different time—time now of rediscovering the whole. Every person is part of the whole spherical One. In the whole spherical One of each planet or sometimes even each family (but usually planet), there are always certain people who do certain things well. Other people don't do those things so well because they were born to do something else.

Now is time of rediscovering the One (planetary One), then become more than that, but start out as *planetary* One. In my time is more like tribal One. In your time, has expanded to be planetary One, and is now a time to rediscover that. So next few years, not much more than that, everybody will discover at some moment or another what is natural for you, what you were born to, skills you were born with—talents, you call them. [You] might not do them full-time, but you will discover them.

If you are in doubt, ask your friends. You might say, "Have you ever noticed anything that I am really good at?" At first you will laugh, but after you get over that joke, then say, "Will you notice me a little bit the next few times we are together and tell me, is there something I'm just good at that you notice or can think of now?" Most people will not need that, but some of you might, and it's okay to say such a thing to your friends.

## Too Much Individuality

***Okay, what was the catalyst? What happened so that suddenly the old way we lived was changed?***

Went too far into individuality. Began thinking of the individual as a sphere in his or her own right, such as each individual being a planet, individuality of each being more important than the whole of all beings. Got to the break point with that. If you went any further, [you] would not be able to keep soul capacity; all souls on the planet at any given moment would not be able to feel, on spiritual level, union with all other souls. If do not feel that way, then mass death

**What Really Happened: The Third Wave**

**1**: The first wave, who wanted to awaken, were previously pulled gently.

**2**: The second wave, who wanted to awaken, were previously *pushed* gently.

**3**: The third wave, peaking on August 11, 1999, do *not* want to awaken, but are being massively pulled *and* pushed, using astrological pressure.

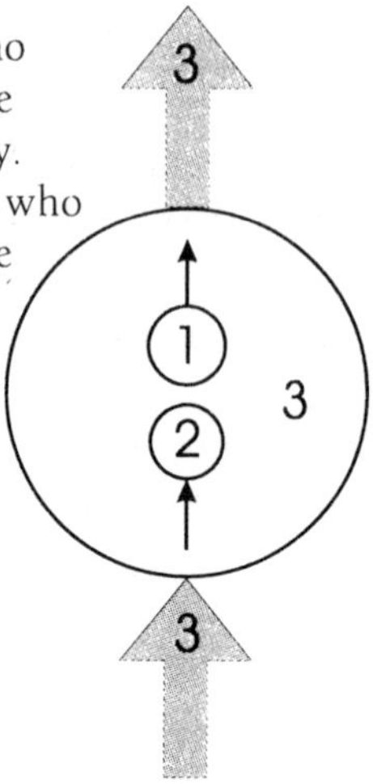


takes place.

***So something happened in August?***

No, has been building to this for hundreds of years.

***And this year . . .***

This year is the time to notice that individuality is not meant to be the goal, but the *means* to the goal: exploring individuality to discover the whole of all beings. Normally one explores the whole of all beings to appreciate that, but in recent years cultures have been exploring individuality. You have gone as far as you can go with that.

***We start perceiving ourselves as part of a greater whole instead of each being an individual whole?***

Yes, but it cannot be philosophical or mental conception. Is not about *thinking* about it that way. It is not symbolic; [you] have been presented with all of that already. Must be something for which there is *physical* evidence. In the past, in disasters people are put into situations. Some people good at climbing, other people good at thinking, some people good at following, other people good at directing and so on. In disasters [you] discover these things very quickly out of necessity, but disaster often causes much harm, and now with more people *everywhere* on the Earth, [it is] not possible to have too many disasters without causing great harm to people. So many people, you know. Must create other kinds of pressures that affect the planet, such as motions of celestial bodies. These things affect the planet, and you, being made up of Mother Earth's body, are also affected. That is why motions of celestial bodies affect *you*. Astrology [is] real.

## August 11, a Trigger to Discovering New Abilities

***So the lineup of planets that will happen in August will trigger this?***

Correct. Because is way to create things without flood, fire, earthquake, volcano.

***So we each feel a pressure to become part of a whole.***

A pressure, exactly. Or circumstances happening more often where your "born-to" talents must come to the surface. If is not pressure on you, is pressure on somebody who knows you or pressure on someone when you happen to be nearby, say, scene of accident. If you have something you are good at (maybe you didn't know it) and someone says to you (here you are, walking by—innocent bystander, eh?) or just says to the crowd, "Run down to that drugstore," says emergency medical technician, "we're all out of something. Run down as fast as you can get there, and run back." Obviously, heart patient does not volunteer, but somebody suddenly gets feeling, drops everything, runs down, runs back, discovers, "Didn't know I could run like that!" That is simplistic example, but could happen. Dramatic example I pick, because is appealing, but ofttimes things are much more subtle.

> **WHAT IT REALLY MEANS**
>
> **After 8-11-99, you will begin to:**
>
> • Use the energy of this astrological push/pull to change, no longer needing crises and catastrophes to shock you into discovering your abilities and unique skills—what you were born to do.
>
> • Leave behind the cultural imperative to be all things to all people, to be a separate individual who has to do everything, even things you're not good at. Become a unique part of the planetary whole, doing what you were born to do.
>
> • Start doing what you are good at, what you love to do; then an explosion of creation and creative energy will lead to such a renaissance in every field, every human endeavor, that 50% of all occupations will be created in the next 3 to 5 years.
>
> • Recycle everything.
>
> • Earth changes will lessen as you reduce Earth's population naturally by committing to having fewer children.
>
> • Create the nucleus of things that have appeared in benevolent science fiction—and the world is re-created like a celebration.

For instance, you are visiting in home of your neighbor who has recently given birth. Child is having problem, crying, coughing, something—not enough to call the doctor, but you get the feeling of what is wrong with the child. "Try this," say you. You not even married, never had any children. Only experience with child is being one yourself. But suddenly you say, "Try this." Person tries that and immediately, baby happy, fine. Person looks at you and says, "How did you know that?" And you say, "I don't know." [Laughs.]

[You] discover hidden talent. Maybe have capacity to . . . it's not thought, it's just something you say immediately. Discover you have a connection to youngsters, babies. Somehow you are able to know what they need as simple, sudden thing. "Oh, do this," and maybe just change position of baby. "Oh-oh, that's okay, that's fine." Then young mother say, "Oh well, my other kids didn't need that, but I guess this one does. Thank you very much. [If] I have another problem, I'm gonna call on you." Everybody joke and laugh, and maybe you think about it later. Where did *that* come from?

***I've got goosebumps.***

See?

***Each human, then, needs to really start focusing on what they call in business their core competency, right?***

Yes, these skills you must know about, because you need to discover you have undiscovered talents, talents that you were born with. But most of you do not know of your talents in such a way as you are using them all the time. Oh, you might say, "Gee, I've always been able to swim really good." Like that. You have discovered the kind of talent that would be discovered in your school system, because the school you went to had a pool. Or maybe you discover you're a good athlete or something because school has good athletic program, or you're good at math or something. But most talents are not discovered in schools. Most of the talents are discovered in circumstances of *life*. [Laughs.]

Now must alter circumstances, change things a little bit so people have the chance to discover talents they didn't know they had, and then can say, "Oh-h-h, I can do *that!*" Very important, because once you discover talent, [you] will be aware of it. [There] might be a circumstance again in the future where such talent is needed, and [you] might have some competence. Doesn't mean that everyone who gets an inspiration *all* the time has that talent, but you will recognize it if it just comes natural, easy, or someone gives you tiny amount of instruction and suddenly you are really good at it—quick learner, they say sometimes.

***Are you saying that we may have been doing things because of circumstances in our life, and they're not what we were born to do?***

They're not what talent you were born with. You just adapted to this because your culture says everybody must do everything. Some people were raised to believe that it was not okay to ask for help. Somebody down the street is good at math; you aren't, but you struggle along with math. You study, study, study, and you get to be adequate. Person down the street hardly studies at all, and they are whiz at math.

***So you should be doing something else—is that what you're saying?***

Probably you were not born to math, you were born to something else. You are a whiz at something else you just don't know about yet. Everybody born for different things. They don't know what they are because the system you live in, the culture, is not set up like ancient cultures, where people's talents are often discovered. They did not have same education for everyone. In your culture, same education for everyone—opportunities very limited to discover [people's talents]. Usually, culture *also* very limited. Get out of school, get a job, get married, have children, like that. Very fixed way of living, not much variety. Not much opportunity to discover what you might be good at because such fixed culture.

***But this is the time when we have to start to do what we love to do. Is that what you're saying?***

Exactly, and what you love to do is very often what you are good at, and *naturally* good at. In circumstances of things being different, [it] has been very important for you this year to be very flexible. People who are rigid this year are having trouble, but if you are flexible, adaptable, [you] will be able to learn this easily and perhaps in ways that are fun. [If you are] rigid and unable to adapt and [are] controlling or living in circumstances of *feeling* very controlled, [you] might require drama. So be more flexible.

***There's the inertia of habit, also. If someone's done something for 20 years, it's hard to start over.***

When they've done it that way, that's right. You don't have to start over. Remember, starting over is too much, if done in the way you have been doing things. Can't do that. "It took me 20 years to learn how to do this so I can do it well now." You understand? But when you discover the thing you are good at, it takes you a week or two to get *really* good at it, not 20 years.

***So you're really talking about every human beginning to do what he wants to do and suddenly enjoying life.***

I am talking about *discovering* what you are good at. Maybe not everybody feels they can do that right away, but [it's an] opportunity to discover. Only a few people on the planet, in terms of percentage—10, 15 percent—are doing what they are naturally good at. Most everybody else [is] doing something that they are just doing. They learned how to be good at it, but [were] not born to it.

***So when someone finds what he is good at, then he needs to have a career change or do it as . . .***

They need to take note that they are good at this thing, they don't necessarily need to throw career away. But they need to consider, "Now I know of at least one thing I am good at that I didn't know about before. I wonder how this could be used in a career. Rack my brain, don't know. [I] think I'll ask my friends, think I'll ask others." In other words, you are now in a position to ask people you will never meet, through telephone, computer, other things, "[I] discovered I was very good at this. Is there a job where this is involved?"

You don't know about it, your friends don't know about it, but somebody on the other side of the Earth says, "Oh yeah, how 'bout *this?*" And you say, "I don't know." This would be the thing you discover you can do. You say, "Oh, how wonderful!" Then because of advice from friends, others, people who live miles away, people you don't even know, you discover, "Here's something *else* that I can do that I didn't know about" similar to the thing you discover. Then somebody else saying, "Well, what about *this?*" Then you discover, "Oh, there's that, too, and it's kinda like what I been doing, yes." Then you discover there is even more.

You understand? You discover things that are related, that have [their] foundation in the thing you discover you can do. Pretty soon you discover all kinds of things that are natural abilities that open up new avenues for you to do in a career that would be easy.

## New Jobs Created, New Designs and Technology

During this time and for the next three to five, maybe seven years, fully half the world's jobs will be created. When people start doing what they are *good* at doing, an *explosion* of creation and creative energy go into this, because when you are happy doing what you are doing, is like a celebration. You no longer are just trying to do the best you can at something that's hard for you. You find that it is easy and fun to do the best you can at something that is fun to do. You can put creative energy into this, and it's not hard, it's simple.

Lots and lots of jobs [will] be invented in all fields, not just technology: medicine, healing, food preparation, lots of new kinds of cooking, making garments, making decorative objects, making furniture. In the next few years, society begins to form the nucleus of things that have appeared as benevolent pictures in science fiction, like futuristic furniture, not just funny-looking stuff that would be uncomfortable to sit in, but things that would be actually comfortable.

For instance, [Robert is] currently sitting in flat chair, but what if chair was shaped like doughnut, but well-padded, so [that] rounded portion of bottom of person kind of hangs a little bit in the chair, and looks beautiful sitting there. Before you sit in it, you say, "This has got to be uncomfortable." Then you stretch back and you discover, "Never found a chair so comfortable in my life." So futuristic-looking things suddenly become designed to be more comfortable and more beautiful. World is re-created like celebration. Everybody wants things, everybody is doing things they enjoy doing. People make lots and lots of money, can buy lots and lots of stuff.

***A renaissance.***

A renaissance, a good word. So this coming now. This is coming for your people and can only happen when people are loving what they do because [it] comes easy, or at least core thing comes easy. Things that are allied to it are also easier than what you've been doing. But if you go too far, you get to point here [makes expansive gesture with arms spread wide]—thing is not quite so easy anymore.

***We went too far.***

That's right, you went too far. [You] don't do that anymore because there is somebody else who does that thing, and you don't have to take the bad with the good. You just know, "Oh, somebody else does this. If I have been discovering this, soon I will meet these people. If I do not know them, I ask friends. If friends do not know these people, then I ask others I don't know on computer. Somebody [will] tell me, 'Oh, this person is doing something like that, too. You two ought to get together.' "

***So this is a very positive thing that happened. What's been building up for all these years, culminating with the astrological configuration in August, is going to change the way we perceive ourselves and the way we live.***

Exactly. So [it] is the beginning of better times. Of course, will not always be so wonderful. Things will still happen [that] make you unhappy, but is the beginning. And remember, sometimes opportunity is disguised as difficulty. Difficulty often means [you] must do things differently, does not mean can't do things anymore. Means do differently, better. May not find different right away for some people, but *will* find. Do different, better way. Then is very easy and won't look at doing that thing with dread like before. Now [you] say, "Oh, fine."

For example, nowadays very often people dread to go to dentist office—"Oh, pain. Somebody fooling around in my mouth, I don't like that." Very soon, without any discomfort—no needles, nothing—go to dentist office [that] not have just current technology, but more that's coming—no pain. [You] just relax, listen to music, watch video, [and] dentist works. Not uncomfortable at all. No needle. Something is put into body with no break on the skin. [An] adaptation of previous invention is coming. So [you'll] see new things coming. Surgery same way pretty soon. No needles, no pain. Having surgery is like having someone work on your car, is fine. "I go [to] doctor, [she] do this thing. I heal up real quick afterward," okay?

## Social Skills

Revolution in such things for other technology also, including interaction with social skills. Right now might want to do something to help people. "These people don't get along with each other. How can I help?" Is hard, go to school, learn many, many ways, takes years and years. You get out, is still a struggle, but some people discover in this time and time to come soon that they are very good mediator, good between people. "Oh, why don't you this? Why don't you do that?" People say, "Oh, yeah, I didn't think of that. Good idea! We can do that, fine." Then, "You over there, why don't you come try this?" "Oh, yeah, I like that."

See, people help each other. Lot of time people want to help each other, they just don't know how to do it because they are trying to do a job they don't find easy. They try to apply what they were taught that worked in some other situation sometime. But application does not work in this situation, so need to have different application not only to the individuals involved, but to the circumstances, both inner and outer, to say nothing of the inspirational moment. If you are good at that, then you go there. You are with those people for just a moment, [and an] inspirational moment happens. You say this and this, [you] try this and this, and everybody says, "Oh, yeah! That's terrific!" because you are good at that.

***That's wonderful!***

## A Period of Birth Control

Then life get easier, more fun to live, no stress. Stress goes away and people live longer, happier, healthier, more comfortably. There will be some things that people won't like. One example: There will be for a time birth control, not unpleasant, not cruel, but will be birth control required by world government for a time. Some people will be very sad, cannot have lots of children, but rational mind will say, "I understand. For one thing, children who don't have parents need to have parents. Maybe one of these children can live with us. Oh, boy! Wonderful!"

Then after that, [you] have to take hard look at civilization. Too many people are enough. "Let's not kill people off in battles. Let's just decide not to have so many children for a while." This comes initially by government enforcement and people will feel very unhappy about it, try to fight it sometimes. That's when unpleasant thing coming. All people will be able to agree in thought, in theory, that this is a good idea, but won't want to give up opportunity to have children. Children will not be taken away from people and redistributed, not that, but [when] couple come together might be that government will say, "Can have no more than one child. Sorry." So couple are allowed to have one child that survives. Maybe accident, child does not survive. Sad, very sad. Grieve for a while, then can have another child. This gradually reduces population in not a cruel way, but necessary.

***This will happen all over the planet, all governments.***

Yes, this having to do with world government. Not coming immediately, but coming. Necessary to shrink population gradually, gently.

## Earth Changes from Digging, Tunneling

***What about the Earth changes? Are they going to continue—the high winds and floods, the volcanoes and the earthquakes?***

There'll be some, but the more you can adapt to these benevolent ways, especially shrink the population gently and make commitment to doing it, and saying, "We make the best of it. If my wife and I cannot have a child or we only have one child, is okay, because almost everybody in the neighborhood has one child. Sometimes many children [get] together and we're with them. We're all kind of sharing each other's children, and this is fun. Then [we] can sometimes be around many children. [It] is fun. [We're] just not responsible for them all, all the time. So is all right, not a terrible sacrifice."

When you do this, then planet can find a way to have these planetary motions without causing catastrophe. But must sometimes do extreme motion in attempt to live with effect of human beings' activities on Earth, such as, primarily, mining, drilling, tunneling. [These] have profoundly damaging effect on the Mother Earth. Much of what you need can simply be taken out of places [where] you have dumped things that you don't need and re-created into things you do need.

***Recycled.***

Yes, recycle. A good place to begin that is to start digging in old dump sites now to retrieve things that have been buried, trash. Take it all out and recycle. We can recycle almost everything except some chemicals, but in time we'll be able to recycle all that, too. Mother Earth now is reacting to all that digging in her body and melting polar icecaps, as you have noticed. Some of this might cause a little problem for a while—water problems, rain problems—but ultimately [this] will give you virgin land. So [it's] not so bad. Just don't dig in Earth. [If] you dig in virgin land, is like poking a needle in a baby. Cruel. If too much cruelty to baby, baby go away. Mother Earth does not feel good about what you are doing in land and virgin land. Her function of going away simply means flooding, as has happened before, or [else she will] take all her water inside her. No water. Everything dry up like that. Not usually done with volcano, usually done on planet like this by water. The Earth change that is to be looked at with the most important eye is water.

***Do you see that people will start listening?***

Must.

***Oh, that's excellent. That's good news. It's so delightful to get good news.***

[It's] good news.

# 39

# Energy Tips

Zoosh
Late July 1999

***Zoosh, people are saying they feel sleepy a lot and at odd times. What is going on?***

It is a compound thing. One, because of such great trauma going on in the Earth right now, tribal warfare and so on, there is a great deal of action with the angelics and with souls departing. Sometimes the angelics are overwhelmed when there are so many souls departing plus the souls coming in. It is a lot, and some of you, not all, will help them out and take over some of their more simple skills while they are so actively participating in this soul coming-and-going on a much more rapid basis. That's part of it.

And also, at least 30 to 50 percent of it has to do with a little more wake-up energy happening for people at large. That's why sometimes you'll meet someone who is also drowsy or, as you like to say, spaced out. So it is a compound thing. The ones who are feeling it most profoundly—when you have to take a nap or you feel compelled to go to bed early and sleep very soundly through the night—are participating with the angelics to a great extent.

***Other questions we get are about people experiencing dizziness, feeling hot or cold or having trouble with their eyes. Is something else happening?***

People need to drink more water and less coffee. Most people are dehydrated most of the time. That's part of the reason for vision problems. The fluids in your bodies are being constantly drained because coffee pulls water *from* your body. It tends to take up the water you drink. This is how diuretics work. They tend to pull not only the water in coffee out of your body, but a little more besides. If people drink one glass of water and five cups of coffee in a day, the diuretic action takes all five cups of coffee plus that one cup of water and maybe a little more. If this goes on indefinitely, you might not get the same symptoms of someone who is parched, but you get similar symptoms. So people need to drink more water. If they can't drink less coffee, they need to drink more water.

# 40

# All Humans Are Being Tested Now—and the Test Is Your Response

Zoosh
April 21, 1999

*"What if Creator had almost finished the universe with materials and energies that all volunteered, but for the last part, no volunteer had what Creator needed, so Creator used some material without its permission? We have tension in the universe because some material was taken without its permission. That's why we have to have thieves—to balance that out."*

## The Origin of Thievery

I brought that up awhile back along the lines of one of Robert's curiosities, and that was my answer to his question. I wanted bring it up because there is a great deal of consternation felt by many people on this planet as to why there need to be certain events or how these events can be justified by any creator. Yet you must remember that when this Creator arrived in the space in which He would create this universe, He'd not had much experience creating universes before. He'd had some, but not much, and just like anyone who does anything, the more you do it, the more you learn about it. So this has been a learning experience for Creator. I can assure you, if Creator had it to do over again, He would not have used that material without its permission.

Consider this: If you had an idea that was inspired unto you and you had visions of great and wonderful things that could be done, with the idea that it would benefit all beings, you'd be sorely tempted to utilize whatever existed in order to bring about the culmination of events that the Explorer Race will bring about [see the Explorer Race books listed on page iv]. So Creator used a small amount of material to bond together elements that don't normally go together. You can compare this with a catalyst that might do the same thing in a chemical reaction, but this has more to do with ideas and experiences. It also has something to do with time and dimensions. For the most part, this material is not functionally operative where you exist on Earth in this dimension, so you don't really experience it. However, somewhere in the universe there needs to be a counterbalancing mechanism, because you cannot create such a usurping of the material of other beings (what was destined to be used elsewhere) without consequences.

Creators are not only *not* above consequences, they are usually *masters* of consequences. However, when this Creator began the creation in which you now reside, He/She was not yet a master of consequences, which, as you know, is quantum mastery. He became that later on. That's why Creator had this regret. Creator realized that the universe, no matter how perfect He designed it to be, would necessarily always be out of balance because He did not have the capacity to create what was needed at the time of the creation in which this material was substituted, and so had to borrow it from elsewhere.

It was not done in a malevolent way, of course. It was done in the nicest way. But even in the most polite way, it was done without the permission of the material, which wished to be elsewhere. This is why the consequence takes place on a planet where such things can take place and with people where such things can happen—specifically, the Explorer Race's planet, where you are surrounded by and consumed with challenges.

Thievery is directly associated with this singular event in the creation of this universe. You might reasonably ask, "Well, Zoosh, didn't thievery exist in other universes before this event?"

No, it didn't. People did utilize materials, but always with their permission. Thievery—taking something without someone's permission—was invented here unintentionally by this Creator, and it was one of His lessons in quantum mastery. At any level of mastery, whatever it is, spiritual, material and so on, toward the end of your learning cycle you begin to be tested.

The tests that are often the most difficult and challenging are tests related to something you are creating or something you are doing that is near and dear to your heart and that you can easily rationalize, going against your normal principles. This is because what you are doing is not only near and dear, but you know it will ultimately benefit all beings. So Creator was being tested and did not, you might say, pass the test.

However, this is not the kind of test where it is simply right or wrong. If you make a choice such as Creator did, you then live with the consequences throughout the cycle or the time that you, as a creator, experience within any creation.

### You Will Create True Heart to Replace the Stolen Material

This is another reason that Creator is looking to you to replace Him. When you take over for Him, because *you* did not (coming from other places) use this material without its permission, you will not only feel uncomfortable with that in the universe, you will set about to correct it at once. Because of your vast experience and because of the help of advisers and teachers and so on, the first thing you will do is create the material that the Creator of this universe did not know how to create. You will find a volunteer and free up that part of the universe which is here without its permission. Where will that volunteer come from? *From yourselves*—the true missing link. You will develop the ability to reproduce True Heart. True Heart will embrace that which was used without its permission and let it go to its true home, and True Heart will take its place.

***And let the other stuff . . .***

Yes. Once that's done, the material will be disseminated to all the places it needs to go. The new material, True Heart, will work better than the material that has been substituting for it; it will take its place and function the way it was intended. The other material will simply be freed up.

You won't send it back home, because where it was from has moved after all this time and experience, of course. The material will probably go directly to where it was headed in the first place, so it is not for you to send it anywhere. But it *will* be for you to release it; this is something you can do. When you do this, thievery will gradually disappear in this universe because there will be no need to balance that act of Creator's.

So you see, many things happen at once. With all the talking we have done about the Explorer Race, eventually things like this can be revealed. We didn't criticize Creator at the beginning because a lot of people would be uncomfortable with it. But at this time, especially for those of you who have gone through a lot of the Explorer Race books, if not all of them, you will be prepared to hear this because you will begin to understand Creator as a personality, which is critical.

### Understanding Creator as a Personality

For you to even consider that you might be a creator someday, with all the rights and responsibilities of a creator, you have to be able to think of or imagine creators as someone rather than some omnipotent thing. The omnipotent idea about creators is a limiting factor. Rather than simply eliminate that idea (which I don't recommend), if you begin to think about Creator as someone with certain personality traits, this idea not only prepares you to become a creator (because *you* are someone with certain personality traits), but it will also tend to release that former idea. It will remove a huge barrier that you have artificially placed between you and Creator that causes you to not only ask, but sometimes demand, that Creator must provide for you. In fact, it was always intended that *you* do the providing.

Many people get upset because Creator doesn't seem to answer their prayers, but in fact Creator does not answer your prayers because Creator knows it is up to *you* to create. And in order to create, you must have a greater sense of personal identity. That personal identity comes about when Creator is someone and has characteristics of someone or when you feel, "Well, *I'm* someone." It does not mean that you automatically qualify to be a creator, but it removes a huge hurdle in your path.

### Thievery

***Does taking something that doesn't belong to you occur only on this planet, or are there other places this has happened?***

It has very occasionally been found in other places, but if it happens, it is usually unintentional, and the crime, as it were, is worked out quite quickly and feelings are soothed. Only on a planet where people such as yourselves are learning the lessons you are learning here in Creator School can you be faced with such an extreme situation. Having something stolen from you is extreme; conversely, when you have to live as a thief, something is stolen from you as well—a great deal of peace of mind, continuity and so on. The perpetual axe is over your head for the time when you get caught and have to deal with your punishment. There is more than one way to look at it, you see.

***Will the end of thievery come long after we, the beings here on the Earth now, leave the planet?***

It will come about most likely when no one on this planet, or conceivably on some other planet, is going through polarized creator training. If people are going through polarized creator training, then it might be used as an option, but not likely, because it can be so destructive. Other things are more destructive, granted, but that can be very destructive.

## The Afterlife Review

***How does it work? Someone is a thief and finishes his natural cycle. He leaves and the personality rejoins the soul. How would you put it?***

After they leave, they will usually have the opportunity to review their life and discover a broader understanding of the consequences of their actions. They will not be told that they are bad for stealing, but they will see the consequences, what happened as a result of that theft and how it affected various peoples, situations and so on. That's how you learn, and you're learning this totally surrounded by unconditional love, which soothes and comforts you. You can learn because of this love, because it is very clear that you are not being chastised. When people are being chastised because others want them to learn, it often doesn't work, because when you are being chastised, it's all you can do to deal with that. You don't really learn different ways from that.

***The personality leaves at death, and it is usually a theme or a part of the soul, right? After it integrates with the soul, what does the soul learn from this? The review happens when you are more connected to the Earth, doesn't it?***

The review happens when you are still thinking about your Earth life, when you are still conscious of it, so that it is fresh.

***Before you've gone through the veils?***

It depends. There is no hard-and-fast rule, but usually it is after you have gone through at least some of the veils. I would have to say that your soul, which occupies the physical self of any individual, is a totality in its own right even though there may be more of your soul elsewhere.

The soul that was part of your life here is what goes through the life review. After the review and after the lessons are understood and perhaps discussed with teachers or guides, then you might begin to infuse some of that into the greater portion of your souls. It has to happen that way so that any such shock or grief is dealt with by the soul that had Earth experience, so that these dramatic feelings are not brought to the part of the soul that cannot handle such feelings. It has to be done gently and carefully.

### Integrating Life Experience into the Greater Soul

It's like this [draws diagram]. The circle represents the soul(s) of a given life. This larger curve is not designed to look like a brain, but we'll make it look like one. It is the greater part of your soul—parts of your soul that may be incarnated elsewhere, certainly outside the context of time—living elsewhere and doing other things.

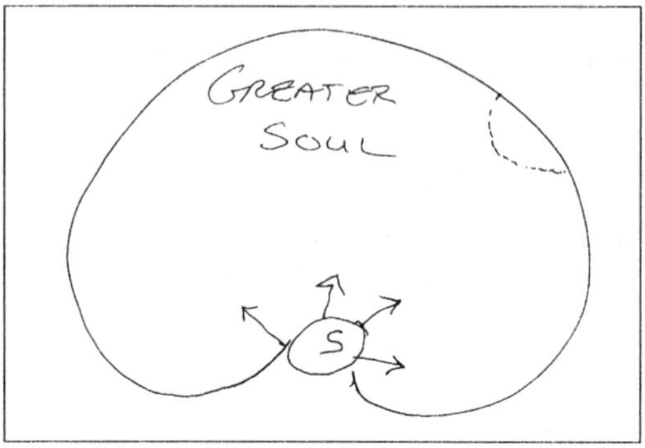


This [circle/soul] part goes through it first because it has already had Earth experience and can handle it, as the kids used to say. Then after a time, that experience will radiate or permeate gradually into the rest of the soul, taking its time easing through. But it will be blocked. (I'm drawing on the same drawing here.) Let's say the soul has another life (outlined by a dotted line) someplace else, such as the Pleiades, where things are gentle. That soul will be protected from experiencing the ramifications of that lesson until that life is over, because the soul is too gentle and is not prepared to deal with such serious consequences.

### "Illusion" from the Viewpoint of Those Who Haven't Experienced Earth Life

***So here we are in lives on Earth going through this extreme negativity, this pain and suffering. The great teachers say it is an illusion, but it's pretty real when we are living it.***

You have to consider what they mean by that. When they say it's an illusion, they are trying to encourage you to change your experience. They are also saying that in the broader picture, it's an illusion. To them, illusion means something slightly different than what you mean. When you think of illusion, you think of a magic trick that a stage magician might do to create illusions.

***Something not real.***

Yes, but to a spirit illusion might also mean something temporary or fleeting that has no lasting effect. When you add that meaning to the word *illusion*, you can see that they are speaking from a more philosophical position rather than a down-to-Earth, day-to-day, practical, grunting-through-life position. You have to take that into account. You cannot just throw your wisdom away. You need to use your wisdom and recognize that such teachers are speaking to you from a plane where such pain and suffering is unknown.

It might be known in terms of their having compassion for those who are suffering, sending love and support to do what they can, but it won't be known as part of their actual experience. What does that suggest?

***That they have never been human.***

What else?

***They are not part of the Explorer Race.***

Yes, and it also suggests that you are learning things here that *they* do not know.

***They will never have the opportunity.***

They might, but they do not know at this point. This does not mean that their advice should be ignored, but it needs to be looked at and experienced within *their* context.

***I really want to pursue this because here, humans are going through wars and shootings and agony and earthquakes and violence, then they leave their bodies. But you are saying that the soul is so gentle, it can't feel all this. So what happens to this experience? What is the value of it if it doesn't go into the data part of our beingness?***

I didn't say it didn't. I said that it has to go in in a certain way. That's what the drawing shows. The part of your soul that lives on Earth will experience it (most likely most souls do) after life in some full and learning type of way, and then, as indicated by the drawing, it is assimilated in some way. It can radiate into the rest of your being, but it has to go through that as a circuit.

## Protecting Other Portions of Your Soul

It's almost as if your Earth soul acts as a filter after life (this is an analogy) to remove the drama of Earth life that would upset the greater portions of your soul—though not all, because some portions are very advanced and can handle anything. The "greater portions" of your soul would cover lots of other lives being lived in lots of other places, maybe even in other universes, where drama and trauma in even the most infinitesimal quantity could turn that entire universe upside down. You would not want to do that, would you?

***No, not really. Will that greater part of the soul, the big picture, join with the other greater parts to become the new creator?***

All of it, including that particular Earth soul, which might at some point merge with the greater soul or, depending on the agenda of that overall soul, might reincarnate quickly. If it doesn't reincarnate quickly, it will probably merge with its total being, but there will be some delay. The delay acts as a safety mechanism to keep from polluting (it would be just like a pollutant, though not poisonous) . . . if you dropped just a drop of blue paint into a jar of white paint, it would change the color, change everything about that white paint.

You might not be able to do that with the totality of your being and still fulfill your intentions or the intentions that others such as your teachers may have—to encourage you to choose. In other words, you might be used to taking on burden after burden after burden and slogging through life and toughing it out—which I am not necessarily saying is good, but it happens. You might then get used to a certain level of pain. You're not conscious of it because you're used to it. That doesn't make it a good thing. Remember that you are not here on Earth in this Creator School to learn about pain. You're here to learn about consequences.

Pain is maybe one of those consequences. It may also be a consequence for one of your teachers and a great many other things, but you're not here to experience pain per se. You are here to understand your responsibilities, your applications, your wisdom—and consequences, in a nutshell.

***Many beings who are human at this time have reincarnated many times, right?***

Yes.

***So there have been waves and waves of that experience slowly permeating into the greater being of those individuals, right?***

Perhaps, depending on how the life went, what they experienced. One does not have life after life of misery.

***It seems that souls often don't understand what goes on in Earth when they set up a human life.***

Exactly.

***At what point do they get it? At what point does what you are doing on Earth affect the greater part of the being?***

You have to remember that the greater soul, which is a direct reflection of a portion of Creator, is going to truly reflect Creator. And we know that Creator cannot feel pain.

So the greater soul will get it when it gets it. I realize that is vague, but it has to be, because I cannot give you the formula. If I gave you the formula, you would all follow it and you wouldn't learn anything. When an Earth soul experiences consequences and has its life review, as it's been called before, that experience will gradually filter into the greater being, and the greater being will learn from it without suffering. As you say, the more of these experiences that happen, the more the soul is likely to learn. But if we had the power to arbitrarily give the greater soul the actual experience of pain, do you know what would happen?

***No.***

The Creator would suddenly feel pain, because those greater souls, each and every one of them, are a direct reflection of this Creator, aside from everything else He was before He got here. We're speaking within the context of the present. This Creator, while It has been shown what pain is, does not feel pain within this creation. It is not intended at this time.

***From various members of the Council of Creators and various outside beings—many, many beings [in first chapter of* The Council of Creators, *unpublished] —it's come up a number of times that the Creator is being ordered to start feeling our discomfort.***

I know that, but "ordered" is a strong term. You don't order creators around, you urge them.

***But due to the nature of these beings who are making the "suggestions," He will listen to them, right?***

He might.

***What is the result?***

## Why You Need Pain

Think about this: What if Creator felt the pain? It's true that Creator would suffer with you, but *you need* pain to learn on this planet the kind of things you are learning. You will simply not respond to some lessons until the pain level is high enough for you to ask for help. When you ask for help, you often may not get it immediately, but you will eventually.

***What is the lesson?***

It could be anything. Do you want an example?

***Yes.***

An example might be that a person is used to doing things on his own and would, as the kids used to say, rather die than ask somebody for help. This kind of pride can survive for a time, but ultimately such an attitude will draw to you experience after experience that will give you the opportunity to ask for help, to be assisted so that things go smoother, work out better, what-have-you.

***So asking for help is one of the lessons coming out of separation.***

What occurs when you *don't* ask for help is that you might experience some pain. Or maybe you don't do it quite right; or maybe you cause injury to yourself and others because you wanted to do it yourself, for whatever reason. Ultimately there will be increasing levels of pain, which you might simply feel as tension. That tension will erupt in various ways within your body until you learn how to ask for help.

Initially, you might ask for it in some grouchy way because you are resenting the people you're asking for help. You're resenting them before the fact, even before they help you. If they don't give you help, you immediately forgive them, but those who help you are not so quickly forgiven. Paradoxical, eh?

***That is a lesson only because we bounced against the wall of separation and we have to start going back to unity, right?***

That is simply an example, which you asked for. Your question really related to why you need pain, and that's an example. Let's say somebody loved to go jogging. He jogged farther and farther and farther every day, and in the process he was spending time away from his family and was actually going past the point where exercise can help the body, actually injuring his body, to say nothing of impacting his personal life. Pain tells you that something is wrong and needs to be corrected. This is an oversimplification, but it is necessary for the explanation.

***Okay, that is the basic use of pain. It's almost like a guidance tool.***

Exactly.

***There is just too much suffering on this planet, and I'm trying to figure out why, other than the fact that I guess we'd forget it when we leave here.***

## Transformation Needs Physicality

You don't forget it entirely, but you release those portions that cause the suffering. When you are out of your body, you do not have the mechanism. The physical body is from Mother Earth and contains the mechanism to transform, but when you are in your soul, just your energy, your spirit, you can learn, but you *cannot transform.* Another reason that souls want to manifest physically is that the physical body, especially when it is made up of a very advanced being such as Mother Earth, will almost always give you the opportunity to transform, to change, to grow, to expand.

I see. That's incredibly important, and it's never been said quite that way before.

That's why souls are lined up to come to this planet. You have a planet who is a spiritual master, a material master, a teaching master, a dimensional master, and she's just about completed quantum mastery. That's a lot, and when your body is made up of those things, you have a great many opportunities to do many things as an applied soul, meaning a soul living within a physical body on a planet where change is not only possible but encouraged. In just a short Earth life you can grow a thousand lifetimes' worth of lives where things are gentle and pleasant because of the powerful capacity here to transform.

***That answers why the soul can't feel it and why we are doing this. Considering everything sacred and requesting—we are learning that. But how do we get from here to there from the separated state?***

The same way you always do with anything. By little incremental steps and by putting it into your day-to-day life. It's okay to add things in a little way. You put in something in a little way that is new to you, and if it works, you keep doing it. If it doesn't work, you try something else until something works. If it feels good to you and produces good results in some way, you add it to your wisdom and keep doing it.

## Shamanic Ways

All shamans are not required to do the exact same job. Some do this, some do that. If you don't do something or if it doesn't feel good to you or isn't part of your wisdom, it means that it is for somebody else.

***Define shaman.***

It is someone, man or woman, possibly even a youngster, who holds all life sacred, knows that everything is alive and seeks ways to interact with that life for the benefit of all beings. This might initially take a form where you do something yourself. Let's say you are talking to a spider or a leaf. It would seem that you are doing that for yourself, but as you learn more about it and feel more confident about it . . . that is important. When you feel confident about your beliefs, you might be more inclined to mention it to other people, people who are interested, perhaps the very young or someone who asks a question. Or you might have opportunities to bring things up with the group of people you work with or even people beyond your own group. Even things you are learning that seem to be for yourself will ultimately serve others as you speak of these matters or demonstrate things to various individuals as opportunities present themselves, things that you know are of benefit to all beings.

***When you use the word "shaman," does it imply that they have great powers?***

No. Many people who have had shamanic training have abilities, things they have learned how to do, but you don't have to have powers to be a shaman. Power, in fact, doesn't enter into it. Power, after all, is seductive. It can easily be used for harm, even unintentionally. So the shaman himself or herself does not have the power. But these powers do exist within the totality of all beings, so the shaman requests that certain things happen. But the shaman does not, in his or her own right, make them happen. The shaman does a lot of requesting. Some people would call it praying.

***Requesting of who? What?***

For instance, the shaman might request in an area that is drought-stricken that rain come, but rather than say, "Rain, please come," the shaman, who might have had training in rain, for instance, would know or remember absolutely how rain felt on his or her body. *You* might say, "I know what it feels like to be in the rain" because you were probably uncomfortable in the rain, but the shaman *trains in rain* in order to become intimate with it, to feel good with it and to notice how his or her body feels while it is being rained on.

For example, in a droughtstricken area, the shaman might recall not only mentally but physically (think about *feeling* that rain, then experience it physically and in the auric field as much as possible). When his experience gets to be heightened to the degree that the shaman feels good about it or feels it is working or performing something or feels it is time to say something (depending on his individual trade), he might say something like, "Welcome, rain." The feeling of welcome is actually present. It is not a definable word, but a feeling stated by "Welcome, rain" while he feels that experience of being rained on and (if possible) while he walks barefooted on the land to remind the land what the rain feels like and how wonderful it is and to involve the land in requesting that rain. And if that rain is required or needed by the land, the *land* is the best being to request the rain. So the shaman gets things started.

***Stimulates the land.***

Yes, he gets things started and welcomes the rain perhaps more than once, perhaps touching the rocks or the stones or whatever is on the surface of the land that can accept this feeling, this experience. Maybe even a tree, but usually it is part of the land itself. The shaman will keep this up until it rains, or if the rain is not forthcoming and the shaman feels that the rain is not supposed to come, he might stop and say thank-you.

You say thank-you because you are thanking all those beings, including the land, who worked with you to bring something about. If it didn't come about, it doesn't mean that they didn't work with you, so you say, "Thank you." You say it, not as words, but as a feeling.

You feel thanks and you say thank-you out loud to make it part of your physical world. You don't think it, you *say* it.

Different cultures might have different ways of saying it. Some might sing it, some might use words. There might be gestures or motions. You might use articles that are significant and meaningful to you that you have used in ceremonies. There are lots of different ways to do it.

## Beginning Shamanic Practices

***How does the average human being living in a technological society and going to work every day begin to bring into his life this respect for all beings and this natural way of living?***

Begin at the beginning. Start by looking at your hands, which most of you have. Then look at some other part of your body. Examine it. Notice it like it was a work of art. Those who have looked at leaves closely can see all its little veins and lines. Begin to appreciate your body as a work of art. Thank your body with downward strokes. "Thank you. Thank you, arm, for your good work."

Begin at the beginning. Begin with your own physical body, using physical touch, lovingly, friendly and truthfully. Don't thump yourself, but stroke gently. Make the strokes downward because the lightbody is often trying to escape outward and upward. If we make the strokes going downward, we please the physical body by communicating with it in its own language and by having good feelings about it. You don't blame it because one arm isn't working well that day. You thank the arm for working as well as it does, and you do that with other parts of your body. Begin at the beginning.

Then the next time you see a spider or an ant, remember that it is an individual first. If you are afraid of spiders or ants, then it is something you are afraid of secondarily, but it is primarily an individual being with an individual personality and an individual soul just like you. Just because they don't talk to you in their own language does not mean that they don't have language, a culture, a philosophy, even a form of religion. But begin at the beginning with your physical body.

## The Colorado School Violence

***I heard about the Colorado school shooting tonight. It was just horrible. It was Hitler's birthday. Were they stimulated in some way to do this?***

Let's just say that a lot of that does have to do with alienation, as sociologists have been warning for years, to say nothing of police departments. It is so difficult for parents to know, because a lot of youngsters go through something similar, or at least it has that outward appearance. Youngsters are very creative, just like at any other time, only there are more things to distract people. For most youngsters, it would have been a phase they went through, got over, then went on with life. How can a parent know? So the parents are not to be blamed. Please, everyone, sympathize with the parents. The parents of the youngsters who did this damage thought their kids were going through a phase. They didn't know they were collecting weaponry to start a small war.

You're in a time now where a great deal of responsibilities for making decisions and value judgments are visited upon the young, the very young. You might say, "Well, the youngsters have parents, and they tell them what to do; they guide them" and so on. Yet television, radio, to say nothing of their conversation with their friends, is a constant stimulation to do other things. Advertising is a major thing. Movies encourage them by giving them heroic figures who are by no means heroic—in other words, beings are put up in the films as being heroic when in fact their behavior is entirely self-destructive. As you know, my description of self-destructive is that which harms yourself or another.

When you are young and not very experienced in life, meaning not very experienced in consequences that have had a direct impact on you or those you care about, you might very easily make judgments or decisions that are not in any way based on a more experienced point of view and that are not particularly profound. You all know that.

***All of this is part of the test.***

That's right. Ultimately, we can't single out Hollywood and say Hollywood isn't making Roy Rogers and Gene Autry movies anymore, where heroes are clearly heroes and bad guys are clearly bad guys, where the heroes are clearly meant to be emulated and the bad guys are clearly meant to be perceived as bad guys. You can't just single out one element and say they're bad. This is all part of the test, as you said yourself.

And it is not easy. Tests are hard, sometimes very hard. If your own Creator in this universe can make a mistake that leads to thievery even with all that Creator's experience, you can understand that this entire universe is set up to be profoundly sensitive. And it is a test, yes. I'm not trying to nimbly step around this story. It is shocking, it is tragic, and ultimately it will probably have a widespread impact. Some of it will be political, some otherwise. Hopefully, there will be some means by which individuals will come together to pay attention to developing crises before they explode.

## Using Sensitives as Troubleshooters

You know, a sensitive person might walk through a room and feel very uncomfortable around a certain individual and assume that the individual is bad, but if a person has been trained in shamanic ways, for example, you might notice your discomfort but then proceed to go through various factors to decide whether that discomfort you are feeling from them has to do with the fact that they don't feel well that day or that they are sick or that they are simply just not compatible with you on a personality level and so on. You go through various issues until you find out what is going on for them.

At some point sensitive people will be trusted, whether they be shamans or not, and those who are suffering within will not be allowed to pursue such paths of self-destructiveness. Ultimately, people who show signs of self-destructiveness will hurt themselves or others.

***So you are saying that along with the increased counseling, they'll actually start using sensitives to help identify those who really need help?***

Not immediately, but someday this will happen because it is something that will have a significantly higher percentage of finding the trouble spots. There is only so much you can do with mental things. Ultimately, things need to be done with feelings. A lot of people in a lot of societies feel shamed, and because they do, they don't speak out when they are hurting on the inside. Then they turn that hurt into some self-destructive pattern, and after a while, because they have gotten used to their pain, they don't feel anymore and they see everything in their world through that veil of pain or distortion, and that self-destructive function will manifest in some way.

This is not so revealing; it is known and understood. Yet, as I say, there is only so much that can be done by the most caring people who function strictly on a mental level or even on an encouraging, nurturing level. Eventually, one must use one of the most profound sensing devices to tell whether people are in pain and don't know how to ask for help: *a trained sensitive*, a person.

Now, some animals can do this. It would be possible to train dogs—not train them, actually, but the person working with the dog or cat would understand the dog's or cat's behavior around a certain person and be able to interpret what it means. There will be some experiments with that, but ultimately, what is needed and what you are always being encouraged to do, is find out how you as individual human beings can use your sensitivity in ways that benefit you and others rather than simply have your sensitivity assailed and feel vulnerable, getting hurt and spiraling down into that.

***Especially as more people become sensitive.***

Yes, but people are born sensitive, so it is a matter of reintegrating something you already have rather than something entirely new happening to you.

***You say that all people are born sensitive.***

Yes. All people, all animals, all plants, everything is born sensitive. Some stay that way and are taught what to do with it, but in a vast amount of your societies, that is not the case. When it is, you won't have such crises develop. This method is not infallible, but when utilized correctly (and some ancient societies are utilizing it today), it will tend to head off 90 to 97 percent of such incidents that would otherwise happen. I'm going to qualify it very specifically that way.

This is not to say that other people aren't doing wonderful work to head off these incidents. Various police departments and so on have been doing a fine job, but there is only so much you can do with the tools you are using. As any workman knows, better tools often do a better job.

***And have better results. The real point here is not the details, but every human on this planet is going through a time of testing, whether it is somebody shooting in schools or a war or an earthquake—anything.***

Or a personal internal conflict.

***So every human on the planet right now has got to focus on the next step, as you say.***

## Use What You Know

No, they have to focus on their current situation and the situation you have defined—being tested. Not every second, but when things come up, use what works for you. If you have been trained in the sensitive skills, use them. If you are a religious person, pray. Use what you know.

***I think everybody should become aware that it is a time of testing. It is not the end of the Earth, it is not millennium tribulation, all those ideas.***

It is the end of what was.

***It is the end of the old way, and there is a little shakiness going into the beginning of the new. We need to face it, right?***

Yes, that's right. If you use what you know, use your wisdom, what actually works for you, not what other people tell you *should* work for you, it would probably be much easier, because everybody has slightly different wisdom. If you can't do something that is needed, there will be somebody else who can. You don't all have to do everything.

***Well, that's important. How long will this period of testing go on?***

I can't give you a year.

***Until a dimensional point is reached? Until a certain event happens?***

Until you get used to doing things in a way that is more benevolent because it feels better and because you can see the benevolent results, if not immediately, then eventually. That's why I say that feelings are everything now. Thoughts are not useless, but feelings will be much more defined, they will be quick. You will be able to tell that something is working.

***The old can almost be defined as mental and separated, and we are moving into feeling and—what, cooperation? A sense that we're all one?***

Yes. Understand that we are talking to the Western world here. Not everybody is like this, but in terms of the Western technological society, which has in recent years become enamored with external solutions, ultimately you will need to go forward with your real strength, which is your feelings, your instincts, and know on the basis of how you feel physically, such as the heat in your chest [see page 230], that something is right for you at that moment. It may not *always* be right for you. You might like macaroni and cheese for dinner but not want it for breakfast, lunch and dinner all the time.

***The testing will be over when we can use our intuition, our heart, our feelings? Is there a point at which we are clear here, or does this keep on until the fourth dimension?***

It's like this: The testing will feel like testing until you have integrated these more benevolent ways of doing the things we have been discussing. When you have integrated them, it won't feel like testing anymore. It will just be things you easily solve using these methods.

***There is an end in sight.***

Yes, it is a change in experience. The testing might get stronger and more powerful, but once you are doing these things, it won't feel like testing anymore. It will just feel like, "Oh, I know what to do about that." You do it and that's that. You do it and then you go on. It just takes a moment.

***So the test is not somebody shooting or the violence or the earthquakes or the war, but how we respond.***

Yes, ultimately that is the test—how you respond. Well said. And many people are responding in wonderful ways.

***Already?***

Yes, and more will be done.

# 41

# Why You're Tired and What to Do About It

Speaks of Many Truths
September 21, 1999

***There seems to be difficulty in connecting to Robert today.***

Is difficult in general these days. The energy distortion is profound.

***What is the cause of the distortion?***

Seems to be caused by the overlays of choices. The past-anchored time line is being held onto by many people; the future-anchored time line is beckoning and some are grasping it, but instead of the straight path to the connection, it creates a jog. There is also another factor going on here. Over the years people have become enamored of individuality, but in fact, as you know, not only are you connected to all things and all beings everywhere but (perhaps more importantly on Earth) you are connected to all human beings—everyone is.

But now the veil (there was a veil in place) that allowed you to function as an individual is being torn away. As a result, all people are feeling connected with all other people. In my time this is how we knew we were connected; this is how we knew when one of our people in our tribe or even other people nearby was suffering or in need of something. We would be tired, or we would have some affliction that we would not normally have. Then we would go around and ask everybody in our tribe if they were all right, and if they were, we would send out emissaries to the nearby tribes or clans and ask them if *they* were all right. If they were not well, we would do what we could to help them, just as they would do what they could to help us if they were feeling uncomfortable.

In your time this experience has been somewhat lost during your struggle to develop your individual creative capacity, but now problems you are facing as the human race are so large and complex that you, as individual creators, need to function in partnership with others. You are all beginning to feel each other again, so you know there are people suffering on your world in your time. Many of you are acting as links to relieve the suffering in whatever way you can, and as a result, many people are feeling excessively tired. I might add, it does not matter whether you are the finest-tuned athlete or a sickly person, everyone has had an increasing experience of fatigue and exhaustion.

Over the past three or four weeks it's been getting more profound, and the comparison between your normal energy as an individual and the amount of energy you have available for you now is on the average of maybe a 5 percent loss for some people to a 30 percent loss for others. But taking all people into account, it is overall about a 20 percent loss on the average. As I say, some people are experiencing a 30 percent loss in their energy and others not so much that they would really notice.

### Breathe Deeply to Increase Your Energy

Now, I'd like to say that this is temporary, but unfortunately I cannot. So it's going to require efforts on your part if you want to increase your energy. I'm going to recommend that people do breathing exercises, which used to be popular years ago. Deep breaths in the morning, especially on rising, and maybe another [session] once or twice during the day. Try to step out of the factory or office wherever you work and into some area where the air is a little fresher and take 10 to 12 deep breaths—slowly. Don't hold your breath and don't pant. Just take 10 or 12 deep breaths, then relax. If that doesn't quite do it, take another 10 deep breaths. That will help.

I grant that there might be many other things that can be done. Certainly it might be useful to do yoga or something like that. Yoga can be demonstrated, but such breathing exercises are well-known to the Eastern studies. This will continue for a time.

***Days, weeks, months, years?***

## Find Ways to Increase Oxygen

I cannot say. It could be as long as three years, but there will be moments when it will get better. One of the potential problems that we cannot overlook, in your time especially, is the significant decrease in available oxygen. It would be a good idea now for people to stop cutting down trees and pay attention to the plankton in the ocean. Even with all the life forms that exhale oxygen, with six billion human beings and many other oxygen breathers on the planet, the demand for oxygen is much greater than the planet can provide. It is just a short time before the industrial complex of many different countries realize that there is going to be a need for more oxygen.

Ultimately, there will be systems in buildings—you will see it probably first in places that are therapeutic, such as hospitals, but you might also see it in places where people have to stay very alert, such as military institutions or places involved in traffic control or perhaps even computer-development facilities—that will take bottled oxygen and bleed it into the air-conditioning system to push the oxygen content within the building up, the outside air not having sufficient oxygen. This will gradually be applied in various ways within people's vehicles, but the oxygen will be created by processing water.

***And that's not good.***

No, it is a short-run solution, because six billion people and others need water. So you will have to come up with something better. Of course, the polar icecaps will melt quite a bit over the next few years, and that will give you a little time to deal with it. Rather than this causing a flood or more water or extremes in weather conditions, as you utilize water for oxygen purposes and perhaps the hydrogen for fuel purposes, there will be some overlap of time in which you will be able to consider other sources. It might be possible to extract some oxygen from stone. That is something that has been looked at for spaceships and so on, but it is perhaps not the best long-range solution.

Atmospheric science is probably going to be a very important field in the coming years, so any young people reading this who have not chosen their scientific major in college, look into atmospheric science, the study of gases and the study of [converting] liquids into gas, and you will be well prepared for making a contribution in the next ten or fifteen years.

***We need the implant that the Zeta talked about, which allows you to amplify the usable gases in the atmosphere. [See the "ET Visitors to Earth Speak" column in***

***the December 1999* Sedona Journal.*]**

## Consult the ETs and the Insects

That's just another reason to prepare yourselves for contact with extraterrestrials, and the best way to do that, of course, is to learn how to get along with each other and with life forms on Earth that you have done battle with—such as insects, who have a great deal to offer you in wisdom. They know how to make the most of the least; when you have a massive population, you must know how to do this.

***What are some other things? We really need to take care of the body. We really have to watch what we eat and exercise and not get too tired. I mean, 20 or 30 percent drain on our energy for years is a . . .***

It's a possibility, but for some it would be 5 percent. It depends. For people who are living out in the countryside or in the mountains or places where a more vigorous lifestyle is occurring, the spread of the numbers would be more like 5 to 15 percent (this is the average, though there will be some people there also at 30 percent). But for people in the cities where there is less clean air, these actions are important, and some breathing exercises will not help them because the air is so foul—for instance, certain California cities that are famous for polluted air. But they are not alone; Brazil and the Asian countries that have emerging technical development are also going to have to deal with that. That is why bottled oxygen—or what will come to be known as oxygen infusion—is going to be not only a developing industry (since it's already started), but a huge industry in the future. It will be everywhere for quite a while.

## Overpopulation

Even though religion will fight it with the best of intentions, it can't be too far off that some form of required birth control takes place. I am not saying this is a good thing; I'm just saying that six billion people is more than Earth can provide for. Why have loss of life through war if it is possible to limit a marriage to one child? It is a sad thing to lose having seven or eight children, but something must bend; if not, everything will break for everyone.

For example, let's say that the population went to twelve billion. At 12 billion, oxygen starvation would be a very serious crisis. Most people would require a unit that you actually wear that infuses extra oxygen into the air you breathe. Twelve billion people would have to live somewhere, and the more people who must have places to live, the more trees are cut down and the more pollution there is in the water and so on. I'm not saying anything that isn't known already.

Earth will try to hold off from interfering in your population. Of course, she could easily interfere by generating, duplicating and spreading part of her natural organisms, which you call germs, but she won't do that any more than is normal. No, she is trying to hold off the best she can to allow you to discover and apply the type of magic necessary for you to adjust your body to live on other gases, which is extremely unlikely. But a lot of people will try to do that or stimulate the Earth to create more oxygen in other ways or use benevolent magic to create needed oxygen.

### Using Benevolent Magic to Create More Oxygen

***How would we go about doing that?***

You wouldn't try to create the materials that would create oxygen. Rather, when you're working with benevolent magic, you must state the need specifically and allow the creative elements of life around you to find their own solution. If you try to lay out the formula based on your understanding of how oxygen is created, you will limit the capacity of creation to produce what's needed. So let's give some homework on that.

In order to create oxygen in larger quantity, I would like you to try this—this is the gesture: The heel of the right hand is in the center of the chest [and the fingertips pointing outward, touch the left palm at 90 degrees]. That gesture can be held for about 10 to 15 seconds. Then say these words (I will give more circumstances in a moment): *"I ask that there be abundant oxygen for all beings on Earth now."*

Keep it simple. You must say "all beings" because you are united with all beings. The best way to do this is to face south. Ideally you would be out in the countryside, but I know many of you cannot be. If you can sit on a rock in the country, that's fine. It's probably better not to sit right on the ground, but you can try that if you wish. At least try to take your shoes off and, at best, your

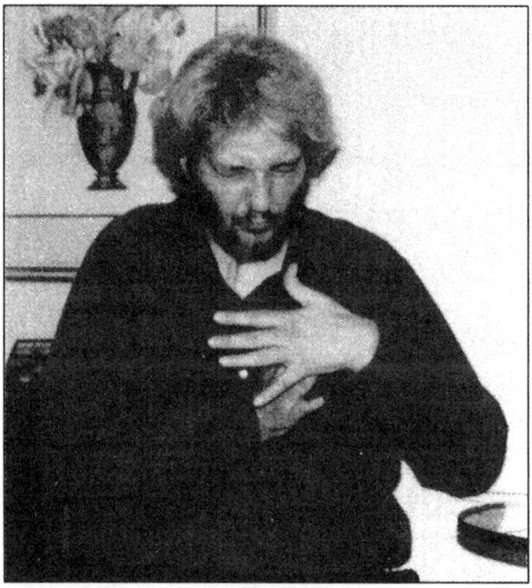

Gesture.

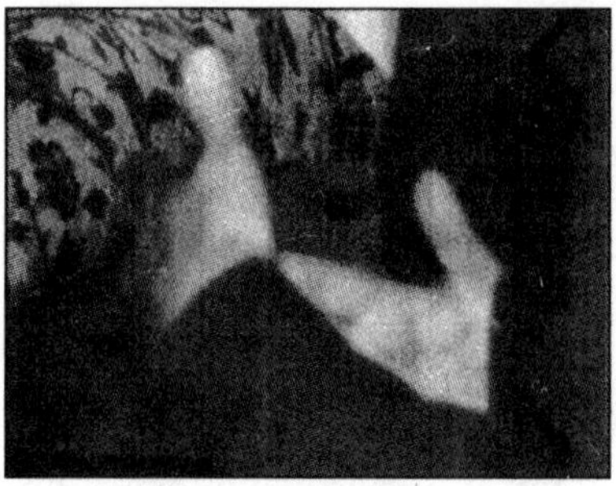

Closeup from his left.

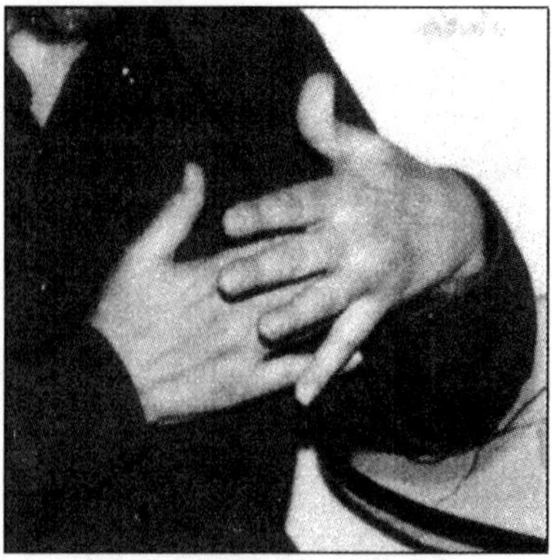

Closeup from his right.

socks off. But you don't have to if it is not easy or convenient. If you are in the city, try to do it outdoors. If you cannot do it outdoors, you might try to do it on the roof. If that's not convenient or possible, do this wherever you can. It will help.

### Individuality

I recommend these things now because so many factors are operating to challenge individuality. It is difficult for you, especially in some societies such as the Western world, where individuality has been held to be a profound right as well as desirable in some cases. But you will discover that many's the time now when you will need to gather. Don't, if you would, use only narrow opportunities to gather, meaning weddings and funerals, church services and parties. Try to find other reasons to gather in groups of three to five or more.

It is a good beginning to prepare you for the spiritual and ceremonial activities that you will do in groups of 20 to 30 thousand in the coming years. Granted, not immediately in the Western world, but in other parts of the world this will probably happen within the next three years, and in some cases it is already happening. The ceremonies will, in some cases, be religious—to pray for better circumstances. But in some cases they will involve some form of benevolent magic to create the best life for all beings on Earth—and eventually you will say, "and everywhere else." And you must say "now." You must always say "now," because if you do not, benevolent magic will spread out that capacity to create in time immemorial. So one must be specific with benevolent magic or you will have to do it over again.

***Are you saying that in the brief 400 years since your time, we've gone from a more heart-and-soul connection to other beings on the planet to this absolute individuality and disassociation?***

It's not absolute individuality, but since this is going out in English at the moment, that is a very relevant concept for English-speaking worlds. Generally speaking, in English-speaking countries that has become a profound characteristic. I grant that there are exceptions—some tribes and some religious groups have sworn an oath, a loving oath, to support and sustain each other, and that's good. But individuality is something that was cherished by people in the past because it was so rare. It was generally granted only to the very wealthy or people in isolated circumstances. Of course you would at times be lonely, but at other times you would appreciate the space around you.

So there was a groundswell of interest in exploring individuality, especially in exploring it in the context of so many people. Could it be done? Could it be maintained? And could it even be guaranteed by law, which is what your country sought to manifest? So one cannot say it is a bad thing. One can only say that it is now an indulgence that you may not be able to continue.

### People with Too Much Energy Can Share Some

You know, we are all familiar with people who have more energy than they know what to do with. It's actually intended that people like this who have abundant energy—even to the point where it makes them nervous and uncomfortable (you all know someone like this)—be around other people who don't have much energy. Not because the people with low energy are supposed to drain the other individual, but people tend to charge the atmosphere with their energy. That's why when teachers of young students are in a classroom, they might get tired from the experience, but they can all acknowledge that the air is charged with energy.

People like this are not meant to be burdened with too much energy, because it agitates them and even has some negative impacts on their physical body. It is meant that people like this be exposed to people who don't have as much energy, not to be drained of it, but just to be in the same physical space for a time. That person who has too much energy will begin to feel more relaxed and comfortable, because he or she emanates that energy. You all tend to serve each other's needs all the time, whether you know it or not. The people who need the energy will simply take it from the atmosphere of the place where the extra-energized person is. At the moment when that extra-energized person feels relaxed and comfortable and not so nervous anymore, he or she will get up and leave, because it is not intended that he be drained.

This is actually a technique used in my time when we needed to keep, for instance, an elder alive because that elder had wisdom the tribe needed and had not yet passed it on to anybody in its completeness. The people with too much energy would go into the space where the elder was and would leave when they felt relaxed. In this way the elder's life might be perpetuated for a few years, giving the elder enough time to pass on his or her wisdom.

***Say more about the next three years. When we're so tired, are we feeling the suffering of everyone else on the planet?***

Of course, the people who are suffering will also be able to draw energy from those who are not. Sometimes when there is a preponderance of a great many people suffering, there are checks built into the system so that you are not exhausted by doing something that requires your absolute attention. Generally, they will be allowed to pull energy from others when the others are in their deep sleep state. Some of you can identify with this experience in recent times: You wake up in the morning after what is usually a restful night's sleep, but you feel exhausted. That is why at times like that you will need to (if you possibly can) take a nap during the day. That will help get you through. You might even have to take a nap after a couple of hours of being awake. If your hours are flexible, try to do that. That will also help, because the people who might pull on your energy when you are in deep sleep can only pull on it then; they cannot pull on it when you are in a light nap, say, for 20 to 40 minutes, when most people do not sink into deep sleep for long.

***How does this work out? Is there some sort of balance in energy after three years or less suffering?***

## When Others Suffer, You Are Unsafe

It might not be three years. It might go on past that point. I am just saying that you need to know, as an individual who might be in a very safe environment with all you need, that *it's not safe, because others are suffering*. It is like an extreme moral lesson. In our time, being tired or afflicted was our method of knowing when people were suffering. We tried to find out who it was, because we were raised to believe it was of value, so that all people, at least in our group and in nearby villages, be as energized as possible for the good of all beings.

But in your time this has been lost somewhat, especially with the overaccentuation on competition. This idea of competition was originally started to bring out the best in the individual, but it has come to be something that is way out of balance in your time. So there needs to be more focus on the fact that you are all united all the time, even when you are in your deepest sleep. It is unavoidable, and you need to be reminded of it. This experience you are having now, however unpleasant, does remind you.

Should you ask, I will give other homework in the future to encourage, support and sustain all beings. Some will be magic; some will be suggestions; some will even be intentions. Very often those who are suffering cannot take care of themselves. You know this; you have all suffered in some way, when you needed others to help you. Perhaps you cannot go to the other side of the world where people are suffering, but there may be things you can do here—practical, grounded things to help. For those of you who are unable to do these things, I will give other exercises in the future that involve magic or ceremony to encourage the betterment of all beings.

***This is to motivate people to start thinking about how suffering can be abated all over the world because, as you said, it's going to affect each of us.***

That's right. It always has in the past, but you haven't noticed it that much. Now you cannot help but notice it. It is not a punishment; it is an urgency to become united as one being to prepare you for the union of all beings everywhere, and it would not happen at this time if Creator had not felt that you were ready to take on such a challenge. There will be many different individuals, and spirits as well, who will comment on what to do or why these things are happening, and many of those comments will be absolutely relevant. But the main thing to focus on is, what can you do to improve the situation for all beings?

## Regaining the Feeling Connection

***Is that a prerequisite for the fourth dimension—that there is a feeling connection amongst all beings on Earth?***

Yes. It's actually a prerequisite for all life, but in this recent time, the sense of disconnection you are experiencing now is an anomaly.

***So all over the planet, even during what we call the ancient times and the Dark Ages, people still had a sense of others on the planet?***

They might not have had that sense, no, but they would have had a strong sense of connection to their own kind, a sense of tribal consciousness and less of a desire for individual freedom. They might have had desires for happiness and wealth and so on within their group, but not as happiness and wealth apart from their group. This is something, I think, that can be historically shown.

***When you presented the information on the effects of the 11 August astronomical pressure for the September [1999] issue, you didn't anticipate this redistribution of energy, this flow of energy to those who are suffering?***

That's right. You cannot anticipate how it's going to affect people. You can know about it, but you don't know what the impact will be. When things like this have occurred in the past, there have been other impacts. It is not a formula: "If this happens and this happens, then this will definitely happen." You never know that in creation. The optimum happening would have been that everyone would have felt profoundly united and there would have been a profound organized effort of everybody helping everybody else. But that is something that will take time because of your competitive societies and other things. So it just takes longer.

That's why certain predictions are not given, because creation is always a surprise, especially to those who do the creating. Do you know that when Creator created this universe, Creator Itself was always surprised at the outcome of Its own creation? It is not unlike cooking, where one puts in ingredients, not by measurement but by feel, and then the stew always tastes a little different each time. So it is in the nature of creation that spontaneity and the unknown manifest. The desire, of course, is that they manifest beautifully, but sometimes it is not as beautiful.

***Is this 5 to 30 percent loss of energy consistent for the next three years?***

I can't guarantee that. It is what I see at the moment.

***It could be more?***

It could be more. Most likely it will be less. It could change tomorrow. Maybe tomorrow you'll feel like jumping out of bed and running around the house. The future is not fixed, because the future has to do with the surprise of creation.

***And all human beings contribute to that surprise.***

All beings, from the smallest beetle or particle to the biggest mountain or sun.

***I thought there was something wrong with me. I didn't want to get out of bed this morning.***

It's not you. As I say, even professional athletes are saying they are exhausted or behaving as if they are, meaning they might get unexpected injuries. That's why people who are managing athletic teams have to be particularly vigilant now. It would be good for them to add a little oxygen to the players' menus—not a lot, just a little. Oxygen has a profound impact on the blood for everybody.

***So the Creator was just looking to accelerate the process?***

It wasn't really Creator's idea to accelerate it, no. This was the idea of all Explorer Race beings who came here. As you know, with human beings—even before you manifest as a human being—there is a tendency to say, "Well, how can we do this quicker?" If it were done in a perfectly balanced state of existence, it would not be so difficult. It would be a challenge, but with all the other challenges you are dealing with as individuals and as a society, it is a bit overdone.

When the next full eclipse of the Sun and full eclipse of the Moon happen, I would like to see that this energy, the impetus energy you are dealing with now, is moderated somewhat. I think it would be all right to spread it out over a few more years so that people are not as exhausted, but that will be up to you.

The animals can handle it, though they will need more rest and food. Since they are decreasing in numbers, many of them, it is more possible for them to deal with it than for you, because they do not have internal conflicts to worry about, with the possible exception of pets that live with people. They have some internal conflicts, meaning what they know to be true. What they know that you, the people they live with, need sometimes creates internal conflicts for pets, and that's why pets get diseases and die off or act strangely and so on.

***So there are conferences and discussions going on among the Creator and His advisors about what just happened?..***

No. There are never discussions, just knowing and paying attention. It is all up to you now. Creator is not going to say, "Let's make this adjustment and make it better." It's up to you to make the adjustment. That's why I'm saying it. I'm giving people a suggestion, and they will have to decide what to do on the basis of their personal needs. If you feel you can get through it, don't change a thing. It will be faster, but at a cost.

***Faster by how many years?***

Maybe by two years.

***Oh, is that all? It doesn't make sense to have this extreme discomfort just to get something done two years faster.***

Some people might think it would. I'm not guaranteeing that any feeling of profound unity will be felt. It's not like you are going through this over many years, maybe three, maybe seven, maybe fifteen, whatever. Maybe it will all be over soon. I'm not saying that when it's over you will all feel totally linked and want to behave as people do in my time. I'm not saying that at all. I have no reason to believe that people in your time will ever behave as people do in my time, because you are living in a profoundly overcomplicated society, from my point of view. So I do not know, nor can I really make any valid prediction at this time.

# 42

# Asking for Energy

Isis
September 21, 1999

Gesture.

Ask that the energy of all creation be fed to you in the most benevolent way for you. Do this, either as people have done in the past [shows position; see top photo] or, if you prefer, this [see alternate gesture]. This [last photo] is not the position. It is to see the position of the fingers only. Goodnight.

Alternate gesture.

Position of fingers in

# 43

# Theoretical Consequences

Robert's Vertical Wisdom
September 21, 1999

***Is gravity becoming greater? [A question asked by Robert.]***

Yes, gravity is relative to the conscious mind's capacity to solve its limitations. As we work through our limitations from the starkly physical to the application of theoretical consequences (which allows a vehicle to travel beyond the speed of light and remain intact), we release gravity's effect. In short, we transform the limiting constriction of gravity and are pulled forward by our own natural capacities, without limits, to remerge with our true spirit selves, or that which is of our true essence.

Conversely, when we allow ourselves to be constrained by the limits of others, the effect of gravity becomes greater and our mass requires greater quantities of energy to propel us. In short, we become "heavier" and have to use greater energy to move.

So we have a choice now. Will we choose the heavy path, burdened by the limiting beliefs found all around us, or will we choose the lighter path, which removes our limits and allows us to be our true selves with all of our true capacities and our unlimited applications? The application of theoretical consequences defines the capacity of one body to exceed the limits of another body when that body is moving in the opposite direction of the first body, as long as both bodies are exceeding their own capacity of forward thrust.

This can happen only in an environment of electromagnetics. In short, picture an armature spinning in one direction surrounded by its opposite field member spinning in the other direction. Add an environment free of friction that might exist in space and the two bound together by a magnetic field, and nothing else can exceed their capacities.

# 44

# Humanity Chooses Species Consciousness

Zoosh
September 22, 1999

All right, Zoosh speaking.

***What is the process of gravity becoming greater? How does our conscious mind create this heavier gravity?***

Your time line is based, or let's say rooted, in the idea that the wider the experience an individual has, the more likely he or she is to be able to solve some problem, whatever line that problem occurs in. If you have your full capacity (if you remember your past lives and experience), the more experience you have, the more likely you are to be able to resolve anything that comes your way. But in your situation, where you do not have access to your past-life wisdom along the horizontal plane or time experience, you are simply laden with an accumulation of experience that has to do with what I call species experience, meaning the human race in your time.

## Species Knowledge

Right now you all have the capacity to have species knowledge, which is the accumulation of knowledge of all human beings alive on the Earth right now (not in the past, not in the future, just in the now). What Speaks of Many Truths was talking about was that in order to have that gift, you also have to have the responsibility—the other side of the situation, in which all parts of the mechanism (if we can call it that) of humanity must be in equal share of all other parts. You cannot have some people who are suffering while other people are, not happy, but oblivious to the suffering. That's the key. That is why your current-events programs are so important, because they get a lot of information out to a lot of people about what's going on in other places—through TV, radio, newspapers, magazines, conversations between people, Internet, telephone calls etc.

All this is important because it is vital that in order to achieve species consciousness of the moment, which is a step toward having species consciousness of past, present and future, you must make an effort to provide physically for the needs of all people. That's why people like President Clinton and others in the United Nations who are making some effort to provide for the well-being of all human beings on Earth are to be saluted and congratulated. Even though the methods, manners and means may not always be the most benevolent, it is a step, an intention, that is necessary for all human beings to pay attention to.

That's why the Internet is so important. People talking to each other around the world are finding out what's really going on for individuals elsewhere, not just countries and political systems.

## Science Will Find Its God in the Heart

The information that is being talked about [above, in chapter 43] purports to give to physicists the potential for physics to become what physics students have known for many years—that physics and spirituality must join in order to achieve the promise of physics. This promise is not just the explanation of what is; it must also, in order to be the true promise, contain the instructions for how to recreate what is in order to make what is more benevolent and benign for all beings. Therefore, spirituality must join physics. This document points the way for physicists and spiritualists, if I might call them that, to join together to deliver the promise of physics.

There is no reason science cannot find its god in the heart rather than in the mind, which allows for painful mistakes. Needless to say, if at the end of WWII it would have been possible for the U.S. or the Allies to drop a bomb on Japan that would have simply radiated energy that created peaceful sensibilities in all beings, they would have done so. But they didn't have that available to their minds. That loving energy which binds all beings together who wish to be joined together, not abstractly or against their will, is the means by which you will solve the impossible physics problems of today. And that is required, because it is these people who have the desire to solve the unsolvable problems.

Yes, to a degree, benevolent magic will help. But it will be necessary for people who want to solve the problems to be able to instruct others in the means to solve them; to have the tools, technology and heart sense to give to others; and to easily be able to instruct others to, for instance, transform toxic waste to something benign.

***How does this relate to what was given to us yesterday, this sudden happening where everyone's energy is being used to bridge to those who are suffering or connect all of us to a unity of consciousness?***

To have *active species consciousness*, you must not only access knowledge that all human beings alive on the Earth have ever known or will ever know, in addition to what all human beings on the Earth now know in this moment, which continues moment to moment, but also you must have the other side of it—responsibility.

***This evidently just happened, and no one knew that it would deplete human's energy so drastically?***

I wouldn't say that no one knew. Some beings did not know, and it was alarming to Speaks of Many Truths, heart-centered being that he is, loving being that he is. It was alarming to him. Understand that. But from my point of view, it is strictly a challenge that you can rise to. Each individual right now must negotiate with your future-anchored existence. It is not actually your future self. If you try to negotiate with your future self, it will be unnecessary.

## Two Easy Remedies

What you need to do is this: For those who have the spiritual ability to extend beyond their physical body, this will be easy. For those people, the quick instructions, which you probably already know, is to not exit the body entirely, but to send out your physical energy to its future, to a point in that future where you feel comfortable. Then bring that comfort back into the physical body you occupy now and notice how it feels. Keep doing that until you can memorize the way your physical body feels under those circumstances, and work toward achieving that feeling all the time. Then you'll have more energy than you'll know what to do with, and you may actually have to moderate that a bit so you can sleep at night. That's the instructions for those who are able along those lines.

Now, for those of you who do not know how to do that, write yourself a letter and say, "Dear Future, I need to feel physically my benevolent future being in my now body. Please allow me to feel it often. The best time for me would be (then you write down the time) between this and this time." For some people it will be just before sleep. For others it will be when you wake up. For others it will be during the time of the day when it is most convenient for you to relax. You could ask for a specific time. Then just relax during that time and try not to think. Try to keep your mind as free of thought as possible and see how you feel. Also, during the time preceding that relaxation time, you can read the letter you wrote.

## Creator School Challenges

I told you a long time ago that the challenges and lessons in Creator School will get greater and greater because Creator believes you have the capacity to achieve positive results. A fairy godmother will not come along with her magic wand and wave it over your heads to make everything hunky-dory. It's not going to be like that, and you know that darn well. It has to be placed upon you in such a way that you will notice. It can't just be a mental conundrum—"How should we do this? Let's discuss it philosophically."

No, it has to hit you in the home spot, and the home spot is your physical body, which is where you reside. You will find that almost all your challenges that come up in the next few years will strike you right smack in the physical body, because that's what you cannot avoid and what you are most likely to take immediate umbrage to—in short, ask about. So don't be surprised. You might also pat yourselves on the backs, saying, "Well, we must be doing something right, or Creator wouldn't be dropping such a problem on us."

***Speaks of Many Truths said that all humans decided this, but it was decided on a higher or broader level than that?***

From Speaks of Many Truths' point of view, he saw it that way, but from my point of view, I do not see anything happening for humans without the Creator's allowance. It may very well be true that at one point all human beings decided that "this is the moment when we are going to make this happen." But Creator always has the capacity to say, "No, wait." But Creator did not. I am not saying that what Speaks of Many Truths said is false. I am just expanding on it a bit more. If the Creator does not interfere, that is by way of Creator saying, "Yes, you are ready for this now."

***Creator would have checked with His friends and advisors for their approval also?***

Theoretically, but Creator did not do that.

***In this instance?***

Correct.

***This was a further result of the astronomical lineup of planets in August, right?***

The astronomical lineup is not separate from this. Everything is planned. Such astronomical lineups like this occur more than once, so you might say that in the larger sense, Creator brings this about from time to time.

***The opportunity.***

. . . the opportunity with such astronomical lineups. The Creator brought it up again, and this time you said, "Okay, let's do it." If you accomplish the challenge, it is likely to shorten the time for the availability of species consciousness, at least in the now, by 16 to 18 months.

***It would've taken x years; now it's going to take 18 months less. What's the time period had we not done this?***

Maybe seven years.

***So it's from seven years to five and a half now?***

Yes, but think about it: How many people would suffer needlessly during that time? It gives you a chance to improve the lot of all beings and to eliminate that much suffering.

***How does this decision by humanity and the Creator speed up the process by achieving unity earlier?***

It will allow you to make the preparatory steps to get to 3.50 dimension. You see, the challenges are not complicated. The formula is stated in a wordy and complicated way, but it's stated that way to be very specific, precise. It's not stated that way to confuse anybody. The words need to be kept absolute—no changes at all. But the challenge in its own right is not complex.

It just means that the Golden Rule needs to be applied across the board to everyone, even if they say something offensive to you. It does not mean that you have to be beaten up or killed and still apply great love. You can defend yourself to some degree. What I'm saying, though, is that it is not all right to remain ignorant of the suffering of other people.

Now, think about what I'm saying. You can be aware of the suffering of other people and you may or may not do something physical about it. Maybe you'll contribute to the Red Cross, maybe you'll organize something on your own or maybe you'll simply say a prayer associated either with your religion or a living prayer: "May all beings be at peace, love and harmony with all other beings now"—such as that or other things that suit the situation. That is what is required: *do what you can.*

It is essential, then, that you know about it. In short, it is no longer acceptable to be ignorant of the suffering of others. You must know about it. You see, if you know about it, in most beings it will automatically create a desire to make it better. So even if you did nothing, but you heard about it and then went to sleep at night, your spirit selves would be instructing your physical selves what to do, whether you did it or not. And at the least, you would talk it up to people and you would likely do something.

### The Redistribution of Humans' Energy Will Force Your Attention to It

***Precisely how is this energy being used or redistributed? What does that mean when 20 or 30 or 5 percent of our energy is being used to bridge to this unity consciousness?***

If you had three generators—one operating at 20 percent, one operating at 30 percent and one operating at 50 percent—that would give you perhaps the 100 percent energy you need in order for your business to function. But suppose the 50 percent-operating generator dropped to 40 percent. Then what needs to happen doesn't happen as well as before, or maybe it gets completely messed up. You need to have that 100 percent of energy. This means that someone somewhere has to bring in a 10 percent generator or else some other means must be found to provide the energy needed.

You all know that the brain and nervous system can be measured for its electrical capacity. The energy that evacuates your body to go to the bodies of others comes directly from the electricity in your nervous system. This usually happens in the most benign way, which is when you are asleep. Think what would happen if energy were being tapped from your mental and neural systems when you were awake. You could have accidents, you could make mistakes—you could, in short, hurt yourself or others. So it has to happen when you are at the deepest levels of sleep, when you can afford to let it go because you are less likely to be injured.

***A percentage of our energy is being sent in sleep to other humans on the planet who need it, and we need to learn how to replenish that by calling for energy from the future time line.***

Yes, that's the temporary solution—and/or you need to resolve the sufferings of people on the Earth. Even saying a simple living prayer will help. You need to *do* something about it.

***This is an attempt to force us to do something about it—not force, but . . .***

No, it's all right. Let's say it: It's an attempt to force your attention on this point. Disease is also an attempt to force your attention onto your physical body.

***How do we focus on this future energy?***

You pull it from . . . what is the present? The present is energy, mass, love, motion, all these things. It is something tangible, something that you can't quite grasp, like the air, but you can feel its effect on you if you move your hand around quickly. In short, it has tangibility. It is easier for you to understand what is the past, having lived it. But it is no easier for you to understand the past in physical terms because you can't go back and grasp the past any easier than you can go forward and grasp the future—unless you know how to do that, as I gave instructions to those who do.

***Isis said to ask for energy from all creation in a way that's benevolent.***

Yes, that's fine. Understand that it is my tendency to speak about things in mental terms. It is Speaks of Many Truths' tendency to speak of things in physical and feeling terms. And it is Isis' tendency to speak in terms of loving spirit.

***I'm concerned about the people who don't know what to do, people whose energy is being used but who don't understand what is happening to them. They're going to feel depleted, but it's not going to cause depression or breakdowns?***

It might.

***What about all the people on the planet who don't understand that there are ways to increase their energy? I'm concerned about them.***

I appreciate your concern, but as it is with all discomforts, the discomfort is not intended to be a punishment; it's intended to be a message, and the response to the message is ASK FOR HELP! If something is giving you difficulty, ask. Eventually someone will tell you. Try many different things. Some will work for a while, others won't.

***At the end of five years instead of seven, we should approach 3.50?***

No, I didn't say that. I said that it's a preparatory step to allow you to approach 3.50. I didn't say it would be the result. You always want the solution, but the solution is not in the answer; the solution is in the process. The answer is obvious once the process has been started or is in the middle or sometimes when the process is completed. But the answer is almost useless in a physical world.

## Apply the Process and Juggle Your Challenges

The process is essential. Thinking about it doesn't accomplish it. So I am less interested in your knowing the answer than in your *applying the process*. You are here in this profoundly physical world, you and everybody else, in order to understand how physicality can make a profound difference in the expansion of all beings. Yes, there are great risks involved, because if one goes the wrong way, it's very easy to create contraction out of necessity. Contraction is essentially going back to the starting point, because the process is going in the wrong direction. If you *don't* go back to the starting point, everything will contract [to understand this remark, see the loop of time illustration on page 168 of *The Explorer Race*]. That's why Creator took such risks. [See *Explorer Race: Origins and the Next 50 Years* and *Explorer Race: Creator and Friends.*] That process is the key to it all.

***Of constantly taking risks?***

Of doing things, of attempting the process, of accomplishing it or at least trying and saying, "Well, that's not for me, but at least I tried. I did what I could do. I couldn't climb to the top of the mountain, but I got partway up. I feel pretty good about that. I know now that I might not be a mountain climber in this life, but I can climb partway up if I ever have to." You, the reader, cannot know that by thinking about it; you can only know that by *doing* it.

***We can look forward to being motivated and responding to this challenge, and at the end of five years, we will create another interesting challenge?***

There is no reason to assume it will take that long. What makes you think it is one at a time? Certainly there are other challenges going on while this one came up. There are always many hats in the air to juggle. To be a creator even on a small scale, such as having children, what is it like having four or five children running around? You have to pay attention and take responsibility. You have to do many things at once. What is it like having uncountable numbers of beings running around, and you have to pay attention to all of them? You are a creator now, but you are taking necessarily slow steps. Why do you think that life is the way it is here? Why do you think that you perpetuate this species by birth rather than by cloning, as happens in many cultures on other worlds? It is so that *you will experience in every moment the responsibility of creation on a detailed scale.*

***The process of creation.***

That's right, a process.

# THE EXPLORER RACE SERIES

## 1 the EXPLORER RACE

This book presents humanity in a new light, as the explorers and problem-solvers of the universe, admired by the other galactic beings for their courage and creativity. Some topics are: **The Genetic Experiment on Earth; The ET in You: Physical Body, Emotion, Thought and Spirit; The Joy, the Glory and the Challenge of Sex; ET Perspectives; The Order: Its Origin and Resolution; Coming of Age in the Fourth Dimension and much more!**

574p $25.00

## 2 ETs and the EXPLORER RACE

In this book Robert channels Joopah, a Zeta Reticulan now in the ninth dimension, who continues the story of the great experiment — the Explorer Race — from the perspective of his race. The Zetas would have been humanity's future selves had not humanity re-created the past and changed the future.

237p $14.95

## 3 Origins and the Next 50 Years

Some chapters are: **THE ORIGINS OF EARTH RACES:** Our Creator and Its Creation, The White Race and the Andromedan Linear Mind, The Asian Race, The African Race, The Fairy Race and the Native Peoples of the North, The Australian Aborigines, The Origin of Souls. **THE NEXT 50 YEARS:** The New Corporate Model, The Practice of Feeling, Benevolent Magic, Future Politics, A Visit to the Creator of All Creators. **ORIGINS OF THE CREATOR:** Creating with Core Resonances; Jesus, the Master Teacher; Recent Events in Explorer Race History; On Zoosh, Creator and the Explorer Race. 339p $14.95

# THE EXPLORER RACE SERIES

## ❻ EXPLORER RACE: EXPLORER RACE and BEYOND

In our continuing exploration of how creation works, we talk to Creator of Pure Feelings and Thoughts, the Liquid Domain, the Double-Diamond Portal, and the other 93% of the Explorer Race. We revisit the Friends of the Creator to discuss their origin and how they see the beyond; we finally reach the root seeds of the Explorer Race (us!) and find we are from a different source than our Creator and have a different goal; and we end up talking to All That Is! 360p $14.95

## Ⓐ EXPLORER RACE: Material Mastery

Secret shamanic techniques to heal particular energy points on Earth, which then feeds healing energy back to humans. $14.95

**AVAILABLE SPRING 2000**

## Ⓑ EXPLORER RACE: Shamanic Secrets for Physical Mastery

Gestures for clearing cellular memory of trauma and pain. $19.95

## ❼ EXPLORER RACE and ISIS

Isis sets the record straight on her interaction with humans – what she set out to do and what actually happened. $14.95

LIGHT TECHNOLOGY PUBLISHING

Former U.S. Naval Intelligence Briefing Team Member reveals information kept secret by our government since the 1940s. UFOs, the J.F.K. assassination, the Secret Government, the war on drugs and more by the world's leading expert on UFOs.

# Behold A Pale Horse

by William Cooper

$25^{00}

Softcover 500p

ISBN 0-929385-22-5

## About the Author

Bill Cooper, former United States Naval Intelligence Briefing Team member, reveals information that remains hidden from the public eye. This information has been kept in top-secret government files since the 1940s.

In 1988 Bill decided to "talk" due to events then taking place worldwide. Since Bill has been "talking," he has correctly predicted the lowering of the Iron Curtain, the fall of the Berlin Wall and the invasion of Panama, all of record well before the events occurred. His information comes from top-secret documents that he read while with the Intelligence Briefing Team and from over 17 years of thorough research.

## Excerpt from pg. 94

*"I read while in Naval Intelligence that at least once a year, maybe more, two nuclear submarines meet beneath the polar icecap and mate together at an airlock. Representatives of the Soviet Union meet with the Policy Committee of the Bilderberg Group. The Russians are given the script for their next performance. Items on the agenda include the combined efforts in the secret space program governing Alternative 3. I now have in my possession official NASA photographs of a moon base in the crater Copernicus."*

## Table of Contents


| | | |
|---|---|---|
| Chapter 1 | Silent Weapons for Quiet Wars | 35 |
| Chapter 2 | Secret Societies and the New World Order | 67 |
| Chapter 3 | Oath of Initiation of an Unidentified Secret Order | 99 |
| Chapter 4 | Secret Treaty of Verona | 103 |
| Chapter 5 | Good-by USA, Hello New World Order | 109 |
| Chapter 6 | H.R. 4079 and FEMA (Federal Emergency Management Agency) | 121 |
| Chapter 7 | Anti-Drug Abuse Act of 1988 H.R. 5210, P.L. 100-690 | 151 |
| Chapter 8 | Are the Sheep Ready to Shear? | 159 |
| Chapter 9 | Anatomy of an Alliance | 163 |
| Chapter 10 | Lessons from Lithuania | 179 |
| Chapter 11 | Coup de Grace | 183 |
| Chapter 12 | The Secret Government | 195 |
| Chapter 13 | Treason in High Places | 239 |
| Chapter 14 | A Proposed Constitutional Model for the Newstates of America | 251 |
| Chapter 15 | Protocols of the Elders of Zion | 267 |
| Chapter 16 | The Story of Jonathan May | 331 |
| Chapter 17 | Documentation: U.S. Army Intelligence Connection with Satanic Church | 361 |
| Appendix A | William Cooper's Military Service Record | 381 |
| Appendix B | UFOs and Area 51 | 397 |
| Appendix C | Alien Implants | 442 |
| Appendix D | AIDS | 445 |
| Appendix E | New World Order | 448 |
| Appendix F | U.S. Government Drug Involvement | 473 |
| Appendix G | Kurzweil vs. Hopkins | 490 |

LIGHT TECHNOLOGY PUBLISHING

## 7 A BEGINNER'S GUIDE TO THE PATH OF ASCENSION

This volume covers the basics of ascension clearly and completely, from the spiritual hierarchy to the angels and star beings, in Dr. Stone's easy-to-read style. From his background in psychology he offers a unique perspective on such issues as karma, the transcendence of the negative ego, the power of the spoken word and the psychology of ascension.

**$14.95 Softcover 166p** ISBN 1-891824-02-3

## 8 GOLDEN KEYS TO ASCENSION AND HEALING

### REVELATIONS OF SAI BABA AND THE ASCENDED MASTERS

This book represents the wisdom of the ascended masters condensed into concise keys that serve as a spiritual guide. These 420 golden keys present the multitude of methods, techniques, affirmations, prayers and insights Dr. Stone has gleaned from his own background in psychology and life conditions and his thorough research of all the ancient and contemporary classics that speak of the path to God realization.

**$14.95 Softcover 206p** ISBN 1-891824-03-1

## 9 MANUAL FOR PLANETARY LEADERSHIP

Here at last is an indispensible book that has been urgently needed in these uncertain times. This book lays out, in an orderly and clear fashion the guidelines for leadership in the world and in one's own life. It serves as a reference manual for moral and spiritual living and offers a vision of a world where strong love and the highest aspirations of humanity triumph.

**$14.95 Softcover 284p** ISBN 1-891824-05-8

## 10 YOUR ASCENSION MISSION

### EMBRACING YOUR PUZZLE PIECE

This book shows how each person's puzzle piece is just as vital and necessary as any other. Fourteen chapters explain in detail all aspects of living the fullest expression of your unique individuality.

**$14.95 Softcover 248p** ISBN 1-891824-09-0

## 11 REVELATIONS OF A MELCHIZEDEK INITIATE

Dr. Stone's spiritual autobiography, beginning with his ascension initiation and progression into the 12th initiation, is filled with insight, tools and information. It will lift you into wondrous planetary and cosmic realms.

**$14.95 Softcover** ISBN 1-891824-10-4

## 12 HOW TO TEACH ASCENSION CLASSES

This book serves as an ideal foundation for teaching ascension classes and presenting workshops. The inner-plane ascended masters have guided Dr. Stone to write this book, using his Easy-to-Read-Encyclopedia of the Spiritual Path as a foundation. It covers an entire one- to two-year program of classes.

**$14.95 Softcover 136p** ISBN 1-891824-15-5

LIGHT TECHNOLOGY PUBLISHING

# more great books!

## HALLIE DEERING

### LIGHT FROM THE ANGELS

**Channeling the Angel Academy**

Now those who cannot attend the Angel Academy in person can meet the Rose Angels who share their metaphysical wisdom and technology in this fascinating book.

**$15.00 Softcover 230p**
ISBN 0-929385-72-1

### DO-IT-YOURSELF POWER TOOLS

Assemble your own glass disks that holographically amplify energy to heal trauma, open the heart & mind, destroy negative thought forms, tune the base chakra and other powerful work. Build 10 angelic instruments worth $700.

**$25.00 Softcover 96p** ISBN 0-929385-63-2

## ALOA STARR

### PRISONERS OF EARTH

**Psychic Possession and Its Release**

Aloa Starr

The symptoms, causes and release techniques in a documented exploration by a practitioner. A fascinating study that demystifies possession.

**$11.95 Softcover 179p**
ISBN 0-929385-37-3

## EDITH BRUCE

### THE KEYS TO THE KINGDOM

This little book is spiritually rich in wisdom and timely in terms of current world changes. Assembled from a series of channeled readings given by The Great Brother/Sisterhood of Light. The author has touched and lifted the lives of thousands with her powerful healing influence and gentle, loving guidance.

**$14.95 Softcover 136p** ISBN 0-929385-94-2

## MARY FRAN KOPPA

### MAYAN CALENDAR BIRTHDAY BOOK

An ephemeris and guide to the Mayan solar glyphs, tones and planets, corresponding to each day of the year. Your birthday glyph represents your soul's purpose for this lifetime, and your tone energy, which affects all that you do and influences your expression.

**$12.95 Softcover 140p** ISBN 1-889965-03-0

## MAURICE CHATELAIN

### OUR COSMIC ANCESTORS

A former NASA expert documents evidence left in codes inscribed on ancient monuments pointing to the existence of an advanced prehistoric civilization regularly visited (and technologically assisted) by ETs.

**$9.95 Softcover 216p** ISBN 0-929686-00-4

LIGHT TECHNOLOGY PUBLISHING

# more great books!

## GUIDE BOOK

**THE NEW AGE PRIMER**
Spiritual Tools for Awakening

A guidebook to the changing reality, it is an overview of the concepts and techniques of mastery by authorities in their fields. Explores reincarnation, belief systems and transformative tools from astrology to crystals.

$11.95 Softcover 206p ISBN 0-929385-48-9

## GABRIEL H. BAIN

**LIVING RAINBOWS**

A fascinating "how-to" manual to make experiencing human, astral, animal and plant auras an everyday event. A series of techniques, exercises and illustrations guide the reader to see and hear aural energy. Spiral-bound workbook.

$14.95 Softcover 134p ISBN 0-929385--42-X

## EILEEN NAUMAN DHM (UK)

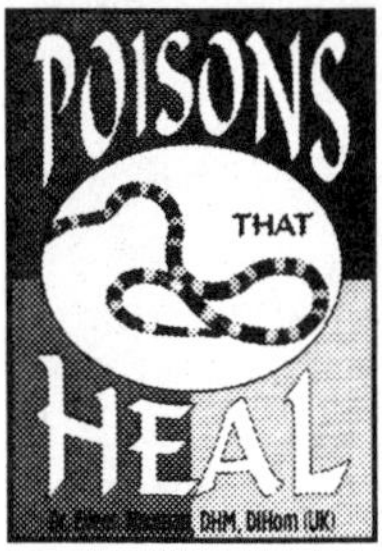


**POISONS THAT HEAL**

Homeopathy is all that remains to protect us from the deadly superbugs and viruses that modern medicine has failed to turn back. Learn how to protect yourself and your family against the coming Ebola virus and other deadly diseases.

$14.95 Softcover 270p ISBN 0-929385-62-4

## AI GVHDI WAYA

**NEW!!!**

**PATH OF THE MYSTIC**
The author shares her own journey through Native American stories of her discovery — and how you can access the many teachers, too. Walk the path of the mystic daily and transform from chrysalis into butterfly. "Our best teachers are inside ourselves."

$11.95 Softcover 114p ISBN 0-929385-47-0

## BY 12 CHANNELS

**THE SEDONA VORTEX GUIDEBOOK**
200-plus pages of channeled, never-before-published information on the vortex energies of Sedona and the techniques to enable you to use the vortexes as multidimensional portals to time, space and other realities.

$14.95 Softcover 236p ISBN 0-929385-25-X

## TAMAR GEORGE

**GUARDIANS OF THE FLAME**

Channeled drama of a golden city in a crystal land tells of Atlantis, the source of humanity's ritual, healing, myth and astrology. Life in Atlantis over 12,000 years ago through the eyes of Persephone, a magician who can become invisible. A story you'll get lost in.

$14.95 Softcover ISBN 0-929385-76-4

LIGHT TECHNOLOGY PUBLISHING

STARCHILD PRESS

A DIVISION OF
LIGHT TECHNOLOGY
PUBLISHING

# for kids
of all ages!

## THE LITTLE ANGEL BOOKS by LEIA STINNETT

**A CIRCLE OF ANGELS**
A workbook. An in-depth teaching tool with exercises and illustrations throughout.
$18.95 (8.5" x 11")
ISBN 0-929385-87-X

**THE 12 UNIVERSAL LAWS**
A workbook for all ages. Learning to live the Universal Laws; exercises and illustrations throughout.
$18.95 (8.5" x 11")
ISBN 0-929385-81-0

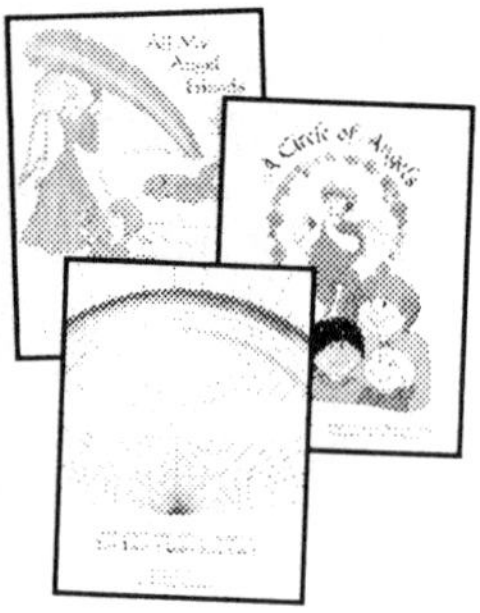

**ALL MY ANGEL FRIENDS**
A coloring book and illustrative learning tool about the angels who lovingly watch over us.
$10.95 (8.5" x 11")
ISBN 929385-80-2

**WHERE IS GOD?**
Story of a child who finds God in himself and teaches others.
$6.95 ISBN 0-929385-90-X

**HAPPY FEET**
A child's guide to foot reflexology, with pictures to guide. $6.95
ISBN 0-929385-88-8

**WHEN THE EARTH WAS NEW**
Teaches ways to protect and care for our Earth.
$6.95 ISBN 0-929385-91-8

**THE ANGEL TOLD ME TO TELL YOU GOOD-BYE**
Near-death experience heals his fear. $6.95
ISBN 0-929385-84-5

**COLOR ME ONE**
Lessons in competition, sharing and separateness.
$6.95 ISBN 0-929385-82-9

**ONE RED ROSE**
Explores discrimination, judgment, and the unity of love.
$6.95 ISBN 0-929385-83-7

**ANIMAL TALES**
Learning about unconditional love, community, patience and change from nature's best teachers, the animals.
$7.95 ISBN 0-929385-96-9

**THE BRIDGE BETWEEN TWO WORLDS**
Comfort for the "Star Children" on Earth.
$6.95 ISBN 0-929385-85-3

**EXPLORING THE CHAKRAS**
Ways to balance energy and feel healthy.
$6.95 ISBN 0-929385-86-1

**CRYSTALS FOR KIDS**
Workbook to teach the care and properties of stones.
$6.95
ISBN 0-929385-92-6

**JUST LIGHTEN UP!**
Playful tools to help you lighten up and see the humor in all experiences you create.
$9.95 (8.5" x 11")
ISBN 0-929385-64-0

**WHO'S AFRAID OF THE DARK?**
Fearful Freddie learns to overcome with love.
$6.95 ISBN 0-929385-89-6